CRITICAL PERSPECTIVES ON USER INVOLVEMENT

Edited by Marian Barnes and Phil Cotterell

First published in Great Britain in 2012 by

The Policy Press
University of Bristol
Fourth Floor
Beacon House
Queen's Road
Bristol BS8 1QU
UK

t: +44 (0)117 331 4054
f: +44 (0)117 331 4093
tpp-info@bristol.ac.uk
www.policypress.co.uk

North America office:
The Policy Press
c/o The University of Chicago Press
1427 East 60th Street
Chicago, IL 60637, USA
t: +1 773 702 7700
f: +1 773 702 9756
sales@press.uchicago.edu
www.press.uchicago.edu

British Library Cataloguing in Publication Data
A catalogue record for this book is available from the British Library.

Library of Congress Cataloging-in-Publication Data
A catalog record for this book has been requested.

ISBN 978 1 84742 750 2 paperback
ISBN 978 1 84742 751 9 hardcover

Cover design by Qube Design Associates.
Front cover: image kindly supplied by istock.com
Printed and bound in Great Britain by Hobbs, Southampton.
The Policy Press uses environmentally responsible print partners.

Contents

Notes on contributors

Rosemary Barber is an honorary senior research fellow at the University of Sheffield, School of Health and Related Research, where she jointly leads a research theme on public involvement in research. She became interested in public involvement through her work as a clinical psychologist in adult mental health. Current research interests include evaluating the impact of public involvement, and working with service user co-investigators to explore acceptable and unacceptable aspects of psychological interventions and ways of improving services for people with long-term depression. She is a member of INVOLVE and the Medical Research Council's Public Panel.

Marian Barnes is currently Professor of Social Policy at the University of Brighton. She has both researched and worked with service user and carer groups for over 20 years and has also studied public participation in different policy contexts.

Peter Beresford OBE Professor of Social Policy and Director of the Centre for Citizen Participation at Brunel University. He is also a long-term user of mental health services and chair of Shaping Our Lives, the national independent service user controlled organisation and network. He has a longstanding involvement in issues of participation and empowerment as writer, researcher, educator, service user and campaigner. He is a member of the Ministerial Reference Group for Adult Social Care, a trustee of the National Skills Academy for Social Care and a member of the Advisory Board of the National Institute for Health Research.

Jonathan Boote is employed by the National Institute for Health Research (NIHR) Research Design Service for Yorkshire and the Humber as a research fellow with particular responsibility for patient and public involvement, and has been involved in a programme of research on patient and public involvement at the University of Sheffield for the last 10 years. He is a member of the NIHR Stroke Research Network's Clinical Studies Group on Patient, Carer and Public Involvement, the Strategic Local Priority Group for Patient and Public Involvement in South Yorkshire, and invoNET.

Geraldine Brady is a senior research fellow at Coventry University in the Applied Research Centre in Sustainable Regeneration. Her substantive area of research has been a range of qualitative research, evaluation and training projects exploring the experiences of pregnant teenagers and young parents. Together with colleagues she has used visual methods to provide insight into the lives of young people and to challenge negative perceptions. Her interest in the experiences of children and young people began with her PhD, which explored perspectives of living with the diagnosis of attention deficit hyperactivity disorder (ADHD). Geraldine is keen to promote links between research, policy and practice, including encouraging reflection on the processes and decisions involved in research.

Louca–Mai Brady was a senior research officer at NCB Research Centre (www.ncb.org.uk/research) and is now a freelance research consultant specialising in research with children and young people and public involvement. She is a member of INVOLVE. Ellie Davis, Amrita Ghosh, Bhavika Surti and Laura Wilson were all members of the NCB PEAR young people's public health research group (www.ncb.org.uk/PEAR).

Fran Branfield has worked within the disability and service user movements for over 20 years. She has a strong track record of managing and undertaking research, evaluation and development work and has published many papers and project reports. For eight years, Fran was Director of Shaping Our Lives, a national service user and disabled people's network. Fran is an experienced diversity, accessibility and equality consultant, drawing on both her own personal experience of impairment and her academic background. At present she is Director of Cairn Community Partnerships Ltd, a consultancy that offers independent facilitation, accessible participation and stakeholder engagement.

Geraldine Brown is a research fellow at Coventry University. She has over 10 years' research experience, which has included undertaking research for the voluntary, community and public sector. Geraldine's research interests include health and social care policy and practice and community engagement and action. Her work has focused on the health and social care needs of teenage parents, black and minority ethnic communities and older people. Her particular focus has been consideration of mechanisms and processes that may contribute to these groups' exclusion and the effectiveness of efforts to challenge it. Geraldine's approach to research aims to promote the voices of those identified within public discourse as marginalised and/ or vulnerable in order to embed their experiences within research and in the development and implementation of policy and practice.

Cindy Cooper is a senior research fellow at the School of Health and Related Research (ScHARR) at the University of Sheffield and Director of the University of Sheffield Clinical Trials Research Unit. She is also chair of the Yorkshire and Humber Research for Patient Benefit (RfPB) Regional

Funding Committee. Cindy has interests in trials methodology, psychosocial aspects of chronic conditions and public involvement in research.

Phil Cotterell is a clinical nurse specialist in palliative care at St Catherine's Hospice, Crawley, West Sussex and a visiting senior research fellow in the Macmillan Survivorship Research Group (MSRG), Faculty of Health Sciences at the University of Southampton. He has a nursing background and his research interests are in cancer survivorship; service user involvement and social movements; and palliative and end of life care practice and provision. He has conducted research with many service user colleagues using a participatory approach examining the nature and impact of service user involvement, is a member of the Central South Coast Cancer Network's Cancer Research Partnership Group, invoNET and is involved with developing service user involvement in the MSRG.

Joe Duffy is a lecturer in social work at Queen's University, Belfast. Joe has a special interest in the area of service user and carer involvement in social work education and public services more broadly. He has coordinated several funded projects that have culminated in the publication of good practice guidance on service user involvement in social work education for both undergraduate and post-qualifying levels in Northern Ireland and he has published guidance on the incorporation of the service user perspective more generally in health and social care contexts. Joe is also particularly interested in creative and innovative approaches to service user and carer involvement in social work education.

Clare Evans MBE is a disabled person and registered social worker now working as an independent disability equality and social care consultant. She was founder and first Director of the Wiltshire and Swindon Users Network from 1991and first chair of the Wiltshire Centre for Independent Living in 2005. She has published widely on user involvement and independent living and has directed three user-controlled research projects.

Michelle Farr is a PhD candidate in the Department of Social and Policy Sciences at the University of Bath. Her research focuses on how employees and service users can work collaboratively to improve public service provision. Previous to her PhD she undertook research projects in the NHS and in community involvement. She has worked extensively within the voluntary sector on environmental community projects, within mental health services and with young people.

Beatrice Gahagan has spent over 14 years as a senior manager at Age Concern Brighton, Hove and Portslade, developing and managing services, quality assurance, training, policy development and research. She has undertaken several joint projects with the University of Brighton and is currently engaged in a partnership research project involving older people in research. Prior to working for Age Concern she did a degree in psychology and a doctorate in the significance of nature as a unique aesthetic realm. She is a Chartered Psychologist and Associate Fellow of the British Psychological Society.

Colin Gell has been involved with the user movement since 1986, initially in Nottingham where the first Patients' Councils were established. Later on he worked in most areas of Great Britain, using the experiences of Nottingham people to help new user organisations to develop. He has worked with local, regional and national organisations to establish user-led projects and statutory organisations such as the National Institute for Mental Health in England (NIMH-E), King's College London and others. Colin has had links with the Sainsbury Centre for Mental Health, the King's Fund, the University of Birmingham, where the successful Suresearch network was established, and the University of Nottingham among many others. Recently he worked with Leicestershire Partnership Trust to develop an Involvement Centre for users and carers and has helped register a social enterprise, Inspired(2009)CIC for users and carers providing training for mental health and other workers.

Andy Gibson is Research Fellow in Patient and Public Involvement (PPI) with the Peninsula Collaboration for Leadership in Applied Health Research and Care (PenCLAHRC) where he has responsibility for developing PPI within all their activities. He has experience of evaluating user involvement in a number of contexts and he previously worked at the Department of Health-funded National Centre for Involvement at Warwick University. He also has experience of coordinating user involvement in research and teaching in the School of Health and Social Studies at Warwick University. His other research interests lie in the area of lay perspectives on health inequalities. His research in this area has drawn on the work of Bourdieu to explore the relationship between health, social status and social capital from the perspective of people living in a 'deprived' community.

Steve Gillard is a senior lecturer in social and community mental health at St George's, University of London with a longstanding interest in supporting and evaluating service user involvement in research. Steve has a background as a mental health researcher in the voluntary sector where he also managed mental health day services. His research has focused on service user experiences of treatment, and on service user involvement in the development and delivery of mental health services. Recent projects have evaluated support for self-care and peer support in mental health services.

Sandy Herron-Marx is currently working as an independent research consultant across a range of European and international universities and patient groups and organisations. Her research focuses on evaluating the effectiveness and efficacy of diverse methods of involvement and the short-term and long-term impact of involvement across a wide range of long-term health conditions. She works with European and international nursing organisations to identify and evaluate opportunities for building capacity and capability for involvement within nurse education, nursing research and nursing practice.

Ray Jones is Professor of Social Work at Kingston University and St George's, University of London. A registered social worker, from 1992 to 2006 he was Director of Social Services in Wiltshire. He is a past chair of the British Association of Social Workers, former Chief Executive of the Social Care Institute for Excellence, and was chair of the Association of Directors of Social Services Disability Network.

Robert Kirkwood is currently employed by Sussex Partnership NHS Foundation Trust where he works within the Child and Adolescent Mental Health Service as both an occupational therapist and a primary mental health worker. Academically, Robert is working towards the completion of a doctorate in occupational therapy at the University of Brighton. His interest in Deaf issues first developed through learning British Sign Language at evening classes while working at a nursing home for disabled young people where some signing was used.

Graham P. Martin is Senior Lecturer in Social Science applied to Health at the University of Leicester. He completed his PhD, on service user involvement in the development of cancer genetics services, at the University of Nottingham, and his research interests cover both patient and public involvement in health, and more general issues of policy, management and organisational change in healthcare. More information on Graham's work can be found at http://leicester.academia.edu/GrahamMartin/

Brendan McKeever draws on his personal experience as a user in the development of user involvement issues. In a professional capacity this knowledge and experience was widened when he led the Family Information Group in Derry, which for 10 years raised issues that affected families of disabled children. As a council member of the Northern Ireland Social Care Council, the regulatory body for social work and social care, for eight years, Brendan gained a strategic insight into social work/care issues. Currently, Brendan works on a part-time occasional basis with Queen's University, University of Ulster (Magee Campus) and Belfast Metropolitan College on a range of user issues. Brendan has written and researched extensively on user and disability issues.

Stephanie McKinley has been the Lead for Service User Involvement in the South London and Maudsley Trust for the last nine years where she has worked tirelessly to promote and strengthen the voice of adult service users – particularly in the field of training. A service user herself, in partnership with another colleague, she set up a service user-led training service: SUITE (Service Users in Training and Education). She has contributed to good practice guides for the education sector as well as presented at various conferences, including internationally. She is the developer of the Changing Minds programme. Since 2009 she has been a member of the Lived Experience Advisory Panel for the National Anti Stigma campaign – Time to Change.

Carole Mockford is a senior research fellow at the University of Warwick. She is currently employed by the Royal College of Nursing Research Institute, based in the School of Health and Social Studies. She was previously a member of a research team at the National Centre of Involvement who conducted a systematic review on the impact of patient and public involvement on healthcare services.

Carolyn Morris is a cancer patient, diagnosed in 1999 and 2009. She is active as a user in local and national cancer services and research and is currently a member of Sussex Cancer Network's Partnership and Research Steering Groups, the National Cancer Research Network Strategy Group for Impact, Compass Research Collaborative's core consumer involvement group and the National Collaborating Centre for Cancer Board. She has worked on evaluations of user involvement for the UK Clinical Research Collaboration and British Paediatric Surveillance Unit, and was a co-researcher on a study focused on the impact of being involved, funded by Macmillan Cancer Support.

Glenys Parry is Professor of Psychological Services Research at the University of Sheffield, School of Health and Related Research and a Consultant Clinical Psychologist and Psychotherapist at the Sheffield Health and Social Care NHS Foundation Trust. She has a longstanding interest in the effective application of research to practice and has led or contributed to a number of Department of Health policy initiatives in psychological therapies. Recent research includes an evaluation of the new model of psychological service delivery, 'Improving Access to Psychological Therapies', and an investigation into research-based methods of improving the quality and effectiveness of psychological services for people with long-term depression.

Rachel Purtell is the Folk.us Director with day-to-day responsibility for Folk.us. This role ensures that service users, patients and carers are able to have a positive and meaningful impact on research, and the structures and processes that support research in health and social care. Rachel works with many people, including people with learning difficulties, people who experience mental distress, people with physical and/or sensory impairments, older people and people who are long-term users of the NHS. Rachel is a freelance trainer in disability equality issues using a social model approach. She holds an MA in disability studies. She has a background in working for inclusive service user-led organisations and delivers training. Rachel is a disabled woman, a disability activist and a service user.

Rebecca Putz gained her Master's degree in public health in 2008. She was a research assistant at the National Centre for Involvement in 2008 and 2009, conducting the National Survey on Patient and Public Involvement for 2009. Her research areas include risk-taking behaviours, health promotion and public mental health. She is currently a PhD student in the Medical School at the University of Warwick, studying the impact of mental wellbeing in community health interventions.

Wendy Rickard is the Folk.us Research Fellow, helping service users, patients and carers to develop research projects that change the culture in which research is produced. Wendy is currently based in the Peninsula School of Medicine and Dentistry at the University of Exeter. Her background was in public health as an associate director of the Institute of Primary Care and Public Health at London South Bank University, where she was Reader in Public Health Research. She also worked closely with the British Library Sound Archive on projects with people with HIV, sex workers, homeless people and other groups.

Patsy Staddon is both a sociologist and an 'ex-alcoholic'. She was awarded her PhD, '"Making whoopee?" An exploration of understandings and responses around women's alcohol use' in August 2009 at the age of 65, which she explains by the years of fieldwork required at a younger age. She is currently editing a book and completing journal articles and book chapters. She is also a Visiting Fellow at the University of Plymouth, a research associate at the University of the West of England and a Director of Shaping Our

Lives, the national service user controlled organisation that campaigns for a social approach to disablement, mental health and substance use issues.

Sophie Staniszewska leads a programme of research on patient and public involvement and patient experiences at the Royal College of Nursing Research Institute, School of Health and Social Studies at the University of Warwick (www2.warwick.ac.uk/fac/soc/shss/rcn/research). She chairs the Evidence, Knowledge and Learning Group of INVOLVE and is a member of the Main Group of INVOLVE. She also chairs the NICE Patient Experiences Guideline Group. Sophie is on the steering group of the Health Technology Assessment International (HTAi) Interest Group for Patient and Citizen Involvement in HTA and a core member of the Working Group on Methods and Impact. Sophie is also a member of the Public Health, Health Services and Primary Care sub-panel of the Research Excellence Framework 2014.

Survivors History Group is an independent survivor-led organisation established in April 2005 to promote the understanding and valuing of the history of action by service users/survivors and their organisations and to work towards the creation of an archive. Members include many who have a long personal history in the movement and who took an active part in writing the group's chapter in this book. These include (among many others) Frank Bangay, organiser of gigs for PROMPT and CAPO and a founder of Survivors Poetry (1991); Anne Plumb, survivor archivist of the movement; Peter Campbell, ex-secretary of Survivors Speak Out, and another founder of Survivors Poetry; Louise Pembroke, founder of the National Self-Harm Network; Clare Ockwell, a pioneer of anorexia research and service user training; Angela Sweeney and other authors of the book *This is survivor research* (2009); and Phil Ruthen of CoolTan Arts. Andrew Roberts, the group secretary and chapter editor, is based at 177 Glenarm Road, London, E5 0NB.

Kati Turner has worked as a service user researcher in the Population Health Sciences and Education Department at St George's, University of London, since 2005, on a variety of different research projects. As part of her role she helped to set up and coordinates the PEER (Peer Expertise in Education and Research) Group, made up of service users interested in contributing to research and education undertaken by the department. Kati has a particular interest in service user involvement and collaborative partnerships and the impact of these on the research process and findings. She is also chair of the service user-led organisation, Emergence, and undertakes freelance work for them and for other organisations such as INVOLVE.

Lizzie Ward is a research fellow in the School of Applied Social Sciences, University of Brighton. Prior to returning to higher education, she worked for over 12 years in the voluntary sector. Her research interests include age and ageing, participatory research and experiential knowledge and care ethics.

Corinne Wilson is a senior lecturer in sociology at Coventry University. Corinne's research interests are focused around the inclusion and promotion of the voices of those who are excluded from traditional approaches and she has worked with young women exploring their experiences of pregnancy and motherhood for the past decade. As a feminist sociologist she is particularly interested in exploring methodological approaches and their accompanying epistemologies.

Katrina Wyatt is a senior research fellow in child health at the Peninsula Medical School. She holds the grant for Folk.us, a Department of Health-funded research programme aimed at securing meaningful service user, patient and carer involvement in research and development. She is also joint lead on a Research Council grant looking at community engagement with research and the role of complexity theory to understand the nature of these relations. Katrina has been involved in several different health service research projects over many years using a variety of research methods, from systematic reviews and randomised controlled trials to longitudinal qualitative research methods, all of which involve service users and carers as partners in the research.

Philippa Yeeles is Deputy Director of INVOLVE (www.invo.org.uk). INVOLVE is funded by the National Institute for Health Research (NIHR) to support public involvement in NHS, public health and social care research. Prior to this, Philippa was joint Director of Operations at the UK Clinical Research Collaboration where she facilitated a programme of public involvement activities (www.ukcrc.org/patientsandpublic/ppi/). Philippa's interest in public involvement in research developed from her experience as a social worker supporting mental health service users to influence and challenge the provision of local services.

Sarah Yiannoullou has been the manager of the National Survivor User Network since March 2009. Her previous experience has included work in the arts, learning disability services, youth services and mental health. Due to her own personal experiences, Sarah has been particularly active in service user/survivor-led initiatives and continues to promote the direct voice of people with experience of distress and service use in the development of policy and service design.

Introduction

From margin to mainstream

Marian Barnes and Phil Cotterell

In this chapter we trace the history of user involvement in health and social care, considering both official initiatives to 'invite' service users and citizens to take part in policy and service delivery processes, and autonomous action by service users and citizen groups to have their voices heard. This will inevitably be a brief and selective history. The aim is to provide some context within which the contributions that comprise the body of this book can be located.

Involving users, patients and the public

Official policy relating to user involvement in health and social care can be traced back to at least the early 1970s. In 1974, community health councils (CHCs) were created in order to represent the 'public interest' in health and health services. They remained in existence until 2002. During their life there were a number of studies that highlighted aspects of their strengths and weaknesses, including the range of functions they fulfilled (such as supporting complaints and undertaking general monitoring of health services) (Insight, 1996). Their limitations as bodies that could 'represent' either the public or specific publics, their ambiguous position vis-à-vis their insider/outsider status within the National Health Service (NHS) and the fact that their composition did not enable them to claim that they were a voice of many of those who use health services, contributed to a growing movement throughout the 1980s and 1990s to develop different and better means of giving a voice to service users within the NHS. CHCs never had a remit for local authority social care services.

The emergence of consumerist ideas during the 1980s affected the public sector in general and the NHS and local authority social care services in particular. The 1988 Griffiths Report (Griffiths, 1988) encouraged the use of market research and consumer satisfaction surveys to assess how well the NHS was meeting the needs and wishes of its customers. By 1990, the influence of what was known as 'new right' thinking resulted in proposals to separate out purchasers from providers in order to increase patient and user choice. The NHS and Community Care Act 1990 introduced the internal market into the NHS, required local authorities to consult over community care plans and also encouraged user involvement in the process of community care assessments. This prompted a number of local authority social services departments to develop initiatives to achieve 'user and carer centered community care' (Goss and Miller, 1995, p 4). The Joseph Rowntree Foundation-funded project *From margin to mainstream* (Goss and Miller, 1995) was intended to support, explore and disseminate good practice in this respect. Similarly, the Birmingham Community Care Special Action Project (CCSAP) sought to embed user and carer involvement in decision-making processes across the local authority and health authorities (see Barnes, 1997a). Prior to the passage of the 1990 Act, the Welsh Office had pioneered 'consumer' participation at all levels in the planning and management of services in the context of the All Wales Strategy for Mental Handicap (using the terminology of the time) (McGrath, 1989).

In 1992, the NHS Management Executive (NHSME, 1992) exhorted healthcare purchasers to become 'champions of the people' by involving them in decisions about what services to purchase (Lupton et al, 1998). An early study of initiatives arising from this identified:

- ways in which public expectations of healthcare provision had been changed through education and public awareness programmes;
- approaches to public participation in priority setting;
- interactive audit of services;
- ways in which the public were being involved in developing core service values;
- ways in which public participation was challenging traditional orthodoxies regarding the nature of services (Heginbotham, 1992).

Health authorities developed a variety of ways of involving local people in determining health needs, setting priorities and acting to improve health and reducing health inequalities (Barnes, 1997b). During the same period, other initiatives were being pursued that were focused on the delivery of health services. The Patient's Charter introduced procedural rights for patients, set standards and published league tables intended to make public levels of performance as a means of increasing accountability. A 'patient subgroup' of the Clinical Outcomes Group was commissioned by the Department of Health to develop good practice in monitoring, evaluating and auditing services and their outcomes throughout the NHS (Kelson, 1995). Individual hospital trusts were developing patients' councils, and so were some general practitioner (GP) practices (eg Brown, 1994). And community development principles were starting to influence thinking about a more broadly based health and wellbeing approach to delivering healthcare (Gaskin and Vincent, 1996).

These developments were given strategic direction by the NHS Executive Patient Partnership Strategy in 1996. This recognised the need for action at a national as well as a local level if the aspirations for change resulting from patient involvement were to be achieved. As its name implies, its focus was on health rather than social care services and in the social care context developments continued to be driven by local rather than national initiatives. Proposals for action at a national level included:

- establishing a central resource to facilitate the production of accessible information for patients;
- providing a resource to support lay people's involvement in national work;
- discussing with royal colleges and others involved in training professionals and managers ways in which the principles of patient partnership could be included within education and training;
- taking forward the Department of Health's work on research and development issues relating to patient participation.

The latter point marked the establishment of another national group that has had an important impact on ways in which user involvement has developed. In 1996, the Standing Advisory Group on Consumer Involvement in the NHS Research and Development Programme was established. This was subsequently called INVOLVE. This led to the publication in 2000 of guidance notes for health researchers about how best to involve members of the public in the research process (Hanley et al, 2000), with a second edition in 2003 that also included social care research. What is now referred to as 'patient and public involvement' in research is now official policy across the range of NHS and social care research funding programmes.

The election of the first New Labour government in 1997 saw an increase in the pace of policy action intended to secure greater involvement of both users of health services (patients) and citizens in general – the 'public'. Structural changes within the NHS meant that primary care groups (PCGs) took over from health authorities as the bodies with main responsibility for health service commissioning at a local level. But PCGs and later primary care trusts were required to have clear arrangements for public involvement. Initiatives designed to improve health and reduce health inequalities (such as Health Action Zones; see Barnes et al, 2005) were also expected to deliver their objectives not only via cross-sectoral partnerships, but also via 'empowering people and giving them the tools to take greater responsibility for their own health' and 'developing strategy and appropriate structures for involving the public on a continuing basis in partnerships for improving health and for monitoring services' (NHSE, 1997, pp 4-5).

One of the tools intended to enable individuals to take responsibility for their own health was the Expert Patients programme. This resulted from a task force that was set up in 1999 and chaired by the then chief medical officer, Sir Liam Donaldson. In 2001, *The expert patient: A new approach to chronic disease management for the 21st century* (DH, 2001b) was published and since then a major industry of self-management programmes has developed to support people who live with long-term medical conditions, with the objectives of increasing their confidence, improving their quality of life and enabling them to better manage their conditions.

By the early 21st century, patient and public involvement had become a duty. The Health and Social Care Act 2001 placed a duty on all NHS organisations to involve patients and the public in planning services, proposals for changes to services and decisions that affect how services operate. A year later, CHCs were abolished and a quasi-independent national Commission for Patient and Public Involvement in Health (CPPIH) was established with local branches attached to every NHS trust. These Patient and Public Involvement Forums (PPI Forums) comprised members appointed by regional offices of CPPIH. Their remit was defined by CPPIH and they had powers relating to accessing and inspecting health services, the right to receive information and the right to refer matters of concerns to Local Authority Overview and Scrutiny Committees and other bodies with the power to scrutinise health services. But they did not last long. In 2007, the Local Government and Public Involvement in Health Act abolished PPI Forums and introduced a statutory duty to involve the public in health issues via the creation of Local Involvement Networks (LINks). These were intended to be more inclusive networks of groups that would gather views and experiences of people in relation not only to health services but also to local authority social care services. But following the creation of the coalition government in 2010, LINks went the way of PPI Forums. In their place it was proposed that 'Healthwatch' organisations would be created, described as a 'citizen's advice bureau for health and social care' (www.dh.gov.uk/en/MediaCentre/Pressreleases/DH_117722).

Most of the developments within the NHS have sought to bring patients and the public into involvement initiatives that are part of the NHS itself. One interpretation of the frequent changes in systems for PPI is that this has been a search for ways of managing such involvement in the context of a highly centralised system. However, the move to LINks suggested that there may have been more recognition of the value of accessing knowledge and perspectives from those outside the healthcare system. Local authorities commissioned third sector organisations to coordinate these networks and 'user involvement' initiatives within the social care system were recognised as a potential source of learning of 'how to do' participation. Voluntary and community groups were also seen as potential ways of accessing the experiences and views of different publics and patient groups in this context. Unlike the centrally determined process and mechanism for establishing

PPI Forums, no mandatory structure was proposed for LINks. It is too early to tell how Healthwatch organisations are likely to operate, although they are intended to retain (and perhaps strengthen) the link between participation in health and social care services and, in rhetoric at least, they are intended to contribute to the local democratic accountability of services via commissioning by local government.

The establishment of the first foundation trusts in 2004 provided another and different context for PPI. One purpose of the foundation trust model was to enhance the local accountability of NHS services. Local people can become members of the trust, have the right to elect representatives on the board of governors and through this role have an influence on its policies and services. Members are divided into three constituencies:

- *the public:* people who live in the trust's area and either have applied for membership or are patients who have been invited by the trust to become public members and have not declined;
- *patients:* people who are or have been patients and either have applied for membership or have been invited by the trust to become patient members and have not declined;
- *staff:* people who work for the trust, including contractors and volunteers.

This process was originally intended to give some sense of a foundation trust being 'owned' by its members and government had originally conceived that ownership would be along a limited liability model, with members being liable for a £1 contribution in the event that the trust became insolvent. This proposal was not implemented, and thus membership imposes no obligations on individuals. The intended expansion of the foundation trust model under the coalition government implies an extension of this context for public involvement in health service decision making.

In addition to these initiatives that were focused primarily on adults who were or might be users of health and social care services, the late 1990s saw legislative commitment to enabling children and young people to have a say about education, health and social services and about their local neighbourhoods (Spicer and Evans, 2005). For example, the cross-departmental Children and Young People's Unit (CYPU) identified children's participation as part of its core strategy: 'the Government wants children and young people to have more opportunities to get involved in the design, provision and evaluation of policies and services that affect them or which they use' (CYPU, 2001, p 2), and defined participation as one of the key principles underpinning the Children's Fund, an initiative launched in 2000 to address social exclusion among children aged five to 13. The involvement of children and young people has been supported via 'Participation Works', a national partnership of agencies that offers information, training and consultancy (www.participationworks.org.uk/).

Other initiatives have focused on older people – not only those who are active users of services, but also older citizens generally. A key initiative was the Better Government for Older People initiative, which ran for 10 years from 1998 to 2008 (Hayden and Boaz, 2000). This resulted in numerous local initiatives for involving older people. At a local level, Older People's Forums and Councils have developed to give older people a voice in health and other services and policies (Barnes, 2005; Barnes et al, 2011). Many of these are supported if not initiated by local authorities and local health organisations in order to provide a focus for consultation with older people.

User movements and patient organisations

The development of user involvement in health and social care cannot be recounted solely as a narrative of official initiatives to give patients, service users and citizens a say in policy and service delivery. Throughout this period, patients' groups, user and carer groups and local community groups have also organised separately, claimed the right to a voice and influenced both policy and practice. They have also pursued other objectives not directly related to health and social care policy and services.

These groups include those who organise on the basis of specific 'conditions': cancer or arthritis for example; umbrella organisations with a broader remit, such as the Long-Term Medical Conditions Alliance; those that relate to specific experiences that are not defined in term of illness, such as women who have experienced sexual abuse, groups that focus on reproductive health issues, carers or people who hear voices; those who identify themselves as part of a broader disability movement; and community-based groups whose focus is on health inequalities and the availability and quality of generic health services.

Baggott et al (2005) have studied a range of such groups, considering variations in political stance, preparedness to work with public officials or to take oppositional positions, their national or local focus, and their size and resources. Some have prioritised advocacy (individual and collective) or political campaigning, others have provided a focus for sharing and exploring experiences, others have developed alternative models of service delivery (such as Independent Living Centres) and some have focused on what can be achieved through user-led research and training. Barnes (2009) has suggested that action among service users and carers is collectively characterised not only by diversity, but also by the challenge they offer to notions of professional expertise and knowledge, the significance of networks between groups that enhance their capacity for influence, and the values that underpin their activities: 'User and carer movements pose questions about the way in which we live together and how we regard fellow citizens. Thus their objectives cannot be understood solely in terms of the production of more sensitive or appropriate services, but concern much broader issues of personal and social life' (Barnes, 2009, p 226).

Both researchers and activists have considered the significance of the collective challenge posed by user groups as evidence that they constitute a social movement or movements (Campbell and Oliver, 1996; Barnes and Bowl, 2001; Kelleher, 2001). For example, one of the most significant impacts of the disabled people's movement has been the refashioning of concepts of disability and the articulation of the social model of disability. This offers an alternative way of viewing disability and disabled people. Instead of disabled people and their impairments being seen as a 'personal tragedy', the social model has enabled disability to be seen as 'culturally produced through the relationship between the mode of production and the central values of the society concerned' (Oliver, 1990, p 23). The social model resulted in a consciousness shift in many disabled people as a consequence of people 'focusing on disabling environments rather than individual impairments' and this 'freed up disabled people's hearts and minds by offering an alternative conceptualisation of the problem' (Campbell and Oliver, 1996, p 20). The impact of taking part in social movement action has both personal and political value, which can be of particular significance for people whose identity and self-esteem have been undermined by the way they are treated – within the health and social care system and more generally (Taylor, 2000; Barnes and Bowl, 2001).

While patient and user groups have different priorities and many groups have fiercely defended their independence from service providers, it is rare for them to refuse to take up opportunities to seek influence that have been created by the official acceptance of patient and public participation. While official discourse often describes such relationships as 'partnerships', experience suggests that this is a problematic notion (Barnes et al, 1999, see also Chapters Two and Four, this volume). The tension between user-led and officially determined participation initiatives has been a feature of 'user involvement' throughout the period we have briefly documented here and this is one of the issues that motivated the conference on which this collection is based. There are a number of aspects to this in addition to the contested notion of partnership that we can simply highlight here:

- action that reflects consumerist ideology and that which promotes the citizenship of disabled people and other service users (Beresford and Croft, 1993);
- multiple sites for participation and choices to be made about where to focus efforts (Barnes, 1999);
- official denigration of user voices by labelling them 'professional users';

- the emotion issue – officially sanctioned ways of deliberating that rule emotions 'out of order' and can make it hard for users to take part (Church, 1996; Barnes, 2008b).

By the mid-2000s, 'user-led organisations' had been officially recognised as key players in the process of delivery of personalisation: 'By 2010 each locality (defined as that area covered by a Council with social services responsibilities) should have a user led organisation modelled on existing Centres for Independent Living' (PMSU, 2005, recommendation 4.3). User-led organisations were given financial support and offered opportunities to take part in capacity-building initiatives. They support disabled people who are in receipt of direct payments or individual budgets and are thus a part of the service delivery system. This is a far cry from the direct action that has been taken by some disabled people and from the explicitly subversive actions of those engaged in, for example, Mad Pride (http://madpride.org.uk/index.php). It demonstrates the success of user organisations in their claims for recognition as legitimate participants in service delivery, but does this also imply a softening of the radical edge of user organisations?

Which identity?

This summary has started to distinguish the different ways in which people who use health and/or social care services might be identified or identify themselves through what we are calling 'user involvement':

- as consumers or users of specialist health and social care services;
- as citizens with rights to fair and equal treatment;
- as experts in their own lives, the conditions they experience and the management of their own treatment;
- as partners in the design and delivery of services;
- as 'ordinary people' (Martin, 2008a) who can bring a lay perspective to health policy making;
- as political activists;
- as researchers involved in the generation of new knowledges.

Here we address some of the complex issues concerning the language of what we have called 'user involvement'.

The language of involvement is wide ranging, confusing and at times seemingly contradictory. Nearly two decades ago, a call for clarification of its meaning was made (Beresford, 1992, p 16). Lindow and Morris (1995, p 1) described a 'service user' as a person who needs some kind of support to live in the community and 'user involvement' in terms of their participation in decisions that affect how much and what kind of support they receive.

Carers, family members, friends and neighbours are also defined as potential service users in their definition and Kelson (1997, p 2) added patient representatives and taxpayers to this list. Language is not neutral and early on an important distinction was made between terms that identified people by reference to their relationship with services (user, consumer, patient) and those that reflected people's identities beyond this. The preferred term here was often 'citizen'.

The term 'service user' requires definition in each context that it is employed to describe. How people 'use' services looks very different if we are considering the occasional visit to a GP by someone who generally experiences good health; the intensive interactions with a range of services that a severely disabled child and their carers will experience; and the experience of compulsory detention in a hospital of someone who has a diagnosis of mental illness. Our use of the term in this book is intended to describe the involvement of people who receive or who are eligible to receive health and social care services and their carers who may be family or close friends. We adopt it because of its broad descriptive utility, while recognising its partial and limited connotations.

One limitation of the term 'user' is that it has a rather passive connotation, but the term 'consumer' carries with it often unacceptable connotations of 'shopping around' in the commercial sector. As we have noted, its adoption was associated with the introduction of markets to the public sector and was intended to emphasise a more active, choice-making relationship between those who provided and those who received services. Official participation discourses within the NHS identify patients as users whose voices should be listened to in order to ensure responsive services. They are not grateful recipients of whatever is offered by a service free at the point of delivery, but rather consumers whose expectations have been raised about the standard of care and treatment. But as a man with experience of psychiatric services quoted by Beresford and Croft (1993, p xv) argued, '[p]eople who use mental health services are no more consumers than wood lice are of Rentokil'. As a consumer a person can choose from a range of services and influence the market via their purchasing power. But many people needing to utilise health and social care services do not have the range of choice available to them and it is not usually a case of taking trade elsewhere. Direct payments or individual budgets are intended to promote opportunities for choice and this might be considered to mark the dominance of consumerist ideas in relation to the ways in which users of services should exercise control over them. For the most part, however, individual service users, although able to take advantage of limited choice and redress in health and social care, cannot tackle wider social exclusion or inequalities of service provision in this way. This suggests that broader-based collective action continues to be an important part of 'user involvement.'

Hanley et al (2000, p 1), in reference to user involvement in research, point out that we are all potential consumers. We all use health services at some point in our lives, we may need support from social care services when we become old and we may find ourselves caring for a disabled friend or relative. However, at the point of service use, the distinction between provider and service user or carer is usually very clear.

But many have preferred to think of initiatives that give a voice to actual or potential users of services as addressing them as citizens. Heater (1999, p 4) distinguished two traditions of citizenship: 'the civic republican style, which places its stress on duties, and the liberal style, which emphasises rights'. He suggested that it was the liberal style with its focus on citizens' rights that was predominant during the 1990s, although New Labour's promotion of 'empowerment' in a variety of contexts linked participation with 'active' or 'responsible' citizenship. The contemporary understanding of what it is to be a citizen invokes notions of rights *and* of responsibilities and duties – including the responsibility to look after one's own health and to take up opportunities to take part in consultations about public services.

Beresford and Croft (1993, p 25) argued that ideas of citizenship can be used to highlight 'people's exclusions and of giving force to arguments and campaigns for their *involvement*'. A focus on people who use services as citizens highlights not only their relationships with the services that they have a right to receive, but also their identity as participants within the society in which they live (Sayce, 2000). Thus, strategies adopted by user groups that are framed within a citizenship discourse are concerned with the relationship between individuals, the state and civil society as well as relationships in the context of service provision and use. They potentially have a more wide-reaching impact than strategies focused on specific services.

In the context of official initiatives from within the NHS, the dual identities of 'patient' and 'member of the public' are acknowledged in the various ways in which potential participants are targeted for involvement (DH, 2001e). 'The public' in general is acknowledged as having an interest in the way in which the NHS develops and citizens as taxpayers and as beneficiaries of publicly funded healthcare are recognised as wanting to have their say about priorities and developments. 'Citizens who have tended to be excluded by poverty, disability and ethnicity deserve particular support in this respect' (DH, 2001e, para 5.11). More collective identities are also summoned: 'communities' are the focus of much action to engage people in relation to health improvement initiatives, while different types of 'public' are evoked in relation to, for example, membership of foundation trusts and lay reviewers of research proposals submitted to National Institute for Health Research (NIHR) programmes.

Claiming the right to define themselves and the nature of the difficulties they face was a key aim of disabled people and people who live with mental health problems in the early stages of these movements. In some instances, derogatory language has been deliberately reclaimed as a means of challenging both professional and public perceptions. For example, Russell (1998) produced a 'Manifesto of an uppity crip' in which she called for participatory democracy at every level. For carers, collective action was a means to creating a distinct identity, and encouraging people to claim that identity remains a key objective of the carers movement: both as a means of ensuring that people can recognise and access benefits and resources to which they are entitled and to make a more collective case about the contribution of carers:

Step one:

Remember you're a carer!

Recognising yourself as a carer is the very first step to getting the support you need. Many of us do not see ourselves as carers straight away: we are mums and dads, husbands, wives, partners, brothers, sisters, friends and neighbours. We are simply doing what anyone would, caring unpaid for a loved one or friend, helping them through when they are unable to do things for themselves. The fact is that you are also a carer, and there are things that you need to know. No one likes to be labelled, but recognising yourself as a carer can be the gateway to getting a range of help and support. (www.carersuk.org/Information/Newtocaring)

Thus, when we think about the language that is used to describe 'user involvement', it is important to be conscious of the purpose this serves, and to recognise that language is one of the sites of struggle in the power relations between those who provide and those who use health and social care services.

Conclusion

This introduction has simply sketched the history and the terrain that this collection seeks to explore. What was radical in the 1980s is now a well-established part of the health and social care system. The aim of the event at which most of the chapters in this book were initially presented was to adopt a critical perspective on user involvement, questioning whether it has achieved the transformations and aspirations claimed for it, but also asking some more fundamental questions about the assumptions on which it is based and what this suggests about how both welfare and wellbeing may be achieved.

From the start there have been critiques of the different ideological positions taken on this issue and questions have been asked about whether it actually makes a real difference to the services people get and their experiences of them. But initially contentions between those adopting consumerist or rights/empowerment approaches were constructed in the context of struggles and campaigns to gain a voice for users in the face of professional and bureaucratic resistance. One perspective is that this struggle has been won and user groups and movements are now confronted with the consequences faced by other successful social movements in terms of an official co-option and possible corruption of their objectives (cf Lovenduski and Randall, 1993). But as the contributions to this volume make clear, there are many different perspectives, understandings and interpretations of user involvement, what it means and what it has achieved. One aim of this collection is to contribute to a better understanding those differences and what we can learn from them.

We have structured contributions in terms of their focus on 'the movement', on action within services, and contributions that reflect on user involvement in research – a process that seeks to both generate new knowledges and change the relations of knowledge production. In each case, we offer a short introduction to the issues and the contributions and conclude by highlighting questions arising from these.

Part One

Introduction: user movements

Marian Barnes and Phil Cotterell

We start this collection with contributions that take different approaches to understanding the nature and significance of collective action among service users themselves, independently of any action to encourage or invite their contribution by public officials and service deliverers. As we suggested in the Introduction, it has sometimes been hard to draw a clear line between autonomous action by service users and official involvement initiatives because official initiatives have led to 'organised' users being invited to take part. Indeed, it has often been the case that involvement has been made possible because service users have developed confidence by taking part in their own organisations and have been supported by their peers in getting involved in officially-led initiatives. This has been particularly important for those users who have previously been regarded as incompetent to have a say on their own behalf – such as people with learning disabilities and those who live with mental health problems. But for all groups, the opportunity to develop their own analysis and ideas separately from service providers can strengthen their capacity to come up with alternative ideas, rather than simply respond to officially-determined agendas (see Barnes and Bennett, 1998, for an example relating to older people).

Thus, one perspective is that self-organisation has enabled official user involvement initiatives to succeed. It has provided a location in which service users can collectively articulate their experiences, and explore responses and solutions to the problems they encounter. It provides spaces in which people can experiment with their voices and can plan and prepare to enter into dialogue with officials who can exert considerable power over their lives. And it provides an easily accessible group that officials can turn to when they want to consult.

Service users offer practical and psychosocial support to each other through independent organisation. For example, one group of mental health service users that organised specifically to provide mental health awareness training to mental health workers and others, developed a way of working that recognised that there would be times when the user-trainers may not be able to deliver a training programme because they were too unwell. Thus, they always planned training sessions with an 'understudy', ready to take on the work if a colleague was unable to do so. This practical response based in a close understanding of the experience of living with mental health difficulties not only minimised the likelihood that training sessions might need to be cancelled, but also provided psychological support to those carrying out the work because they shared the development of the training with a peer, and were not subject to the pressure of knowing that if they were unwell the training would not take place and perceptions of the 'unreliableness' of people with mental health problems would be reinforced. This group effectively modelled the sort of support that mental health service users value in the way they worked with each other.

The personal growth that comes from developing skills as trainers, as researchers, as contributors to the development of a collective voice has been vital to the growth of service user movements and reflects experiences in other social movements of people who have been marginalised or stigmatised (eg Taylor, 2000). Thus, another way of understanding the significance of user-led action is the impact it has had on those people who have become members of user groups – both individually and collectively. People have gained recognition and a sense of self-worth, and developed skills that can be applied in speaking on their own and peers' behalf and in other contexts (Barnes and Gell, Chapter Two). Collectively, this has challenged the way in which disabled people, older people and others whose identities have often been constructed around their use of health or welfare services are seen by the rest of society. Claiming the right to identify *themselves* has been an important objective of user movements and this is illustrated in the importance attached to claiming the right to tell their own history of that movement (Survivors History Group, Chapter One).

Ultimately, such groups are about seeking changes in health and welfare services, in social relations generally and in realising equal rights as citizens. Thus, although members may experience direct benefit from taking part within the user movement, a collective sense of the possibility of change is important to sustaining action. At both local and national levels, organisations such as People First, which promotes and supports self-advocacy for people with learning disabilities, the National Survivor User Network of people with mental health problems, the National Centre for Independent Living and local independent living networks provide a collective focus for action that gives service users a voice in policy making and service delivery, and which champions their rights as citizens. As Beresford and Branfield (Chapter Three) describe, many different groups of service users have found it valuable to come together to share common experiences and maximise the possibility for change. Collective action is intended to make a difference to the way in which users are treated in their day-to-day interactions with services, *and* to the way they can live their lives beyond health and social care services.

Throughout the development of user involvement as policy and practice, there have been tensions between the ideologies and objectives of officially sanctioned involvement initiatives, and the priorities and positions of user-led groups (Campbell and Oliver, 1996; Barnes, 1999; Martin, this volume). The increasing confidence and effectiveness of service users who have experienced the support of such organisations has also led to questions being posed about their 'representativeness'. The term 'professional user' has sometimes been used to undermine the credibility and legitimacy of those who speak on behalf of their peers, while officials have also sometimes attempted to bypass disabled people's organisations when they do not like what they have to say, claiming that they need to get to the 'real users' (Barnes, 2002). The credibility attached to user groups by health and social care officials has also been related to criteria that have more to do with state bureaucracies than with user organisations (Harrison et al, 1997).

Collective action by disabled people has achieved significant successes in influencing policies and the way in which services are provided. Perhaps the most significant impact has been in the adoption of direct payments and personal budgets as means of giving service users control over the services they receive. But many have expressed ambivalence when government and statutory service providers appear to adopt arguments and slogans with which user movements have campaigned. For example, following the publication of the coalition government's White Paper on the NHS, *Equity and excellence: Liberating the NHS* (DH, 2010a), Sue Bott, chief executive of the National Council for Independent Living (NCIL), wrote in her blog:

> Yesterday the Secretary of State for Health announced his plans for the future of the NHS with the launch of the White Paper 'Equity and Excellence – Liberating the NHS'. I was particularly struck by one of the phrases he used. He said of patients that there will be 'no decision about me without me'. It is an adaption of the phrase 'Nothing about Us Without Us' which is the term that has been adopted by the international disability movement.... When disabled people adopted the term it was very much in the spirit of the originators. It was a message of the need to redress the balance of power and in that sense has always been a strong political statement. I wonder whether the Secretary of State has the same shift in power relationships in mind? I have my doubts not least because shifts in power always have their basis in grassroots movements. (http://suebott.wordpress.com/2010/07/13/should-we-worry-when-government-adopts-our-language/)

The purpose and significance of user movements go beyond ensuring a user voice within decision making about services and policies and some avoid contact with service providers, preferring to focus on alternative ways of supporting their members (such as groups in which members can explore what hearing voices means to them), or on promoting the distinct identity of disabled people, mental health service users and others through arts and performance, for example. Thus, while it is important to understand the relationship between autonomous action by service users and officially-sponsored involvement initiatives, such relationships do not completely define either the nature or the purpose of such organisation.

Up to now we have been primarily discussing movements among disabled people and mental health service users. It is in these contexts that user movements are most developed and it is important to recognise and reflect on why this might be the case, and the implications for other groups of people who might be defined as users of health and social care services. Briefly, we can suggest four reasons why it is among these groups that autonomous action has been most developed:

- Experience of services was often that they were oppressive and demeaning and a challenge to professional dominance of services was seen as necessary to enable people to regain control over their lives.
- Linked to this, services were often provided and received collectively and this provided a focus and opportunity for developing a collective analysis of the nature of the problem.
- The experience of living with disability or mental illness was/is also one of discrimination and in some cases stigmatisation and thus service users were seeking change in social relations more broadly.
- And linked to this, the experience of living with disability or mental illness is one in which personal identities are bound up with professional 'diagnoses' or other ways of defining the condition. Thus, reclaiming the right to define people's own identity has been an important aspect of collective action.

In the context of social care in particular, we can identify a similar movement among carers for whom collective action has been a way of asserting their distinct identity, offering support to each other and influencing policy and service delivery (Barnes, 2011). However, collective action among older people, who constitute the biggest single group of users of social care services, has tended not to include those who are most dependent on such services for regular support and quality of life. Nationally, the National Pensioners Convention campaigns in relation to pensions, health services and other issues that have particular significance for older people, but activists are not primarily users of social care services (although like the population in general and older people in particular they can be identified as users of health services). At the local level there is now a substantial network of older people's forums that are often supported by local health and social care agencies, but led by older people, and which provide a focus for consultation and involvement on a broad range of policy issues, including health and social care. But once again these are led primarily by older people who are not substantial users of social care services, and there are questions about the assumptions they may make about the capacity of older service users to speak out on the own behalf (Barnes et al, 2011).

The situation in relation to young people is different again. The National Association of Young People in Care (NAYPIC) and later A National Voice provided a voice for young people in the care system. But much of the activity around young people's involvement in decision making is currently promoted by voluntary organisations via the Participation Works partnership (www.participationworks.org.uk/).

As we noted in the Introduction to this volume, Baggott et al (2005) have researched a broad range of health consumer groups that represent people with different health conditions and collectively can be considered to constitute a health consumer movement. Martin (Chapter Four) focuses on action by people who live with cancer, working within the context of a third sector organisation that is not user led, but is committed to giving a voice to those affected by cancer. Cotterell and Morris (Chapter Five), coincidentally also placed in the context of cancer services, focus on service user knowledge and its place and position in relation to official involvement initiatives. One of the characteristics of social movements is their diversity and one aspect of that diversity in this context is the extent to which participants understand their activism as part of a political project or one that is more narrowly focused on service delivery. The contributions in Part One offer a partial view of the range of autonomous action that has developed since the 1970s/1980s, but offer important insights into the motivations and experiences of service users who have taken action on their own and others' behalf, not only to improve health and social care services, but also to change public perceptions and the everyday life experiences of service users.

one

Survivors History Group takes a critical look at historians

Survivors History Group

Introduction

Survivors History Group is run by mental health service users/survivors who value the history of the survivor movement. Membership is open to anyone, survivor or not, who shares our interest. Historians in our sense are people who write or tell history, for whatever reason, not just people who are experts at doing so. We welcome all histories of the movement. This chapter is an introduction to some of the stories about the United Kingdom (UK) movement that have already been told. Several of the authors discussed are members of the group. The group started in 2005 and much of our work will be found in our website archive and history (http://studymore.org.uk/mpu.htm), referred to in this chapter as 'Survivors History'.

If history is a story that purports to be true, we should ask how the story relates to the evidence about what happened. We document ways in which some alleged facts in published histories do not correspond with evidence from the archives and some of the stories conflict with memories of those who took part in the events, and suggest that our collective archiving and storytelling works towards the creation of an objective history that is true to the memories of many different people and fits the evidence in preserved records.

We identify and discuss the significance of two features tending to make survivor histories different from other people's histories. One that stands out is that our histories are usually descriptive rather than theoretical. Less obvious, but important, is that survivor research has focused on the continuity of survivor action instead of considering it a by-product of intellectual trends, such as Laingian anti-psychiatry. We argue that this corresponds more closely to the reality of what happened. As Louise Pembroke, founder of the National Self-Harm Network has said, we were not 'sitting around talking about Laing' – 'our role models were each other' (personal communication, 20 July 2009).

We review the main printed academic works on the general history of the UK survivor movement, focusing on empirical credibility, and conclude with a discussion of our own project. The works we review are:

- Peter Sedgwick's (1982) *Psycho politics*;
- Anne Rogers and David Pilgrim's (1991) '"Pulling down churches": accounting for the British mental health users' movement';
- Nick Crossley's (1999, 2006) 'Fish, field, habitus and madness' and *Contesting psychiatry*;
- Marian Barnes and Ric Bowl's (2001) *Taking over the asylum*;
- Jan Wallcraft, Jim Read and Angela Sweeney's (2003) *On our own terms*;
- Helen Spandler's (2006) *Asylum to action*.

Of these writers, only Wallcraft, Read and Sweeney are self-declared survivors.

Peter Sedgwick

Sedgwick's (1982) *Psycho politics* contains a concisely written survey of 'movements among the mentally ill' in Belgium, England, France, Germany, Holland, Scotland and the United States (US). In this, the English mental patients' movement is described in a few paragraphs (pp 227-8), the accuracy and relevance of which should have made them the point from which subsequent historians began their researches.

Psycho politics has two parts: a critical review of anti-psychiatry and a review of mental health movements and issues. It deals with the mental patients' movement as a movement in its own right, making no attempt to relate it to the theorists (Foucault, Goffman, Laing and Szasz) identified as anti-psychiatry.

Sedgwick's account is based on documents, rather than the interviews favoured by some later historians, but he has the advantage of living through the period and taking an interest in events as they happened. The documents he references are the 'Declaration of intent of the Mental Patients Union' (MPU; MPU, 1973), a (substantial) English magazine interview with MPU activists (MPU Hackney, 1975) and the international issue of the radical French magazine *Gardes fous* in April 1975. The precedence of the Scottish union, two years before England, is mentioned and Sedgwick recognises that the MPU was a 'federation' and not a single group. In contrast to Crossley, he deals with the documents and activities of the actual unions, rather than 'The need for a Mental Patients' Union' (Irwin et al, 1972) (see under Crossley), which was never a union document. He deals with the establishment of an autonomous and recognised union in Hackney Hospital in 1974, and the publication of the *Directory of psychiatric drugs* (Hill et al: 1975), but not with Manchester MPU's *Your rights in mental hospital* (MPU Manchester, 1979). As well as being carefully researched, accurate, well referenced and clearly separating theory and fact, Sedgwick has the virtue of discussing a movement, which is more than the organisations carried along in its stream. He is aware of the movement towards solidarity among patients of which the various organisations are expressions and evidence.

In 1982, the evidence that Sedgwick saw for the stream was only 'sporadic and unpredictable appearances in the far left press' (Sedgwick, 1982, p 228). History and subsequent research (Survivors History) have demonstrated that in this period between the MPUs and 1985, the waters were gathering force and reshaping. In Bristol, Glasgow, London and Yorkshire, critical women's groups were forming (Women in Mind, 1986). In Lancashire and London, patients were entering local Mind organisations. A new wave of 'Mental Health Action Groups' appeared in which patients and radical allies struggled to change established services and/or establish local, user-run services. And a very small and very vocal group called PROMPT (Preservation of the Rights of Mental Patients in Therapy) were reviving and revising the left-wing document, 'The need for a Mental Patients' Union' (Irwin et al, 1972), which the MPUs had rejected as radical and revolutionary, and integrating it with the MPU's declaration to make their own explosive manifesto.

A cultural reshaping of the movement was in the making. Probably unknown to one another, patients meeting in the National Schizophrenia Association in Westminster and PROMPT published collections of poems. In 1984, survivor poet Frank Bangay launched the first PROMPT music and poetry gig at the Metropolitan Tavern in Farringdon, London. Rhythm and lyrics, as performance or printed page, brought the movement together in new and more powerful ways (Survivors History).

Anne Rogers and David Pilgrim

By the time the next academic foray into describing the movement appeared in 1991, the vibrant underground activity of the early 1980s had combined with the desire of the government to consult over the structure of community care (replacing the old-style hospitals) and movement organisations had expanded rapidly with assistance from national charities and progressive professionals. Two professionals, Anne Rogers and David Pilgrim, joined the London Alliance for Mental Health Action to carry out participant observation for what became "'Pulling down churches': accounting for the British mental health users' movement' (Rogers and Pilgrim, 1991). This article in a sociological journal put mental health users on the academic map as a 'new social movement' or 'newly emergent movement' (1991, p 129).

Empirically, the article contains a brief history and a substantial snapshot of movement organisations in the late 1980s. Although the authors list Sedgwick in their bibliography, their history is almost exclusively about Holland and the US. Sedgwick documented aspects of MPU activity, which were 'a model for some of the European movements', but Rogers and Pilgrim argued that 'well documented accounts of developments' in Europe and North America indicate 'the extent of the establishment of patient groups in other countries' in contrast to 'the relative delay' of its emergence in Britain (1991, p 130).

To Andrew Roberts, living at the main MPU address for many years, it appeared that similar organisations emerged at about the same time in various parts of North America and Western Europe, and that we saw ourselves as part of one movement. This international, mutual support grew stronger during the period in the early 1980s, often interpreted as a hiatus in the development of the British movement.

Rogers and Pilgrim state that the 'Mental Patients Union and "People not Psychiatry" in this country ... as campaigning organisations in the 1970s, gained some media recognition but failed to develop', the MPU 'collapsing with the death of a key individual within the organisation' (1991, pp 130-1). We have not been able to identify either the organisation that collapsed or the individual who died. We think, however, that the existence of several unions in England and Scotland (mentioned by Sedgwick) should have cast doubt on the idea that one death could end the union.

Rogers and Pilgrim's survey of organisations is an important record, which we have used in our web history. They interviewed 10 people (seven users and three professionals) between autumn 1988 and 1989, identified (as follows) only by the names of organisations they belonged to:

- Mind/Survivors Speak Out (SSO);
- London Alliance for Mental Health Action;
- Voices;
- CAPO/LAMHA;
- Mind Link.

Voices was not a member of the London Alliance for Mental Health Action; the others were. This circumscribes the claim that the sample represents the 'British' movement, but two interviewees we have identified (Peter Campbell and Jan Wallcraft) believe that the survey is a good representation of what they experienced in London. Rogers and Pilgrim are very critical of Voices. Survivors History has given Voices members the space to reply, and this has added depth to our history. Voices is now The National Perceptions Forum, and its ex-chair, Chris Barchard, has written on its history and its contribution to the movement.

Similar surveys to Rogers and Pilgrim, but carried out by survivors, have received less attention. Chamberlin and Unzicker (1990) identified their sources, which makes the historian's task much easier. The anonymity of survivor sources in Rogers and Pilgrim's and Crossley's histories limits our ability to assess their interpretations. Although adopted for ethical reasons, we suspect that it was unnecessary. In similar circumstances, Helen Spandler included the names of all her interviewees, with the exception of one professional who asked to be anonymous, and preserved their evidence in a national archive.

Chamberlin and Unzicker were conscious of their geographical limitations, but unacknowledged London centricity is a distortion to most academic histories. The significance of Scotland has been almost completely ignored in the generation of the UK movement (Roberts, 2009), and it is impossible to make credible sense of the history of the movement without discussing the leading parts played, at different times, by Bristol, Leeds, Manchester, Nottingham, Sheffield and other centres. In just one, significant, example, we quote Colin Gell, who has written: 'One of the main reasons for the spread of practical user involvement, as opposed to theoretical, was the work of people from Nottingham going around the country in the early 1990s and supporting others to get started' (personal communication, 1 August 2008); (see Chapter Two, this volume).

Nick Crossley

Crossley's (1999) article, 'Fish, field, habitus and madness: the first wave mental health users' movement', is arguably the first significant academic study of the MPU. Habitus (like habit) relates to the way we do things and Crossley describes changes in the way the movement does things. His article was followed in 2006 by the book, *Contesting psychiatry*. His work moves beyond Rogers and Pilgrim to provide a story of the development of the movement in two waves, from the formation of the MPU in 1973 to SSO in 1986. The result is of considerable empirical value, but survivors whose memories and archives he uses, have found significant aspects discordant with what they experienced, and can substantiate this from documents.

We have made considerable use of Crossley's (1999, p 652) concept of 'continuity'. Here, we consider first the empirical issue of whether there was continuity between patient activities before and after 1973, and then the related theoretical issue of what one means by continuity. Crossley (2006: p 144) writes:

> The MPU were predated slightly by the Scottish Union of Mental Patients (SUMP), who formed in 1971, but this group folded relatively quickly and although its founder did later link up with

some MPU members there is no direct line of influence from SUMP to the MPU, as there is from the MPU to many of the groups still active today. In this respect the birth of MPU was the birth of the modern survivor movement.

In fact, continuity between SUMP and the MPU was strong. Tommie Ritchie, the founder of SUMP (Roberts, 2009), left Scotland for London in June 1972. He, and fellow member Robin Farquharson, took part in the founding meetings of the union in March and April 1973, when Tommie signed himself 'RICHIE – LONDON – SEX –SUPERSTAR'. Robin died, tragically, between the two meetings, but Tommie was a very active member of an MPU house for two years and he lodged the records of SUMP with the MPU. Extracts were published in *MPU news* in February 1974. The Scottish experience fed directly into MPU practice. Crossley's mistake, also made by Helen Spandler, is to confuse the union with the four people who wrote 'The need for a Mental Patients' Union' (Irwin et al, 1972), known as the 'fish pamphlet' from its cover illustration. Eric Irwin was the only self-declared patient of the four authors. Two other patients (Andrew and Valerie Roberts) joined in its distribution (see Crossley, 2006, p 146). The MPU, initially based on a patient membership of almost a hundred, referred to the fish group as 'the pilot committee' and, to the annoyance of Eric Irwin, dissociated the union from the fish pamphlet.

Instead of tracing continuity from previous patient activity, Crossley seeks continuities from anti-psychiatry to the MPU, qualifying this by saying that the MPU was 'shaped by the anti psychiatric effect … without being reducible to it' (Crossley, 2006, p 144). He argues (2006, p 160) that the fish pamphlet was 'framed' by two 'key discourses': Marxism and anti-psychiatry. By anti-psychiatry (chapter 5) he means the activities of Laing and his associates. If we include Szasz and Goffman, who he occasionally mentions, it is reasonable to describe anti-psychiatry and Marxism as prominent features of the fish pamphlet. But although part of the context of the MPU, they were not its substance. Unions contained patients with diverse views on psychiatry and politics, as one would expect when the constitution entitled any mental patient to full membership. Union activity was primarily a coming together of patients in solidarity. The same point needs to be made with respect to the second wave of survivor activity in the 1980s. SSO initially contained a sizeable minority of 'allies' who were not patients, and, as Peter Campbell, its first secretary, points out in an email to Crossley 'anti psychiatry … may have been more important to the allies' (personal communication, 12 June 2009). Most of the patient members were, as Louise Pembroke has argued, learning from each other.

What constitutes continuity? With Tommie Ritchie we traced it physically through the same individual being active. Similarly, Valerie Argent and

Andrew Roberts progressed from the Ingrebourne Society of patients in a therapeutic community in 1963, through an informal network of patients from different hospitals, to the MPU in 1973 (Survivors History). But continuity can also be traced, empirically, through inspiration. Members of the Ingrebourne network read, discussed and annotated a book about a Rampton Hospital patient (Peter Whitehead), recording how, in 1955, he encouraged about 20 patients in Rampton to write letters and get them out to Members of Parliament, the National Council for Civil Liberties and others (Roxan, 1958, p 218). Rampton, one of the three hospitals at the time for mental patients thought to require prison-like security, could not have been further removed from the neurosis centre that was Ingrebourne, but continuity of patient activity stretched through the printed page, and Peter Whitehead was a role model for Ingrebourne and MPU activists. In the MPU, ex-patients from Rampton and Broadmoor lived in the same house as ex-Ingrebourne patients.

Andrew Roberts, Crossley's interview source 2 ('patient and MPU activist', Crossley, 2006, pp 147, 150, 151, 155, 156), finds that the main way in which *Contesting psychiatry* conflicts with his experience is not what it says, but what it omits. It focuses on events preceding the formation of English unions, hardly mentioning the history of the unions themselves. The account omits most of what relates to the activities of mental patients inside and outside hospitals in the years 1973 to 1977 that contain most union activity.

Peter Campbell, Crossley's interview source 9 ('survivor activist', Crossley, 2006, pp 175, 180, 188), relates his own experiences to the generation of SSO (January 1986); Mind Link, Mind's user network (1988); and the UK Advocacy Network (UKAN) in 1991. Voices (the National Voices Forum), a user group supported by the National Schizophrenia Fellowship, was initially London based (November 1986). It developed as a national network in the early 1990s.

Before these events, Peter Campbell and other mental health service users were involved in a professional-led London group called the British Network of Alternatives to Psychiatry. Some of these professionals were associated with Laingian anti-psychiatry. Another professional led group with users, based around the *Asylum* magazine in Sheffield, was associated with the 'democratic psychiatry' of the Italian psychiatrist Franco Basaglia. These two trends within psychiatry are a prominent feature of Crossley's analysis, and they were clearly important as part of the context of second-wave patient/survivor solidarity. However, as Peter comments in an email to Crossley:

> I think you could deal more fully with the worker/survivor split in the 1980s. You don't really say that many survivors felt at the time that the only way to counteract professional dominance was to have survivor only groups. Perhaps it is relevant that anti psychiatry and

democratic psychiatry were very much professionally led enterprises (in my opinion!!). (personal communication, 12 June 2009)

Professionals were much more influential in generating the survivor movement of the late 1980s than in the generation of MPUs in the 1970s. But in the 1980s, as in the 1970s, *Contesting psychiatry* underplayed users' desires and work for autonomy and solidarity in favour of documenting the intellectual developments of professionals.

The MPU from 1973 to 1976 and, more effectively, SSO from 1986, linked otherwise fragmented (Chamberlin and Unzicker, 1990) people and groups throughout the country. It may be the presence or absence of such coordinating centres that some observers have perceived as the presence or absence of the movement.

Crossley correctly pays attention to the origins of both the MPU and SSO. Unfortunately, with respect to the events preceding SSO (Crossley, 2006, pp 180-1), it is difficult to relate the account to our memories because two conferences are mistaken for one, and the conference he describes has elements of both. The World Federation for Mental Health Conference in Brighton in the summer of 1985 excluded most English users. It was gatecrashed by one English group (CAPO: Campaign Against Psychiatric Oppression, previously PROMPT) who linked with invited users from other countries in taking over one of the themes of the conference. This user-led revolution inside a conference was part of the impetus for professionals within Mind to make the Mind Annual Conference in the autumn a user-centred one. After this conference there was a meeting that led to the formation of SSO in January 1986 (Survivors History).

Peter Campbell, first secretary of SSO, and one of the authors of this chapter, suggests that *Contesting psychiatry* would need to pay more attention to the sequence of subsequent events in order to understand the way survivor-led organisations developed. He considers it important that SSO formed in January 1986 and had a clear field before Mind established its user network in 1988. During this period, the strength of survivors within SSO increased and solidarity between survivors was built at the Edale conference in September 1987. Edale, when almost 100 survivors met in a Peak District youth hostel, was really the beginning of what Terry Simpson, first coordinator (in 1993) of UKAN, has called the 'grassroots movement'. It was a strong survivor-led organisation that established complete survivor control in the years of constitution building from 1987 to 1990. Mind Link formed in an environment that already had an autonomous user movement organisation. Terry considers Edale a key moment in establishing the next phase of the movement, which led to the creation of UKAN some years later (Survivors History and clarifying personal communication, 21 March 2010). Crossley (2006, pp 14-15) relates the interplay between organisations to resource mobilisation theory, which stresses competition for resources. A quotation from Peter Campbell (Crossley, 2006, p 188) supports this emphasis. Anne Plumb, another SSO activist and an author of this chapter, stresses cooperation rather than competition. As SSO was joined by Mind Link, by the developing national network of Voices and by UKAN, it became possible for users with different perspectives to find a group congenial to them, and through that group to work together with other groups. It was this underlying structure of user-led organisations that enabled a genuine survivor movement, with hardly a professional in sight, to engage with government in the Mental Health User Task Force from 1993, with three representatives each from SSO, UKAN and Mind Link.

Marian Barnes and Ric Bowl

During the 1990s, the survivor movement and government policy engaged with one another. This is reflected in *Taking over the asylum: Empowerment and mental health* by Barnes and Bowl (2001). Their focus on social policy and user involvement provides a framework for people wishing to relate the history of the movement to public policy. Chapter two, 'From lunatics to survivors', attempts such a 'sparsely documented' (2001, p 26) history, mainly using existing published sources, such as Rogers and Pilgrim (1991). Not everything is based on secondary sources, and exploring the relationship between Nottingham Advocacy Group (2001, pp 35-6), with which Marian Barnes has worked, and user involvement in public policy would provide a useful starting point for a history of the practical issues that Colin Gell of Nottingham Advocacy Group referred to earlier in this chapter. In a PhD thesis, survivor historian David Armes (2006) has built on this and the next work we review, by analysing different movement responses to the forces of involvement, consultation and service provision.

Jan Wallcraft, Jim Read and Angela Sweeney

The most important printed empirical contribution to the academic history of the survivor movement so far is Jan Wallcraft, Jim Read and Angela Sweeney's (2003) *On our own terms*. This work is the background to our own work. Preparation for this research began in 2000 under Diana Rose at the Sainsbury Centre for Mental Health. A large user reference or steering group, with strong black and minority ethnic representation, was formed to supervise the study. Jan Wallcraft took the proposal forward when she took over from Diana Rose in 2001, and a team of survivor researchers was brought together to 'describe and analyse the mental health service user/survivor movement in England'. Their report notes that Rogers and Pilgrim had described this as a 'new social movement' in 1991, but that 'no systematic attempt has been made until now to find out the extent and scope of this movement' (Wallcraft et al, 2003, p 1).

A core of the report is an analysis of 318 questionnaires returned by user groups in England. Chapter three of the report is entitled the 'Development of the movement'. It begins with a table (table 4) of 'Key developments in the service user/survivor movement in England'. This appears to have been constructed by the research team and steering group, including many of the survivors active in the movement since the early 1980s, pooling their experiences. Survivor History Group later used this as one of the starting points for its web history of the movement.

The report includes a chart of the years that groups started. One suspects that this is heavily biased towards recent years, because groups that have closed are not included. However, the curve of the chart suggests the points at which growth in the number of movement organisations was greatest. The authors claim that 'the figures confirm that there was a rapid expansion of local groups from the 1980s onwards, with the majority set up in the last ten to fifteen years' and that 'the postal survey shows that 75% of groups were set up since 1992, which seems to confirm that the NHS and Community Care Act' [1990] had a strong impact' (Wallcraft et al, 2003 p 12).

As well as the questionnaires, a selection of group representatives were interviewed. The questions included ones devised to secure information about the history of the movement: 'Most do think the movement is growing. They point out a number of reasons, including social changes, political changes, individual efforts by survivors and allies, and recent collective actions to put forward survivor agendas such as self management' (2003, p 12). Each of these suggested causes is then explored in more detail (2003, pp 12-14).

Helen Spandler

Helen Spandler's (2006) *Asylum to action* includes a detailed study of the continuity between joint staff/patient action to preserve Paddington Day Hospital as a therapeutic community (Durkin, 1972) and the origin of the MPU in 1973. Spandler argues that the democracy of therapeutic communities contributed to the activation of patients. Roberts (2009) has related this to his own experience of coming into the movement through another therapeutic community in the 1960s. However, although it resonates with the memories of some activists, *Asylum to action*'s thesis is limited. The archives of SUMP, already referred to, lie very close to ones that Spandler used for previous research. We have used them to argue that the movement originated at least as firmly within old-style asylums as it did within therapeutic communities: a qualification that Spandler is happy to accept.

Survivors History Group

We have argued that parts of the story told by Rogers and Pilgrim, and Crossley, should be modified by the evidence of participants' memories and archives. Such a relationship between survivor and academic history is collaborative. There is, however, a difference between the importance that most survivor historians place on how well a story fits with memory and data, and that of many academics. Academics have suggested that in the broad sweep of history, the details we raise are trifling. From our point of view, it is essential that the accounts relate credibly to our memories and to the records. The academic historian/sociologist may only be concerned to find some rough fit between theoretical models and data, whereas the detail of history matters to us because it bears on our lives and our heritage.

Survivors History Group shares Crossley's (2006, p 6) belief in stories and archives as foundations of research. His work with material collected from survivors, although flawed, is also valuable. We use our own stories (memories) and archives to create a collective history of the movement we identify with. Weaving together the stories that different survivors tell of our own lives, we use our archives to check and enrich them. Many people have contributed their stories, providing a strong base for checking narratives against one another. Our aim is a history that relates individual biographies to the movements of history in a way that is both subjectively meaningful and subject to the ever-ongoing test of falsification by the data.

Archives alone are lifeless. Stories bring them to life. But we have found that stories without archives do not have enough substance to make good history. Few of us recall accurate dates for our stories, and without dates it is difficult to relate different people's narratives, or to weave individual accounts into collective history. Written archives often provide the dates. Anne Plumb, for example, has listed events from magazines to provide a framework of dates we can relate our memories to (Survivors History. See, for example, her *Asylum magazine* index).

Crossley (1999, pp 6, 22) speaks of 'movement myths', which may be true in themselves, but not in connections we imply when we use them to raise movement morale. An argument that our involvement will lead us to use history as propaganda, while detached historians seek the truth, is plausible But we do not believe that objectivity belongs to the detached academic in this way. Because the story is our story, the credibility and detail of it matters to us in a different way than it does to the academic historian. This can mean that we are more, not less, concerned about objectivity. We have been less concerned about theory, but our narratives have been researched and told (on the web) in a way that makes interpretations and data open to continuous critical evaluation and correction. Our tapestry of interwoven stories and archives is publicly available (Survivors History). We encourage input in a diversity of ways, including website feedback, a (very lively) internet forum, group meetings, workshops at conferences, exhibitions of books and archives, and special events such as our recent 'Pageant of Survivor History' (Survivors History, 19 March 2010). Our history is always, of necessity, incomplete because it is an ongoing process. Our history too is flawed, but we think that the way we work facilitates criticism of the flaws, and amendment of the stories we tell.

Collective authorship

This chapter is collective work developing aspects of a Survivors History Group conference with historians in 2008, the report of which is listed in the References (Survivors History Group, 2008), and should also be credited to the group. As group secretary, Andrew Roberts drafted both the 2008 report and this chapter on the basis of many members' work. Both articles were circulated widely for comment and correction. We thank everyone, including the historians commented on, for generous help in many forms.

two

The Nottingham Advocacy Group: a short history

Marian Barnes and Colin Gell

The Nottingham Advocacy Group (NAG) was one of the first mental health service user groups to be established in England. It emerged during the mid-1980s, well before user involvement in mental health services became accepted by professionals or policy makers. In this chapter we tell the story of NAG's development and consider the significance of the group for those who have taken part in it and for the development of the mental health service user movement more broadly.[1]

Origins and early years

In 1985, Wouter van der Graaf spoke at the World Mental Health Conference in Brighton about the development of Patients' Councils in Holland. Participants at the conference invited van der Graaf to Nottingham and this led to a small steering group of people from MIND, the local law centre, the University of Loughborough, Colin Gell, Glenys Brocklebank and other service users constituting themselves as the Nottingham Patients' Council Support Group (NPCSG). Members of this group visited Saxondale Hospital, then the county psychiatric hospital, to speak to patients about the idea of setting up a Patients' Council. Service users responded immediately, and the first user-led ward meeting took place at that visit in January 1986. Patient advocacy was on its way.

One of the first tasks for the new group was to work with patients to help prepare for the closure of the hospital and their move to community facilities. The Mental Health Unit manager was supportive but, in April 1986, NPCSG was banned from the hospital because a consultant psychiatrist objected to the group meeting with 'his' patients.

In September 1986, the first Patients' Council meeting took place in Mapperley, the Nottingham City hospital. Group members described how patients came out of the wards into the long corridor that ran along the hospital and marched along it towards the meeting room, an image reminiscent of workers downing tools in a factory and marching to trades union meetings.

By 1987, plans were being made for NPCSG to become a completely independent, user-run organisation and NAG was launched as an independent limited company in 1987.

NAG continued to act as the support group for the Patients' Council at Mapperley Hospital until the hospital was closed. It provided support for patients at ward level and individual patient advocacy, usually working with service users on one-off issues of concern. It also provided longer-term citizen advocacy involving ongoing one-to-one relationships. The latter was seen to be the 'least troublesome' aspect of its work and the easiest for which to secure funding. Jenny Haywood, the first citizen advocacy coordinator, was appointed in 1987, the same year that the group moved into its first independent premises.

By 1988, NAG members were receiving invitations to visit other places where similar initiatives were starting to emerge. At a national level, Survivors Speak Out (SSO) was providing a platform for both individuals and groups to lobby and demonstrate. In 1988, Mind Link was established to ensure an independent user voice within Mind and, in 1991, the UK Advocacy Network (UKAN) was established to support the growing number of local advocacy groups following a conference organised by NAG.

By 1989, NAG had obtained funding for a user involvement support worker – Colin Gell's first paid job for NAG. During 1990/91, user groups were established within community mental health teams and, in spite of some resistance from professionals, the group achieved a good balance in terms of both independence from, but also credibility with, service providers. It had funding from national Mind, and from the Mansfield Brewery to support individual advocacy. John Price was appointed to coordinate these services, and Simon Marritt started an Information and Advice Centre at Mapperley Hospital.

Becoming established

The early 1990s was a period of positive growth for NAG. A conference was held in 1991 to mark NAG's fifth year. Colin Gell renewed contact with the Dutch users' movement that year when he visited Holland, and NAG was supporting other emergent advocacy groups in Birmingham, Lowestoft and Wales.

In 1992, the first City Wide Patients' Council took place in Nottingham. This created a forum in which issues raised by users in different services could be discussed with managers. Invitations followed to NAG to send representatives to various provider-level committees. Some NAG members felt that they had to fight hard to be taken seriously in these forums, and there was a sense in which some people felt that they were being used. But, overall, the view was that this was a positive indication of how far service users had come in the six years since the NPCSG was first established.

The year 1993 saw the first Mental Health Awareness Week in Nottingham organised by NAG to challenge the stigma with which mental illness was viewed by the general population. One method used in this process was a 'Stress Game' designed to make the link between mental health problems and the stresses everyone feels at some stage as part of everyday life. NAG had also taken ownership of a caravan on a campsite in Skegness to offer cheap holidays for service users, their families and friends. Another way in which NAG was looking beyond the mental health system was through the development of Ecoworks. Ecoworks was the brainchild of Brian Davey, and was designed to develop opportunities for people living with mental health problems to get involved in activities to create a more sustainable lifestyle. Much of the activity was focused on allotments where service users and other local residents could grow food for an affordable healthy diet, and contribute to environmentally friendly food production.

By 1994/95, NAG was receiving funding from statutory health and social care services and from private firms. While much of this was short term and fragile, it enabled NAG to support Patients' Councils and user groups in both hospital and community settings, to provide individual advocacy, to take part in joint planning, to establish a Purchasing for Users Group (PUG), to provide training for mental health workers and to initiate projects such as self-assessment by users of their own needs.

Workers and volunteers recognised an important link between individual and collective advocacy. Everyday contact with service users leading to immediate action to improve experiences of services was core to NAG's approach. But NAG's objectives extended beyond improving mental health services and, at a time when 'patients' were being reconstructed as 'consumers', NAG saw people with mental health problems as citizens with contributions to make to their communities as well as rights to fair treatment within and outside the mental health system.

NAG's *Annual report* of 1995/96 was upbeat. By then, NAG had seven waged staff and 24 full-time or nearly full-time volunteers working to support service users in a wide range of services. It was seeking funding to develop new services (such as a young people's advocacy development worker) and had achieved agreement with the health authority for a specification for advocacy services with funding agreed on an annually renewable basis. It had purchased a second caravan, invested in information technology equipment and established an information centre to improve both internal functioning and its services to users. There were plans for Ecoworks to move into small-scale self-build projects.

The group held a 10th anniversary conference, which spurred participants to continue the fight for recognition for service users, but Colin Gell also identified a worrying lack of interest among mental health workers for this event, suggesting that user involvement was being taken for granted and they had stopped working at it.

This greater familiarity with user involvement was reflected in national developments to which NAG members were making a significant contribution. The Department of Health set up a Mental Health Task Force in the mid-1990s to support the development of mental health services nationwide, and the three key national user organisations – SSO, UKAN and Mind Link – were all represented on this. Colin Gell had a substantial role in establishing new local groups and stronger links between users and the Department of Health. He also worked with the Centre for Mental Health Service Development at King's College, University of London to develop user involvement training in more than 60 areas.

Facing challenges

As NAG moved into its second decade it started to face a number of challenges and those who reflected back on this period described it as a very painful time. One problem was the increased size and complexity of the organisation. NAG had funding from different sources and its internal financial management systems had not kept pace with the size and complexity of its activities. Tensions emerged about the role and place of volunteers and the extent to which they felt that they were trained, supported and valued for the work they did. And underpinning these debates were differences in views about the centrality of advocacy in comparison with other aspects of NAG's work, a difference that was underpinned by different conceptions of empowerment.

In his report on Ecoworks in the 1995/96 *Annual report*, Brian Davey reflected a position that underpinned the approach he had been developing in and through Ecoworks:

> Advocacy is always to get someone else (the mental health services, the housing office, the employment services) to do something for you, or something different. Where advocacy doesn't get you any further the only solution is to get together with other people with similar problems, teach yourself and do it yourself.

The May 1997 issue of *Advocateur* (the group's magazine) contained an item about a self-help group for women who self-harm. This had been started by a woman volunteer working with NAG and she looked to NAG for funding to support the group. However, NAG was not able to fund this because the income it received was all tied to specific advocacy projects. This led to a sense of volunteer initiatives not being supported. Differences within

NAG led to a decision to create two divisions under the NAG umbrella: one would take forward the core advocacy work of NAG, while the other would concentrate on service developments. Each division would have its own management committee.

But in spite of these internal challenges, NAG not only continued to provide advocacy support, but also became involved in new initiatives. For example, a spate of suicides among people in contact with mental health services led to NAG calling for an independent inquiry and a Suicide Review Group was established on which NAG was represented; Ecoworks developed Eco textiles and crafts projects and secured funding to organise weekend activities on the allotments; training for patient advocates was established; and Colin Gell worked with Nottingham University to review the content of student nurse training.

Thus, alongside reports of 'turmoil', of 'emotions boiling over' at committee meetings and of fears of 'despondency' setting in among volunteers, NAG continued to do what it had been set up to do. Although there was a high turnover of people in leading roles within NAG during this period, key individuals remained and sustained their commitment to ensuring support for mental health service users and proper treatment from service providers.

By 1998, the new structure was in place, but differences still remained and in 1999 Ecoworks, which had always been seen by both Brian Davey and others to have a somewhat arm's-length relationship with NAG, finally broke away and became a separate organisation.

Into the new millennium

As the millennium drew to a close, the group was recovering from what had been an emotionally difficult time. The difficulties had affected funders' confidence and budget cutbacks led, among other things, to a move into cheaper accommodation. A number of volunteers left and NAG needed to recruit new volunteers. Action was being taken to improve internal communication, group supervision and training. Alongside reflections on the difficulties that NAG had been going through, people also reflected on their achievements, which included:

- planning and monitoring of self-assessment;
- progress in developing a crisis house and helpline;
- involvement in interviewing and recruiting mental health workers;
- consultation on patient partnership;
- advising the local school of nursing about nurse training;
- consultation on the review of the 1983 Mental Health Act;
- involvement in a service quality questionnaire survey.

They were also setting out future plans, which would see NAG responding to developments within health services, such as establishing advocacy within primary care; strengthening its links with groups it had been less successful in including within NAG – such as young people and people from minority ethnic groups; and pursuing new issues such as advanced directives and mental health and homelessness.

By 2001/02, NAG had concluded a formal advocacy agreement with the Nottinghamshire Healthcare NHS Trust. A new post of 'co coordinator and business development worker' was created and Mervyn Goring was appointed to this post. Alongside the continuing development of advocacy in an increasing range of settings and contexts, NAG was also developing its relationships with the business and voluntary sectors and seeking ways of ensuring better financial viability for its activities. For example, 'Experts by Experience' – a pilot for a regional service for people considered to have personality disorder – was set up as a not-for-profit limited company, and *Nag Mag* – successor to *Advocateur* – was relaunched to become income generating.

In 2004, many of the activities and issues in which NAG was involved remained familiar, including the City Wide Patients' Council and an annual Mental Health Awareness fortnight. NAG continued to adapt in order to respond to developments within the National Health Service (NHS) – the reorganisation to primary care trusts and the amalgamation of trusts to create a county-wide Nottinghamshire Healthcare NHS Trust. NAG maintained its links with the NHS beyond Nottingham via the National Institute for Mental Health in England (NIMHE) East Midlands and it was part of a Nottinghamshire-wide advocacy forum.

Colin Gell moved on from NAG in 2004 to take up two user involvement development posts with Suresearch at the University of Birmingham and NIMHE East Midlands. Unfortunately, due to ill-health in early 2005 he had to take retirement. Following treatment he is now active in Leicestershire with the People's Forum and in 2009 established a service user-led social enterprise named Inspired Community Interest Company, which provides training to mental health services.

NAG continued to develop special projects. Experts by Experience provided training opportunities in information and communications technology and advocacy, and was on its way to becoming self-funding. NSURE was set up as a group of service users who were interested in influencing mental health services via involvement in research. NAG was also involved in developing the STAR project, a supported housing initiative where it was providing advocacy; and providing advocacy for a new personality disorder service run by the Nottinghamshire Healthcare NHS Trust.

But by 2006, things were very different. Towards the end of 2005, the advocacy contract came up for retendering. NAG was unsuccessful and the contract went to an organisation that provided advocacy in a number of other parts of the country. NAG had bid to continue to provide mental health advocacy in Nottingham, but the Nottinghamshire Healthcare NHS Trust wanted to commission generic advocacy services (including for people with learning difficulties) across the whole county.

Because NAG had previously successfully argued to have the advocacy contract for the STAR project included in the overall contract, this meant that it lost this service as well. By mid-2006, the only advocacy contract that remained was for the personality disorder service. This loss was devastating. It meant that most of its income disappeared and it was only able to employ one advocate. The remaining personality disorder contract continued to cover some administration and pay the office rent, but the manager's post was likely to disappear. In 2006, NAG's income was as low as it had ever been.

The pessimism that resulted from this affected other aspects of NAG's work. The situation elsewhere was described as 'death by inactivity'. While the City Wide Council continued to meet monthly, NAG members said that they were lucky if anyone from the Nottinghamshire Healthcare NHS Trust or from social services turned up. The remaining volunteers still offered collective advocacy through Patients' Council meetings, but there was no funding to pay volunteers' expenses.

The caravan project was also coming to an end and the caravans were sold. This contributed to a sense that NAG had reached a point where new ideas and new initiatives were necessary if it was going to continue into its third decade. By 2010, when we were writing this chapter, NAG was still listed as an advocacy provider in Nottingham, but an email to the provided address bounced back as 'non-existent'.

Individual stories of NAG

The chronology outlined above is one way of thinking about the NAG. Another approach is to understand what NAG has meant to those who have been involved in it. These are some of the things that NAG members said about what being involved in NAG had meant to them in research carried out in the early 1990s:

> In some ways it turned out to be a positive step for me. It changed my life around from something that was killing me, virtually, to something that I finally got some kind of reward in. (Barnes and Shardlow, 1996, p 125)

It's given me a life and without it I wouldn't have dreamed of doing half the things I do now. It's given me confidence, assurance ... I get up now and speak at a conference quite happily. A few years ago I would have no more done that than fly! (Barnes et al, 1999, p 94)

Interviews carried out during the compilation of the history of NAG presented in this chapter demonstrate more about what being involved in NAG meant to volunteers and workers. Here are just two examples, the first told in 2004 and the second in 2006.

Kim's first contact with NAG was when she needed an advocate to support her through a problem with her general practitioner. She said, "when I came in, the environment was so friendly and welcoming that I asked questions and spoke to Colin ... I was asking questions and wanted to know more, and then eventually started doing some voluntary work for them." Her early experience reinforced a sense of the teamwork that characterised the group. Feeling she was providing a service made Kim feel good – particularly as she had not been working for over four years. She became an advocate and joined the management committee. In spite of the difficulties during the late 1990s, she was determined to stick with NAG – she was committed to the services being provided and to the people she was working with. She went on to join the Patients' Council Support Group and became a volunteer on hospital wards and in a day centre.

She described the differences between meetings in those different contexts. On the acute wards, there was a turnover of patients so they never knew who they would see when they arrived to hold a meeting: "it was just me going round introducing myself to everybody, trying to get people excited enough to attend a meeting. We used to have very good meetings but you'd never know how it would go because you didn't know who was going to be there or what was going to be brought up." Many of the issues came up time and time again and Kim talked of the frustration she experienced because of the length of time it took to achieve change. She thought that it was easier to achieve results on people's individual issues – about medication, the way people were treated by staff, attacks from other patients and issues to do with visitors, for example – than it was to achieve more general changes in the quality of mental health services. She was convinced from both her own personal experience and her subsequent experience as an advocate that it makes a real difference to have an advocate to ensure that people are listened to.

In the day centre, people attended for a long period so it was much easier to get to know service users in that context. The focus for discussion in these meetings included broader issues reflecting NAG's position in national debates about mental health, as well as its concern to improve the day-to-day experiences of service users.

Kim eventually became a paid advocate in 2002, providing advocacy support in the STAR project. NAG was a partner in the service but Kim said that her role was clearly different from the rest of the staff and service users were confident that she was in a position to take up issues on their behalf. Her direct involvement in the service also enabled her to get to know what was going on behind the scenes – it was harder for staff to hide what was going on.

Kim talked of what her involvement in NAG meant to her:

> 'It is supporting people so that they're heard, and to do that is just really fulfilling. That's stage one and if you see that something has changed because of that, that's great. So it's just nice for people to be heard and I love that. I love putting that across. And then when things actually change for that person, you get terrific satisfaction.... [It's been] huge for my own personal self-esteem. I've started very small and suddenly realised that I was capable of a bit more and a bit more and a bit more, and now that I'm working full time it's just lovely, it really is.'

Kim's sense of being able to take on responsibilities in a supportive environment is a crucial way in which user/survivor groups can not only give service users a voice, but also model the supportive relationships that can enable people who experience mental health problems to move into or back into employment.

By 2006, Simon Marritt had been involved with NAG for 16 years. He started out as volunteer, but had also worked in a paid capacity for NAG – first in administrative roles and then on collective advocacy, and recruiting, training and supporting volunteers. He also acted in an unpaid capacity as the NAG company secretary for about 10 years.

Simon learnt about advocacy by going with Colin Gell to visit services. He gradually took on some of this work as Colin took on other roles beyond Nottingham. Simon had been ill for 20 years and his agoraphobia meant that he had become isolated. His early experience of NAG was of a lively place with lots of people around. It was a supportive environment, but he was also aware of different factions and of conflict. He observed people who he had encouraged to join up as volunteers trying to 'take over'. But by this time he was highly committed and was not prepared for others to "take over the organisation and ruin it".

His role in recruiting and supporting volunteers meant that he had a key role in introducing people who subsequently took up paid jobs with NAG. He enjoyed providing training and talked of being able to use his own experience to design training that suited others who also had experience of mental health difficulties. He described his approach as highly interactive and based on a collective ethos also evident in collective advocacy.

Simon preferred working on collective advocacy, but also offered some individual advocacy. He was involved in setting up a number of projects, including the caravan project, Mental Health Awareness Week and Experts by Experience. Like others, Simon's involvement with NAG was the source of new skills, confidence and commitments. Speaking at conferences, chairing meetings, negotiating with service providers and managing accounts were all things he had learnt and that he put down to the confidence that had come through his involvement in NAG. Prior to NAG he described himself as having been "in the wilderness" for 20 years – "NAG helped me get my life back together." Speaking in September 2006, he talked of his sadness at the uncertain future, but also felt he was ready for someone to take over the 'burden' of keeping NAG going.

NAG, the user movement and mental health services

There is not space here to offer a full analysis of the role that NAG played within the user/survivor movement, nor to consider how it was viewed from within mental health services at different stages of its history. But in concluding this history we do want to offer some observations on key aspects of these relationships.

Peter Campbell, a founder member of SSO, characterised the early years of the user movement in England and Wales as a period when:

> As there were so few people involved, people might be involved in a number of groups. It was likely that you would know many/most of the activists personally. This was also a pioneering period when people from SSO and NAG and some other groups would go out to meetings around the country to spread the word. Local groups often grew out of these meetings and were supported by NAG and SSO etc within our very limited means. (personal communication, September 2005)

NAG played a role in the establishment of UKAN and supported the development of other local groups. There was a sense that the local service culture in Nottingham was more supportive than in other places and that Nottingham prided itself on the progressive nature of its mental health services. It may have been that starting with the collective advocacy of patients' councils and then the city wide group was seen as less threatening than individual advocacy, which came later in the group's development. Securing funding for the services it provided also required NAG to establish itself organisationally in a way that other groups may not have needed to do.

NAG's involvement alongside other groups at the national level was crucial to securing influence on the broad direction of mental health service development. During the second half of the 1980s and early 1990s, SSO, UKAN and Mind Link were all involved in campaigning and other umbrella groups, such as the Hearing Voices network, developed in an atmosphere that was increasingly supportive of user organisations.

The NAG experience reflects the diversity of the way in which the mental health user movement has developed. The relationship between NAG and Ecoworks was never entirely comfortable. The origins of NAG were in a commitment to enabling service users to have a voice within the mental health system and this developed through an increasingly diverse range of individual and collective advocacy initiatives. Ecoworks looked beyond the mental health system to the social, economic and political factors that disempower people who live with mental distress and others who are 'different'. Other user/survivor groups have developed around shared experiences, such as of self-harm, of hearing voices or of living with bipolar disorder. Some groups prioritise offering services – not only advocacy but also drop-in, crisis and support services, while others pursue their objectives through training, research and consultancy. Mad Pride provides a focus for campaigning against discrimination among those who celebrate their mad identities through arts, poetry as well as radical political action. The diversity of the user movement means that there are differences and sometimes conflicts among those who consider themselves to be part of it. Not all those who contribute to groups such as NAG consider themselves to be part of a movement. For some, it is about being able to develop skills in a supportive environment, and they may not be aware of the existence of other user groups or want to get involved beyond the very local level.

Different strategies have consequences for the way in which groups seek to achieve change. Adopting individual and collective advocacy as the major strategy for change meant that NAG needed to develop and maintain good relationships with service providers, ensuring that they retained credibility and were not seen as overly confrontational, at the same time as being able to challenge policies and practices that were not in users' interests. Its success in building such relationships meant that is was able to establish itself as *the* provider of advocacy in Nottingham and to achieve important changes as a result. But this also meant that it was vulnerable to changes in policy and organisation within statutory services.

The negotiation of agreements for advocacy services shifted advocacy from an activity that was grudgingly accepted by service providers, to one that became part of the mainstream. However, defining advocacy as a service to be commissioned by the provider organisation eventually led to the decision to buy the service elsewhere. Fears that NAG would become too dependent on statutory sector funding proved justified.

A key change in the nature of the relationship between NAG and service providers came with the advent of 'partnership' as a means of delivering services. NAG's involvement in the STAR project offered a challenge to the principles of independent advocacy because it was involved in designing the service with advocacy 'built in' from the start. Kim, one of the interviewees described earlier, spoke positively about the nature of the relationship she had established with other staff working in this unit, emphasising that partnership required listening to others' viewpoints and the difficulty of keeping anything hidden when they all worked together. But NAG also remained in the position of having to negotiate agreements to provide services and was also embroiled in competitive tendering processes. There is a clear tension between the notion that NAG was a 'partner' and that it had to compete with others to continue to provide advocacy.

Even in the early 1990s, the concept of 'partnership' was being invoked, mainly by 'officials', to describe the changing relationships between service users and providers. Post the election of the New Labour government in 1997, partnership became a central theme of public policy. But the widespread adoption of the term does not mean that equality has been achieved, and NAG's experience demonstrates the incompatibility of claims to work in partnership with service providers' power to control how advocacy – and user involvement more generally – happens.

NAG's experiences are fairly common to successful social movements. The argument that users should be able to have their say about services has been won – to the extent that it is now official policy within the NHS. One consequence is that NHS organisations have 'user involvement' written into their responsibilities and individuals have job descriptions that require them to put this into practice – in ways determined by the service, rather than by user groups. In 2006, NAG activists were experiencing Nottinghamshire Healthcare NHS Trust managers 'reinventing the wheel', and saw user involvement hijacked by large charities able and willing to enter into contracts on terms laid down by the Trust. They described hearing Trust managers talk about activities – such as Mental Health Awareness Fortnight – as something run by the Trust, without acknowledging NAG's role in starting this. They saw the demise of user groups in service settings that were highly significant in the development of advocacy in Nottingham, and the City Wide Council – the key forum that has provided a focus for a Nottingham-wide and Nottingham-focused dialogue between service users and providers – was withering through lack of interest from providers.

Conclusion

One success of NAG and other groups that collectively comprise the mental health service user movement is that not only is such action no longer exceptional, it is also official Department of Health policy. For many of those who have been part of these developments during the last 20 years or more, this involvement has had a transformative effect. They have not only survived but also flourished as a result of being part of a movement that has recognised the value of their strengths and experiences, that has modelled a way of relating to others that acknowledges vulnerability without assuming that this implies lack of competence and that has enabled them to use their own experiences and understandings to help others find a way through what is often a frightening and painful experience. But the success of user-led groups has also contributed to a process that appears to be undermining them. If advocacy is something that can be commissioned, then it can become part of broader commissioning strategies that do not prioritise or privilege any particular group or organisation. Certainly, it appears that, if NAG does still exist, it is very different from the way it looked during its heyday in the 1990s.

Note

[1] For a longer version of this history, see Barnes (2007).

three

Building solidarity, ensuring diversity: lessons from service users' and disabled people's movements

Peter Beresford and Fran Branfield

Introduction

The focus of this chapter is the relationship of solidarity and diversity in user involvement and service user organisations and movements. There is a much wider discussion that has suggested that the move to seek more inclusive and diverse action and organisation has weakened solidarity and distracted from people's efforts to work together effectively collectively (Todd and Taylor, 2004a). There has also been a discussion related to service users and service user involvement, which has highlighted the limitations of such developments to address diversity adequately, resulting sometimes in narrow and hierarchical involvement that can actually exclude many people and groups, particularly members of black and minority ethnic communities, people with high support needs and people who communicate non-verbally (Hernandez et al, 2008).

We are going to suggest instead, drawing on our involvement in a national service user organisation, Shaping Our Lives, that it is through working together, acknowledging and celebrating difference, that we are likely to achieve both service user solidarity and effective involvement.

The broader political and ideological context

The idea and practice of user involvement, which developed during the 1980s, needs to be seen in the broader context of a renewed interest in public and citizen participation. This found early expression in specific spheres, such as community development and civic planning, as well as in broader political thinking, ideology and grassroots action (Barnes and Wistow, 1992; Beresford and Croft, 1993; Barnes, 1997a). As might be expected from this, user involvement has subsequently been a complex mixture of state and service user-led initiatives, with, as Barnes (1999) has argued, self-

33

organisation among users of social care and welfare services preceding the consumerist developments of the 1980s and early 1990s.

However, the service users' movements that emerged from the 1960s to the 1980s were themselves not an isolated development. Some of the pioneers involved in their development have highlighted their ideological and social relations with broader political and cultural changes. They have explored both the nature of their movements and the origins and concerns of their early founders and related these to wider developments concerned with activism, protest and democratisation (Campbell and Oliver, 1996; Charlton, 1998). These developments are particularly pertinent to this chapter because they offer helpful insights relating to its concern with service users, solidarity, diversity and inclusion. It is the tensions between solidarity, diversity and inclusion; and service users' experience of these and what we can learn from their movements; that are the central focus of this chapter.

During the last third of the 20th century, not only dominant party politics but also oppositional politics came in for radical challenge. Both were criticised for being based on narrow economistic views of politics. Class-based systems of political representation and of political opposition were seen as wanting, because they did not address many of the barriers, inequalities, disempowerments and exclusions that people faced. Representative democracy was seen to be in crisis – irrelevant, unrepresentative, unresponsive and offering little choice (Todd and Taylor, 2004a, p 2). For example, the political sociologist, Claus Offe (1985, p 817), challenged the dichotomy of 'state' and 'civil society' and divides between 'political' and 'private' concerns'. Thus, the traditional political division of life into public and private spheres was called into question. This was highlighted by the feminist slogan, 'the personal is political'. Feminists argued that prevailing politics ignored the unequal access to the public sphere experienced by some groups, notably women, because of responsibilities and restrictions constraining them within the private sphere (Lister, 2003; Charles, 2004).

Instead, issues and identities became key bases for political and social action. Such issues are reflected in the animal rights, peace and anti-war, environmental and anti-globalisation movements. Identity has been the focus of the women's, black civil rights, gay, lesbian, bisexual and transgender and older people's/'grey power' movements (Larana et al, 1994). As Todd and Taylor (2004a, p 19) have put it: 'so called "old" social movements attempted to gain access to the state through parliamentary politics and focused mainly on economic redistribution, "new" social movements focus increasingly (although not exclusively) on issues like social identity, culture, lifestyle and human rights concerns.'

A shift has been identified from modernism, which followed largely from 18th-century enlightenment ideas and theories, and current 'postmodern' times characterised by uncertainty and the decline of traditional left/right divides (Heywood, 2007). This has been associated with a new enthusiasm for participatory or 'direct' democracy, in which people can be actively involved, campaigning and working for local and global issues that concern them both because of their particular standpoints resulting from who they are and their broader collective sense of social responsibility for their society and the planet (Todd and Taylor, 2004b).

The Identification of new difficulties

However, such political developments have also been seen as posing new difficulties. As Heywood (2007, p 337) has observed, 'ideological developments have become increasingly fragmented', creating different, competing discourses, rather than unifying ideas and action. Broader concerns are raised about fragmentation and lack of representation (Best, 2002). According to Best and Kellner, these new ideological developments have resulted in:

> Fragmentation, as the 'movement' of the 1960s splintered into various competing struggles for rights and liberties. The previous emphasis on transforming the public sphere and institutions of domination gave way to new emphases on culture, personal identity, and everyday life, as macropolitics were replaced by the micropolitics of local transformation and changes in subjectivity. (http://negotiationisover.com/2010/03/13/postmodern-politics-fragmentation-or-alliance/)

The result is seen as a weakening of solidarity, with campaigns and movements becoming preoccupied with their own issues and situation. Such campaigns do not pay adequate attention to and sometimes divert attention from broader social and economic forces and constraints. The discussion is framed in terms of specific groups struggling for their own rights, potentially at the expense of the collective/overall whole, reflecting broader power inequalities and exclusions in the process. Commentators such as Furedi (2004, p xvii) have questioned how representative such new forms of protest are. They have raised concerns about 'consumer activism', which undermines effective democratic opposition and social change. As Todd and Taylor (2004a, p 20) state:

> What mandate do NSMs [new social movements] have in a democratic society? Who do they speak for? Who provides legitimacy for the actions of such groups? Overall there is a concern that while NSMs may appear to enhance participation in politics

… they do this in an inequitable way by furthering particularistic interests and not the interests of the collective body.

This discussion offers a helpful lens through which to consider service users, their collective action and issues of diversity and solidarity. At the same time, it may help us to get a clearer idea of the broader potential and limitations of the new politics of which they may be seen as part.

The emergence of user movements

The service user organisations and groups that have developed internationally since the late 1960s and early 1970s, beginning with disabled people's, have come to see themselves as part of a movement (please refer to the Introduction of this text). Over the years since then, such organisations of people with learning difficulties, older people, mental health service users, looked-after young people in state care, people living with HIV/AIDS and other groups have emerged. There are local, regional, national, European and international organisations (Beresford, 1999). While they vary in nature and purpose, they are frequently formally democratically constituted organisations. They have also been seen as an expression of broader movements of disabled people and service users. These have developed in the developing world as well as in Western societies (Charlton, 1998; Stone, 1999). These have variously been identified as liberation and new social movements. Certainly, they exhibit the characteristics that have come to be associated with new social movements (Touraine, 1981; Davis, 1993; Shakespeare, 1993; Oliver and Barnes, 1998).

These groups and organisations have developed their own theories, notably those of 'independent living' and the 'social model of disability'; ways of working, cultures, arts, literature and discourses (Beresford and Campbell, 1994, Thomas, 2007; Oliver, 2009). Service users have long emphasised and evidenced the value of such user-controlled organisations as key to both personal development and empowerment and the making of wider social and political change (Campbell and Oliver, 1996). Service users have argued that they are a crucial starting point for effective and broad-based participation and partnerships, providing a workable basis for it.

An isolating and segregated past

However, this is very different to how things once were – and not that long ago. To make sense of the background to today's rights-based, self-organising disabled people's and service users' movement(s), it is helpful to look to the past. There are many ways in which such history can be constructed (please see Chapter One), for example through medical sociology, social history and, more recently, disability studies. Here we track such history through disabled people's and service users' own efforts to explore it. What emerges is a history characterised by segregation, isolation and exclusion. This seems to be the case regardless of what 'kind' of service user or disabled person we are concerned with. The history seems primarily to be a shared one of oppression, disempowerment, impoverishment and coercion. We are aware that there are different understandings of this past and we are not suggesting that they are deficient. Our concern is to focus on the often-neglected history that draws directly on people's own experience and analysis. Ours can only be a brief account. Much fuller and more detailed accounts are available, notably Barnes (1994), Campbell (1996) and Campbell and Oliver (1996), and we have drawn on these.

Writings from within the disabled people's movement highlight an early yet significant cultural shift in understandings of disability with the advent of the Industrial Revolution. This of course was also associated with the 18th-century 'enlightenment' or 'age of reason', with its new emphasis on science and positivism. It was then, disabled commentators such as Finkelstein (1980, 1993) and Oliver (1990) argue, that disabled people were first systematically categorised, incarcerated and excluded. From then, theirs has been a history of exclusion (Swain et al, 1993). It is then that we start to see for the first time on a grand scale, the rise of the asylums, the segregation of the 'morally defective', homes for 'incurables', the sanatoriums and the 'specialist' hospitals and 'special' schools. However, it was not only that disabled people and service users were removed from the rest of 'normal' society. Disabled people, those judged 'abnormal' and 'defective', were also 'scientifically' removed from each other. Thus, 'the insane' and 'the mad' were taken to different spaces from 'the blind' or 'the deaf', who in turn had their own spaces. People with physical impairments were separated from those with sensory impairments and those with learning difficulties were locked away and kept hidden from all. Within these different spaces, people were further medicalised. 'The blind' were distinguished from 'the partially sighted'; 'the deaf' from the 'deaf mute'; the 'manic' from the 'psychotic'. The segregation, isolation and degradation – unintentional or otherwise – of disabled people and service users, were routinised and became the norm. It was what could happen if you were seen to be 'defective' and to have an impairment and lacked family members to protect you from being swept up into this massive network of distant institutions. It also paved the way for how disability is still significantly understood and perceived today.

Many of the institutions that survive to the present day were born out of this period of massive social, cultural and economic change. Large charities, such as the Royal National Institute for the Blind, founded in 1868, Scope (formerly The Spastic Society) and the Royal National Institute for the Deaf aptly illustrate the new classification and medicalisation of disability and disabled people that then developed. After the Second World War, the medicalisation of disability was further consolidated by charitable organisations that prioritised the funding of medical research in order to 'treat' and find a 'cure' for specific impairments.

Thus, the history of disabled people and service users, which culminated in them establishing their own movements in Britain during the last part of the 20th century, is one that is typified by fragmentation and segregation. The legacy of this 'impairment-specific' past persists today. The legislation, policy and procedural guidelines that are specifically concerned with disabled people (in their broadest definition) are still significantly based on impairment groups, such as, for example, people with learning difficulties, mental health service users and more recently also people with autism. Yet we know from more recent broader legislation, such as anti-discrimination and equalities legislation, and from the accounts of disabled people themselves, that what crucially has been problematic for them in society are the shared barriers and exclusions that they have faced.

Traditional tendencies to segregate different impairment groups and see them differently have also been reflected in their different histories. For example, the first trade union for blind people – the National League of the Blind – was formed in 1899 and blind and visually impaired people have a history of being active in fighting for better working conditions and better pay. Mental health service users/survivors are still having to struggle against prevailing media and political perceptions of them as threatening and dangerous, as well as the increasing use of compulsory hospitalisation, enforced treatment and the extension of control into the community. It is not difficult to understand, then, why some mental health service users/ survivors are reluctant to identify with the broader disabled people's/service users' movement. They have tended to follow a different path to self-empowerment and liberatory politics (Barnes et al, 1999; Beresford, 2008). Yet their experience of segregation and medicalisation has been very similar to that of people with physical, sensory and intellectual impairments. The fragmenting effect of service users' disempowering past is still influential.

While it is clear that some of the modern impairment-specific charities do helpful work, for example Arthritis Care, Diabetes UK, Mencap and Mind, at the same time they perpetuate the idea that people with different impairments, who use different health and social care services, are separate and distinct from each other and are best served by their own separate organisations. This has long been challenged as divisive by the disabled people's movement. Such a medicalised, impairment-specific understanding of disability suggests that the problems that different groups experience are quite different, yet we know that crucially they have faced common barriers that have stood in the way of their full and equal participation in society (Swain et al, 1993; Campbell and Oliver, 1996; Oliver and Barnes, 1998).

Given their own strong criticisms of the status quo, it is perhaps not surprising, when the modern disabled people's movement was first emerging, that it was subject to attack for its own homogeneity. And indeed pioneers such as Ken Davies, John Evans, Vic Finkelstein, Paul Hunt and Phillip Mason were all white, male, wheelchair users. They came in for frequent public criticism from service providers and traditional organisations for disabled people, controlled by non-disabled people, for what was seen as their embodiment of an implicit hierarchy of impairment. There were notable exceptions: Nasa Begum, Jane Campbell, Kath Gillespie-Sells, Chris Harrison, Rachel Hurst, Michelin Mason, Tom Shakespeare and others, but even so, the new disability movement was predominantly the domain of white, male, wheelchair users.

The need for inclusion

The disability movement of the early 1980s was quick to recognise the need to address inclusivity and diversity. Alliances were forged with other impairment groups, with black and minority ethnic community groups and disabled women's groups. By the late 1980s, the British Council of Organisations of Disabled People (BCODP), as it then was, the umbrella organisation for user-controlled organisations, included the Association of Blind Asians and the Asian Disabled People's Alliance. The disabled people's movement strove to include groups specifically for gay, lesbian, bisexual and transgendered disabled people, residential service users and other excluded groups. However, addressing truly meaningful inclusion and diversity within the disabled people's movement was and remains a contested area. There have been long-term concerns that it has been based on a narrow interpretation of disability, which has tended to leave out people with learning difficulties, mental health service users/survivors, older disabled people and people with life-limiting and chronic conditions that are disabling and associated with impairments (Shakespeare, 2006; Thomas, 2007).

The emergence of broader service users' movements is perhaps a reflection of this. It also reflects the unwillingness, which we have already touched on, of some groups, notably mental health service users/survivors, to identify as disabled people.

An early criticism made of service users' groups and organisation was that they were not 'representative' (Beresford and Croft, 1990). Over the years, this has tended to be used as a stick with which to beat service users' and disabled people's self-organisation (Beresford and Campbell, 1994). Significantly, however, pre-existing power holders, such as service providers, policy makers and professionals, have rarely been subjected to the same criticism. While the issue of how representative or not service users and their organisations are may be a red herring, the issue of how *diverse* and *inclusive* they are, certainly is important. If they fail to reflect the range of experience and perspectives that go to make up their constituencies, then, arguably, they are merely mirroring dominant barriers and exclusions and failing to reflect the interests of service users and disabled people more generally.

Several dimensions of diversity can be identified that need to be addressed if disabled people's and service users' organisations and activities are to be inclusive. These include:

- equality issues – whether people are included and can take part on equal terms regardless of their gender, race/ethnicity, sexuality, age, class, disability, belief, culture and so on;
- however people communicate, whether they use sign language, they do not use speech, they have speech aids or English is not their first language;
- wherever they live, whether they are Travellers, homeless, refugees or asylum seekers, live in the country, are in the prison and criminal justice system or in residential services;
- regardless of the nature, complexity or extent of their impairments;
- whether or not they are affiliated to disabled people's/service users' or other organisations;
- regardless of their responsibilities, for example as parents, supporting family members, in full-time employment or education and so on.

In recent years there has been a growing concern, particularly within state organisations and the service system, that many service users are being left out of participatory activities and initiatives. New terms have been coined such as 'hard-to-reach' groups and 'seldom-heard voices' to reflect this issue and there has been a growing emphasis on it in mainstream publications and discussions (eg Begum, 2006; Moriarty et al, 2007; Duffy, 2008; CQC, 2009).

Shaping Our Lives

In Shaping Our Lives, the national service user-controlled organisation and network in which we are involved, we have made comprehensive and systematic efforts to address such issues of inclusion. We have sought to do this both in how we work and in our objectives. As well as learning a lot through this, we have also extended our evidence base through undertaking related research projects. Thus, Shaping Our Lives offers some helpful insights into understanding issues around addressing diversity and its implications for service users' solidarity.

Shaping Our Lives was established in 1997. It works closely with local service users and their organisations, as well as with government and other bodies, to increase the say and control that people have, as long-term health and social care service users, over their lives and the support they receive.

One of the features that distinguishes Shaping Our Lives as an organisation and which has helped it in its efforts to address diversity, is that it is made up of and works across a very wide range of service users, including older people, mental health service users/survivors, people with physical and/or sensory impairments, people with learning difficulties, people who have had problems with alcohol and drugs, people with chronic and life-limiting illnesses and conditions, people living with HIV/AIDS and people with experience as children and young people of being in state care. Shaping Our Lives has also developed links with groups of homeless people, Travellers and people with experience of prison and the criminal justice system.

To achieve its commitment to inclusion, Shaping Our Lives places an emphasis on *access*. It sees access as an equality issue and identifies three key areas for access. These are:

- physical/environmental access;
- cultural access;
- communication access.

Shaping Our Lives identifies as part of the broader disabled people's and service users' movements. It works to develop effective ways to ensure the involvement of groups facing particular barriers (so-called 'hard-to-reach' groups), as well as addressing diversity in all the expressions we identified earlier. It has developed policies and practices to do this. Such diversity is reflected in the make-up of both its management and its national user groups.

Two pieces of work that Shaping Our Lives has undertaken in recent years offer insights into the relationships that service users see between diversity, inclusion and solidarity, while highlighting some of the problems that service users, disabled people and their organisations see facing them.

Relationships matter: building our knowledge and networks

For this project, carried out in 2008 and funded by the Equalities and Human Rights Commission, Shaping Our Lives recruited five user-controlled organisations that were interested in and could organise regional events to find out more about involving service users, addressing diversity and equality issues. The aim was to enable user-controlled organisations in their areas to come together and share experiences and knowledge. These 'get-togethers' themselves included a diverse range of service users. They were successful. Key findings from the project included:

- Service users had limited opportunities to network with other user organisations. They often did not know what service user organisations

existed. This was frequently because of service user organisations' overall lack of capacity, with:
  – too small and overworked a workforce to allow for networking;
  – insufficient and insecure funds to network adequately;
  – having to be funding led for their very survival, which discouraged collaboration and networking;
  – the lack of information about and promotion of different user groups.

• Service users identified a lack of knowledge about other service user groups as a barrier to networking with each other. They had not realised the common ground shared by so many different groups until they attended the networking events. Then they recognised that many of the barriers they encountered were shared by other groups of disabled people and service users, for example, in relation to:
  – language and communication;
  – stigma;
  – fear and apprehension;
  – cultural assumptions;
  – financial constraints;
  – lack of accessible public transport.

• Service users felt that it was essential to recognise the common issues that all service users face. They highlighted the importance of actively supporting a diverse range of long-term users of health and social care services to network with each other. Such networking was seen as crucial.

• The project made it possible for long-term users of health and social care services to share experiences and consolidate their identity as service users. This allowed service users from diverse backgrounds and understandings to recognise shared barriers to equality and full human rights.

• The empowerment this offered made it more possible for groups to work together to influence change and promote good relations among and between groups.

This work was consistent with and reinforced the findings of a national research study on service user networking and knowledge, which Shaping Our Lives had earlier carried out supported by the Joseph Rowntree Foundation (Branfield et al, 2006).

Beyond the usual suspects; developing diversity in involvement

This three-year national research and development project was supported by the Department of Health. Its aim was to extend user involvement beyond a narrow group of activists and find out how to enable a highly diverse range of service users and disabled people to be effectively and equally involved. We wanted to hear from them what the barriers were in the way of their involvement and what worked to overcome them (Branfield and Beresford, 2011).

The project worked with three groups of service users. These were black and minority ethnic mental health service users, a mixed group of people with learning difficulties and women who used alcohol services. We also wanted to address different dimensions of difference within these groups, so participants included service users who communicated differently, older people, unaffiliated service users and people using residential services. Key messages from the project included:

- There was no evidence that groups who tended not to get involved were any less interested in doing so. They simply seemed to face more barriers.
- All groups could participate and contribute in some way if that was supported and made possible.
- People's basic access needs continued routinely not to be met.
- It was the stigmatising and negative stereotyping of some groups that discouraged them from getting involved.
- Self-appointed gatekeepers restricted some service users' involvement, particularly those who were most disempowered, for example people living in residential services or relying long term on services.
- Service users were keen to highlight the complexity of their identity. There could be many aspects to who they were. They might also face barriers and discrimination from within their 'own' group. So, for example, a disabled lesbian might find that she experiences discrimination from the disabled community because she is a lesbian, but she might find that she is also excluded from the lesbian community because she is disabled.
- Some service users felt that the 'diversity agenda' was used by agencies to replace more politicised service users with those who had less skills and experience. Diversity should mean including the usual suspects, as well as opening up involvement to others, not debarring them.

The findings from this project and the 'Relationships matter' project were closely consistent. They highlighted the importance to achieving diverse involvement of:

- undertaking outreach and development work: going out to service users rather than expecting them to come to you;
- recognising that inclusive involvement is possible, but demands additional resources to support it, including skills, funding and infrastructural support;
- understanding that the key is moving beyond traditional meeting/written approaches to involvement, developing instead ones that are innovative, flexible, comfortable for different individuals and groups and which connect with their ordinary and existing cultures and experience;
- appreciating the importance of issues of fear and stigma, which mean that methods that enable people to retain their anonymity, get involved on their own and communicate in different ways, for example through the telephone, texting and the internet, are important.

Conclusion

Participants in both these projects welcomed and valued the broader involvement of a diverse range of service users. This did not only go for those who had previous experience of being involved, but equally for those whose past experience had been of exclusion, rather than involvement. Both projects also highlighted that service users and their organisations are uniquely positioned to 'build bridges' with other less-networked individuals as they understand and share many similar barriers. The broad range of service users who participated in these projects emphasises that service users could identify with each other over common and similar experiences from different viewpoints and identities. A general non-specific fear and apprehension of getting involved was particularly highlighted as something that only fellow service users seemed likely completely to understand and help overcome.

This has also been our experience in Shaping Our Lives. As we have worked to become more inclusive in what we do and gained skills and experience in addressing access and diversity, we have come to work in different, more accessible ways. These help make it possible for everybody to be part of meetings, discussions and decision making, regardless of how they communicate or whether, for example, they have learning difficulties. We can work better this way. Our different ways of working make it more possible for what we do to be inclusive and to be of benefit to all. It acknowledges, values and helps each person understand better, issues of sexuality, class and other areas of discrimination, and for us all to overcome the negative consequences of being institutionalised and disempowered. Working together in this way strengthens solidarity because it challenges all forms of discrimination and external pressures to 'divide and rule'. The following compilation of comments frequently made by people involved in Shaping Our Lives sums up the results:

You can feel comfortable at meetings. We use a series of ground rules, which we have worked out to do things together in respectful and inclusive ways. We start off all our meetings with them. There is support for people before meetings so that they can take part properly. You can be open about who you are. You can be yourself. I like being involved. The way we do things may seem slower. We try and make sure everyone knows what is going on and can say what they want. But you see that we get things done. We do what needs to be done.

Our experience is unquestionably that addressing diversity and working in more inclusive ways helps us to strengthen our solidarity. It means that different movements work together and gain strength from each other. It means that we learn about the overlaps between service users and carers, service workers and users, and encourages understanding and alliances – pointing us to a broader solidarity. The evidence from research projects we have carried out supports this.

Given longstanding criticisms of service users and their organisations for being 'unrepresentative', it is significant that the pressure and precedents for such inclusive ways of working and organising have come primarily from people's own self-organisations. Their movements are now a global phenomenon, developing apace in the majority world and not just in the 'developed' and richer nations. Service users' and disabled people's self-organisation points to a different and more inclusive kind of politics that challenges prejudices and discriminations about age, disability and other equality issues. Service users are still significantly excluded from conventional political involvement and that is still true even at the level of reduced substantive citizen and voting rights and engagement (Beresford, 2010). However, their movements and organisations have offered them a new route to involvement, and a starting point for engaging with and influencing traditional approaches both to politics and to policy making. They offer exemplars and insights with much wider application for understanding and developing democracy and policy.

four

Service users and the third sector: opportunities, challenges and potentials in influencing the governance of public services

Graham P. Martin

Introduction

As the contributions throughout this collection highlight in different ways, the user involvement movement has scored many successes over the last few decades. In its transition from 'margin to mainstream' (see Introduction, this volume), it has secured increasing influence in the delivery of mental and physical healthcare, social services and other fields of public service provision. However, as many of the contributions also indicate, in many cases this influence has come at a cost. The mainstreaming of user involvement is seen by some as a deradicalisation, and even a co-optation to dominant managerial, professional and, indeed, academic ways of thinking and doing (see, for example, Chapter Fifteen, this volume). This has given rise to questions over whether the increasing recognition and legitimacy afforded to the voices of service users are compatible with the independence that autonomous user movements have traditionally valued and, if not, then how much of the latter should be sacrificed in pursuit of the former.

This chapter considers this dilemma in relation to the increasing *opportunities* for influencing the governance, management and delivery of public services enjoyed by 'third sector' organisations. As bodies that are made up of, or seek in some way to represent, service users, such organisations have been taken increasingly seriously by successive governments over recent decades. Many voluntary sector organisations are viewed by government as partners in the planning, management and delivery of public services, and have a seat at the table at the highest level of policy development. A growing body of literature has, however, highlighted some of the *challenges* that this brings for such organisations, as they attempt to reconcile their need to defend their independence with the possibilities for contributing to real changes in service delivery given to them. This chapter seeks to provide a review of this literature, with a particular emphasis on the practical implications of this for those grappling with such issues, many of which apply not only to third sector organisations that have the ears of policy makers, but also to those engaging with lower-level state organisations, such as healthcare providers and local authorities. I illustrate some of these with examples from my own research (see also Martin, 2008b, 2009, 2011). While not seeking directly to address the question of how to square autonomy with influence, or whether partnership with state institutions is more a noble compromise or a Faustian pact, I seek to make my contribution as useful as possible in informing those faced with such dilemmas, by highlighting the *potentials* as well as the dangers of such opportunities.

Following this introduction, the chapter is structured by five further sections. First, I review the rise to influence of the third sector as a conduit for users' voices over the last few decades. After this, I consider three linked sets of issues that face voluntary organisations when constituted as partners by the state: the various (potentially conflicting) roles that such organisations are expected to fulfil; the implications of this for the way in which third sector organisations gather and represent the views of users to state bodies; and the outcomes in terms of service user influence on the design, management and delivery of public services. A brief conclusion follows.

The rise to influence of the third sector[1]

At the same time as the principle of user involvement in the management and provision of care and other services has been making its journey from margin to mainstream in policy discourse, so too has the third sector. Following the Second World War, voluntary organisations, which had previously been central to the delivery of welfare, became more marginal as the state came to dominate welfare provision, although they remained important in areas neglected by publicly provided services (Davis Smith et al, 1995). Policies pursued by Conservative governments in the 1980s, such as quasi-markets in welfare provision, saw a renewed role for not-for-profit organisations, now cast as competitors (with for-profit businesses) for contracts from the state to provide public services. While this meant new opportunities for third sector organisations to generate revenue, it also created new challenges for them. Many authors find that being constituted as competitors in a marketplace can give rise to fundamental shifts in the nature of a voluntary organisation (Bode, 2003). Forced to view their value in increasingly economistic terms, they may start to look like private sector businesses (Owen and Kearns, 2006), with an increasingly conventional relationship between voluntary (or employed) staff and service users, as 'consumers of welfare delivered by a professionalised workforce' (Fyfe and Milligan, 2003, p 407).

These difficulties were to some extent recognised by the state, and in the early 1990s, the UK government set up an inquiry into the changing relationship between the state and the third sector. This recommended the creation of a 'compact' between government and the voluntary sector, with a view to protecting the independence of the voluntary sector, demarcating boundaries and setting up a framework for 'partnership' without co-optation (Morison, 2000; Plowden, 2003). This fitted well with the vision of the incoming Labour government, which accepted the inquiry's recommendations in 1997. The new government's vision for the 'modernisation' of public services included a central role for the third sector, and not just as a contractor in the welfare quasi-market, but as a key stakeholder in the design, delivery and management of public services (Johnson and Osborne, 2003). Labour sought to create a renewed role for the third sector, drawing on the close relationship with and knowledge of the needs of service users that it was still seen to have (notwithstanding the way in which market reforms had transformed this relationship). In sum, policy from 1997 held that:

> the specialist knowledge held by TS [third sector] organizations bestows capacity on them to represent users and provide the means to express their views, thereby empowering users to voice their concerns and needs....Accordingly, New Labour posited that as part of the 'new way of doing things', TS organizations would work in partnership with central and local government to make use of the sector's specialist knowledge and innovative expertise when dealing with service users. (Kelly, 2007, p 1010)

Yet as with other facets of its public policy, there were continuities with as well as breaks from Conservative policies in Labour's approach to the relationship with the third sector. As well as this role as partner in the governance of public services, in most fields of welfare, voluntary sector organisations retained a role in the delivery of public services under contract from central and local government (Osborne and McLaughlin, 2004). As we see in the next section, this multiplicity of roles creates significant challenges for third sector organisations as they attempt simultaneously to fulfil this new, representative function, and to conform to the economistic requirements of the competitive market.

The challenges of multiple roles

Since 1997, then, there have been increasing opportunities for third sector organisations to engage with the state as *partners* in the development of welfare policy, as well as contractors in the delivery of service provision. This reflects the situation in Continental Europe, where third sector organisations have long played a much more prominent role in different levels of the design, management and delivery of public services. Brandsen and Pestoff (2006, pp 496-8) present a useful distinction between three levels of involvement for the third sector: 'co governance', 'in which the third sector participates in the planning and delivery of public services'; 'co management', 'in which third sector organizations produce services in collaboration with the state'; and 'co production', involving 'a more restricted service delivery role for VCOs [voluntary and community organisations] in collaboration with the state'. Each of these roles presents a different set of expectations about what a third sector organisation should be doing, and there are potential conflicts between these. For example, Pestoff et al (2006, p 593) find 'a trade off between co management and co governance', because co-optation into the management of public service delivery is seen to reduce the ability of third sector organisations to act as autonomous, critical partners in the overall governance of welfare, and as advocates for the service users for whom they seek to speak.[2]

Such tensions were apparent in my own research, which covered the involvement of service users in a programme of National Health Service (NHS) pilot cancer genetics services. These were co-funded by the Department of Health and Macmillan Cancer Support, a third sector organisation with a long history of collaboration with the NHS (Rossi, 2009). As a large charity (with an income of £120 million in 2008), Macmillan had traditionally focused its efforts on partnerships with the NHS to pump prime new facilities for cancer treatment and care, and new specialist cancer posts (such as the well-known Macmillan nurses). In recent years, however, Macmillan had sought to increase its capacity to represent the views of service users to government and to the NHS, merging with another charity, Cancer Voices, which was dedicated to drawing on the experiences of service users to influence change, and initiating various activities to increase the involvement of service users in its own work and that of the NHS. This included user involvement in these pilot cancer genetics services, where Macmillan insisted that each funded pilot service should include some form of site-level user involvement process, and convened its own programme-level, cross-pilot National User Reference Group. This group allowed involved users from each pilot to come together separately from staff and, with assistance from Macmillan officers, work together to make a programme-level user contribution. Macmillan convened parallel programme-level events for all those involved in the pilots, and through these sought to facilitate collaboration between sites, improved user involvement processes and the sharing of good practice.

In Brandsen and Pestoff's (2006) terms, then, Macmillan was involved in the co-governance of the pilot programme (as a partner to the Department of Health) and its co-management (through the programme-level events for users and others), but not co-production (since service delivery remained the responsibility of NHS staff who had won funding to set up the pilots). As a trusted partner of the Department of Health in policy development and in funding the programme, the organisation was perhaps ideally placed to ensure that user involvement had real influence within and beyond the pilot programme, linking involvement both into the way in which pilots were delivered and into the development of policy around cancer genetics in the future. But how far was it able to balance the competing pressures on third sector organisations in such positions highlighted by Brandsen and Pestoff (2006) and others mentioned earlier?

Consequences for effective user involvement and advocacy

The multiple roles of co-production, co-management and co-governance, then, can impede the ability of third sector organisations to relate to and speak for service users. Where organisations are involved in the delivery of services under contract from the state under co-production arrangements, new barriers can be erected between staff and service users, replicating the professional–client relationship of the state sector or even the business–customer relationship of the private sector (Fyfe and Milligan, 2003; Fyfe, 2005; Jenkins, 2005; Brandsen and van Hout, 2006). This is seen as undermining the very value that third sector organisations bring to welfare delivery, by destroying the trust and social capital shared by service users and voluntary sector staff (Fyfe, 2005).

Co-management and co-governance give rise to somewhat different, but no less pressing, challenges to third sector organisations seeking to retain their distinctiveness, stay true to their missions and thus remain able to speak for those they seek to represent. On the face of it, they may present new opportunities for third sector organisations to bring the views of users to bear on the design and management of services. In practice, this is not always the case. Partnership with the state does not always mean significant extra influence for third sector organisations or involved service users (Lowndes and Sullivan, 2004). Moreover, as we have seen, partnership brings with it the risk of co-optation, and this can mean an increasingly narrow role for user involvement mechanisms, too. In their far-reaching study of various forms of public participation in local government, housing, health and other fields, Barnes et al (2007) found that frequently, when enticed into the 'invited spaces of governance', previously independent user groups found themselves increasingly constrained by much narrower terms of reference. (Often limited) influence comes at the cost of ceding control of agendas to the state rather than holding onto autonomy. Other groups retained a more arm's-length relationship with state organisations, but while these 'parallel discursive arenas', as Barnes et al (2007) termed them, were places where a much wider array of ideas, views and identities could be expressed, they also often had less influence on service provision.

Yet is it possible to retain sufficient autonomy and control over purpose and identity while also gaining greater influence on the governance and management of public services? In my own research, the National User Reference Group that Macmillan facilitated seemed, at times, to offer such an opportunity. Convened, as noted previously, to provide an opportunity for involved service users to come together away from the pilot sites with which they were involved, it offered a space for users to talk expansively about their roles, their contributions, their hopes for how services might develop. Many users found the Reference Group an environment in which they felt more comfortable than their local, site-level groups, where the concerns of professionals and managers seemed to dominate proceedings. In the Reference Group, they were given space to explore ideas and views in detail by Macmillan facilitators, and used this to arrive at a coherent view about what they were doing as involved users in the programme and what they might achieve. But the presence of Macmillan facilitators also brought with it the potential to influence the design and management of the programme of cancer genetics pilots at a high level. From the start, the facilitators were keen to ensure that the deliberations of the users at the Reference Group were 'steered' towards contributions that might stand a chance of being valued by those leading individual pilots, and the programme as a whole. At the same time as offering a place for *expansive* discussions about the identities and roles of involved users in the programme, then, the Reference Group was also a place where these could be *focused* and moulded into something that might have a tangible effect on the way in which the programme and pilots were operating.

The Reference Group, then, seemed to occupy an intermediate space between a 'parallel discursive arena', where influence might be limited, and an 'invited space of governance', where discussions might be constrained. The role of Macmillan as a third sector organisation seemed crucial in finding this gap, and at times, its dual role in the co-governance of the programme and in facilitating the 'service user voice' seemed to work well in reconciling independence with influence. In differing contexts, others too have found that third sector organisations can sometimes mediate the conflicting pressures presented by multiple roles. Carey et al (2009), for example, found that despite the professionalisation of a third sector organisation brought by government contracts to provide care services, it continued to provide a 'community space' for service users and staff alike to share, opening up 'new possibilities for relationships between third sector organizations, their community groups and the State' (Carey et al, 2009, p 643).

Implications for influence

Despite the pressures on their identities, purposes and relationships with service users brought by new roles, then, there are signs from the literature that sometimes, third sector organisations can reconcile these new roles with an ability to stay true to their core missions and, in the process, offer new opportunities for service users to influence the state. This gives the third sector a potentially important role in ensuring a user voice in the design, management and delivery of public services, especially given the deficiencies often found in the way the state itself goes about involving service users. Many studies (eg Mort et al, 1996; Milewa, 1997; Tritter et al, 2003; Barnes et al, 2007) have found that the way in which public servants such as managers and health and social care professionals pursue user involvement is more about self-legitimisation rather than valuing the views of service users, playing 'the user card' (Mort et al, 1996) to assist them in pursuing their own goals. This is often seen as resulting in a 'black boxing' of user involvement, whereby (selected) outcomes from deliberations are pursued by managers and professionals while others are sidelined, and the potential benefit of the richness of the process of deliberation is lost to services.

With its Reference Group, Macmillan attempted to avoid this kind of black boxing. It was keen, as we have seen, to ensure that the discussions that went on in the Reference Group resulted in contributions to the management of the programme and pilots that stood a chance of being utilised by those in charge. Consequently, Macmillan facilitators were eager to work with involved users to steer their deliberations towards clear messages that could inform the decisions made by pilot-and programme-level managers, since they were conscious that for all their richness, the discussions in themselves were not something that these managers would draw on. However, the facilitators sought to achieve this 'distillation' into key messages in a way that involved the users themselves throughout, combining the managerial expertise in gaining influence in the NHS of the facilitators with the knowledge, experience and ideas of the users.

Sometimes this worked well, with the Reference Group producing a variety of outputs that were made available to pilot- and programme-level managers: summaries of what users most valued in service provision, for example, and 'best practice' guidance about how to do pilot-level user involvement as effectively as possible. However, there was a sense in which Macmillan's place in the co-governance and co-management of the pilot programme somehow prevented it from acting as an unencumbered advocate for all that the involved service users at the Reference Group wanted. As a co-funder of the programme and partner to the Department of Health in policy development, Macmillan itself had to act as a mediator between various sets of interests rather than solely as an advocate for its involved users. While it was willing, then, to facilitate the user involvement process and translate users' ideas into 'useable' products for managers, it was not willing to use its influence and place in the funding and governance of the pilot programme to force individual pilots to increase the resources they devoted to user involvement, as some of the users at the Reference Group desired (see Martin, 2011, for more detail). Ironically, then, the central role of Macmillan in the co-governance of the pilot programme reduced its ability to advance the views of the users it involved through the Reference Group, as it also had other responsibilities, roles and priorities to consider.

Concluding remarks

The literature, and my own research, present a mixed view of the opportunities, challenges and potentials offered to user involvement by the increasingly prominent place given to third sector organisations in the co-production, co-management and co-governance of public services. Third sector organisations tend to offer more open possibilities for user influence than state organisations often do, and at their best they can reconcile independence and influence in a novel way, combining the best aspects of both 'parallel discursive arenas' and 'invited spaces of governance'. However, there are sometimes conflicts between the roles and relationships brought by partnership with the state, and the potential to act unencumbered as an organisation that advances the views and needs of users. If nothing else, what the literature shows is that the extent to which these pressures compromise the 'user voice' is contingent on a number of factors:

- the characteristics of the organisation itself;
- the place in co-production, co-management and co-governance it has secured for itself;
- the relationships with other powerful stakeholders that result from this positioning;
- the skill of facilitators and users themselves in negotiating these challenges.

There is a need, then, to consider what these new roles do *to* the third sector organisations themselves:

- Do they change their priorities?
- Do they place them in networks where relationships with other powerful stakeholders become more important than relationships with users?
- Do they change the nature of the relationship with users themselves, making it more professionalised, bureaucratic or business-like?

New roles for the third sector undoubtedly bring with them potential for new influence for service users on the design, management and delivery of public services, but their potential to change in the very nature and purpose of third sector organisations means that they must be dealt with carefully. Above all, it should not be assumed that 'partnership' equates to influence: rather, careful consideration needs to be given to what involved users will get out of such opportunities and how, and ensuring that the structures of co-governance and co-management support this.

Notes

[1] While there is not space in this chapter to explore the heterogeneity of the enormous numbers of organisations (big and small, formal and informal, representative and user controlled) that are collectively labelled as 'the third sector', this variety should at least be acknowledged. See, for example, Kendall and Knapp (1995) for more detail. The discussion in this chapter consequently refers to the third sector in a generic way, which does not do justice to this diversity, and the issues it presents will not apply equally to all of them. It should be noted, however, that the third sector organisation with which my own research was concerned – Macmillan Cancer Support – is a large charity rather than a small voluntary or user-led organisation.

[2] It is also important to note that this 'advocacy' or 'representation' function is itself not uncontested within the user involvement movement. Many third sector organisations have long claimed to 'speak for' service users, but not all have involved service users effectively themselves in their management, governance or even policy development. Few are led or controlled by service users themselves.

five

The capacity, impact and challenge of service users' experiential knowledge

Phil Cotterell and Carolyn Morris

Introduction

In this chapter we will explore experiential knowledge, including claims for such knowledge, and where it exists, evidence of impact. Additionally, we will consider the major challenges that service users and professionals may face when accessing or working with this knowledge. We have two main aims: to explore some of the thinking behind experiential knowledge and to consider how experiential knowledge is embodied in service design and research. For the first aim we draw on work from four distinct settings. This is only a brief introduction to these issues, but we hope it will be helpful to see where such thinking has been enacted. For the second aim we use the setting of cancer care as an example and believe that this can offer insights that are transferable to other settings. We have co-written this chapter with Phil broadly leading on the next section and Carolyn broadly leading on the subsequent section. Our method of working, and the finished chapter, reflects our sharing of types of knowledge: an interchange of experiences and understandings. A conversation that has taken place over time and in which we have learned from each other.

Ramon (2003, p 16) has argued that service user involvement in research 'has been developed as a method of creating new knowledge, hitherto hidden and often described as invalid by professionals'. If the knowledge that service users bring to involvement activities is a 'new knowledge', what form does this take and what value can there be in utilising this within professional practice, policy and/or research? In this chapter we use the term 'service user' to describe those people who make use of health and social care services (including carers and family members); and 'service user involvement' to describe processes where the views and priorities of service users inform the delivery of services and/or research. We reflect further on terminologies later in the chapter.

Experiential knowledge refers to the possession of a knowledge that originates through living an experience or experiences (Hill Collins, 1990, p 233). It is a knowledge that has originated from direct experience. It contrasts with other types of knowledge: 'Experiential knowledge is truth learned from personal experience with a phenomenon rather than truth acquired by discursive reasoning, observation, or reflection on information provided by others' (Borkman, 1976, p 446). Such knowledge might be particularly harnessed in areas where people have had experiences of common interest and organised themselves in relation to it. This may be an experience of a particular practice, system or organisation, for instance, such as when a group of people are motivated to act in reaction to a poor experience of a particular service, or to share personal experiences of their condition.

Collective action by service users has enabled the articulation of new forms of knowledge. Two important elements of experiential knowledge have been highlighted. First, that experiential knowledge arises from personal participation in the phenomenon and incorporates a reflective stance on this experience. The second element concerns the individual's belief about the validity and trust in this knowledge, based on their experience of the phenomenon in question (Borkman, 1976). Beresford (2003, p 22) hypothesises that knowledge originating from this direct experience delivers more reliable knowledge: 'The greater the distance between direct experience and its interpretation, then the more likely resulting knowledge is to be inaccurate, unreliable and distorted.'

However, knowledge claims are contested, and a hierarchical structure operates when claims are asserted for differing types of knowledge (see Chapter Eleven, this volume). An inequality in knowledge production exists, where particular forms of knowledge are granted importance and others a marginal status. As we will see later in this chapter, those in marginalised positions need to struggle for acknowledgement of theirs as a credible knowledge (for example service users), and those traditionally in a privileged knowledge position will need to shift significantly to accept knowledge in different forms (for example health and social care professionals); different ways of knowing the world. In the next section, we briefly review different stances to knowledge outlined by key thinkers in the social sciences.

Key knowledge claims

In this section we outline different approaches to understanding the world from which experiential knowledge claims originate. In order to explore the assumptions that knowledge claims are based on, we describe the differing knowledge claims raised by critical theorists, feminists, emancipatory researchers and an educationalist. These positions are multifaceted and each perspective encompasses differences as well as common features. We do not focus on the differences within these approaches but what we attempt to do here is identify the contribution made by each to an understanding of experiential knowledge and its significance.

Our choice of approaches is not exclusive – there will be others that can inform us on the nature of experiential knowledge – but we argue that those presented here are helpful to our understanding of the building blocks of experiential knowledge. Their inclusion is based on their common aims of challenging knowledge based on a view of people as 'objects', and of promoting the voices of marginalised groups.

A contribution from feminism

Feminist thought challenges a view of people as singular objects in the way that traditional science can do, and it also sees the development of this 'scientific' knowledge as a means of domination by privileged groups in society. Feminism contests science's claims of neutrality and objectivity and emphasises the importance of social relations in general and gender relations in particular (Letherby, 2003, p 20). This has been summarised as follows: 'The personal is the political. The personal and the everyday are both important and interesting and ought to be the subject of inquiry. It is important not to downgrade other people's realities. It is necessary to reject the "scientist/person" dichotomy' (Stanley and Wise, 1993, p 118).

Feminist thought is part of a political struggle with a central debate being about the significance of being a woman, the place of female experience and gender difference in knowing, and knowledge making. Feminist research is often concerned with changing people's situation rather than simply understanding their situation (Maynard, 1994). Knowledge is seen to originate from people's lives; it is shaped by society, transformed from the personal or individual to the collective (Harding, 1993, p 63). Further to this, in a claim for 'strong objectivity', a reflexive position is taken that is aware of the social situation of knowledge generation, how knowledge is produced and the 'unknowing' of researchers (Harding, 1993, p 69). The unexamined shared assumptions and beliefs between researchers and the researched are at the centre of attention here.

Feminist thought argues that many individual voices and many forms of knowledge arise and form collective knowledge. Tanesini (1999, p 156) suggests that these different forms of knowledge need to be invited, in a participatory way, to be heard, in order that all experiences are taken into account. Hill Collins (1990, p 236) points out how each group will speak from and share its own partial and situated knowledge. Here, the suggestion is that with marginalised knowledge accepted, with no one group claiming dominant knowledge, groups can move to consider the varied world, the common thread that connects us all. Connected to this, Beresford (2003, p 49) has highlighted how a history of being marginal, of being unheard and of being discredited takes a great deal of effort to overcome as does seeing one's own experience and knowledge as important and equal to others in more dominant groups.

A contribution from Paulo Freire

The work of Paulo Freire has been influential in the development of critical inquiry. Freire's work has largely been concerned with raising awareness about the empowerment of the oppressed. A symbiotic relationship between oppressed and oppressor is suggested, with each dependent on the other, but only the oppressed is able to act to change their and their oppressor's situations. As with an emancipatory research approach (discussed later in this chapter), Freire (1972, p 30) talks of action, for him in terms of educational initiatives, *with* not *for* the oppressed.

It can be difficult to access the knowledge that marginal groups possess, as people in such a position may feel their knowledge to be unworthy and question the legitimacy of articulating their own knowledge. For Freire (1972, p 40), only a critical consciousness of the knowledge in one's possession can in turn lead to action and transformation. There is a clear link between Freire's work and emancipatory research and critical theory. All share an interest in people's political context, empowerment agendas and equality issues.

For Freire, dialogue becomes the precursor to action and liberation. Dialogue takes the form of critical thinking, with educator and educated working together equally on their knowledge-raising journey. Humphries and colleagues (2000, p 9) discuss the links between the work of Freire and feminist knowledge production. Both are concerned with the transformative and consciousness-raising capacity of knowledge.

A contribution from critical theory

Critical theory is 'critical' in terms of its stance in challenging claims made by scientific or traditional knowledges. It aims to unmask beliefs and practices that restrain freedom, justice and democracy in some way. Critical theory does not claim to emphasise service user involvement but, in terms of experiential knowledge, Habermas (1972, p 308) has argued that the knowledge interest involved in critical theory is emancipatory – concerned with unmasking ideologies that maintain the status quo by restricting the access of marginalised groups to the knowledge that oppresses them. Further to this, traditional science is just one source of valid knowledge but one that has subsumed other valid sources of knowledge.

Habermas (1972) characterises instrumental knowledge as a concrete, objective, cause-and-effect knowledge derived from empirical scientific methodologies. In contrast, practical or communicative action is the interpretative, interpersonal knowledge of society, culture and human relations generated through language and mutual understanding. It is group bound or culture bound and pertains to the social norms within which we live. Emancipatory knowledge is the personal, subjective knowledge of one's self, acquired through critical self-reflection. It leads to personal empowerment. Through emancipatory knowledge, we free ourselves from the constraints of uncritical assumptions and this can lead to a transformed consciousness.

Usher (1996, p 23) argues that critical theory refutes the possibility of a 'neutral or disinterested perspective because everyone is socially located and thus the knowledge that is produced will be influenced always by a social interest'. The aim of critical theorists is to delve beneath the accepted processes and structures that underpin society and shape everyday lives in an inquiring and critical way. They see knowledge as not only about finding out about the world, but also about changing it.

A contribution from emancipatory research

The disabled people's movement itself developed as a response and a challenge to the existing dominance of the traditional medical model of knowledge, and its expression within health and welfare. Rather than this traditional perspective, which placed the onus on individuals' 'limitations' and 'impairments', the developing 'social model of disability' (SMD) saw explanations of disability clearly lying with society itself (Oliver, 1990, p 11). Emancipatory research is often implicitly linked to and developed from action within the disabled people's movement, and is consequently often referred to as emancipatory disability research (Oliver, 1992; Barnes, 2003).

The new way of viewing disability and the issues disabled people faced, enabled by the SMD, has necessitated a new way of researching the issues and a new form of research relationship that is congruent with the social model. This relationship between disabled people's organisations, the SMD and research must ensure that emancipatory research is relevant to the people who are the focus of the research and ensure that their voice/knowledge comes to the fore (Stone and Priestley, 1996).

Emancipatory research is primarily concerned with the way research is conducted (social relations) and with control of the resources available for research (material relations). In discussing feminism's contribution to research with disabled people, Morris (1992) points to the need to move from alienating research to emancipatory research that enables people to take ownership of 'the definition of oppression'. Holding onto one's own knowledge is essential. In discussing feminists' interest in new ways of thinking and doing research, Gill (in Henwood et al, 1998, p 39) suggests that all knowledge production is socially situated, partial, explicitly political and claims that 'ethics, values and political commitments suffuse the entire research process'.

What is common to these different perspectives is the significance of knowledge rooted in experience. This is a knowledge that originates from the lives of people, from their perspectives, and which may often be subjugated, underprivileged, misinterpreted and/or oppressed. This knowledge is not part of 'mainstream' or traditional knowledge. This is not to suggest that such knowledge should be privileged above others, or that an oppressed knowledge is truer than others. The pursuit of an oppressed knowledge is concerned with rectifying an imbalance, to give voice to this knowledge that is often silenced and given less authority.

It is increasingly recognised that people with longstanding or chronic health conditions possess considerable knowledge and experience about their own conditions (DH, 2001b), and it is argued that experiential knowledge is in fact complementary to scientific knowledge (Entwistle et al, 1998; Goodare and Lockwood, 1999; Caron-Flinterman et al, 2005). However, such knowledge and experience have often been given an inferior status (Popay and Williams, 1996; Prior, 2003).

Approaches to collectivise knowledge production, and in particular to highlight the role of experiential knowledge, are attempts to extend the influence of service users within statutory organisations in participatory ways that are far removed from more consumerist approaches to gather views and to seek opinions. In the setting of cancer care, a more co-productive approach to service user involvement has been strived for that seeks to implicitly involve service users in planning and decision making.

Experiential knowledge in the setting of cancer care

We now move on to consider the context of cancer care, which is the basis for this section.

Overview and evaluations

National Health Service (NHS) cancer services and cancer research have been developing patient and public involvement (PPI) with successive cancer policy initiatives influential in this area (DH, 1995, 2000, 2007a; NAW, 2001; Scottish Executive Health Department, 2001; NCRI, 2008). Service user involvement now forms part of cancer core standards (NICE, 2004). Service user involvement is also a component of the Quality Measures against which cancer services are peer reviewed (a system of quality assurance). Service users are also a vital and integral part of the peer review process; 'it is important to show how users contribute to internal peer review processes' (NCAT, 2008).

Cancer services are delivered within 28 regional cancer networks that coordinate and provide a range of cancer services across England. One of the early vehicles for involvement in cancer services was the Cancer Partnership Project. It provided an infrastructure in which people affected by cancer, and professionals working in cancer services, worked together in groups to influence local cancer service development (see also Chapter Four). Evaluation of this project highlighted the complex range of activities that groups were engaged in. It also identified tensions between involved service users and professional members, tensions concerned with motivation and commitment to groups, emotional attachment to groups and disclosure of personal experiences (Sitzia et al, 2006). We will discuss this last 'tension' later in the chapter.

Consumer Research Panels, groups of people affected by cancer who work with cancer researchers to improve the relevance, quality and conduct of cancer research, have been shown to be making progress towards meaningful involvement in research (Cooper et al, 2005; Brown et al, 2006). Additionally, there is a relatively long history in the United Kingdom (UK) of involvement within clinical drug trials (Hubbard et al, 2008).

Leading national cancer research organisations, the National Cancer Research Institute (NCRI) and the National Cancer Research Network (NCRN), are overtly committed to service user involvement in research. The NCRI hosts a Consumer Liaison Group (CLG) consisting of some 70 people affected by cancer. Members of this group sit on the 23 Clinical Studies Groups, each of which covers a specific cancer site (for instance lung cancer) or area of interest (for instance radiotherapy). These groups develop new clinical studies that go forward to bid for funding. The CLG acts as a mechanism to facilitate involvement in every study developed by the Clinical Studies Groups; the majority of national, multi-centred clinical trials in the UK. The CLG adds the perspective of people affected by cancer, constructively challenges aspects of trial design and ensures that patient benefit is maximised. It is now a Quality Measure that service users are members of cancer research network management groups.

What's in a name?

Writing from the perspective of a patient, I [CM] wonder how to refer to myself. 'Cancer patient' will not do, true though it is, it leaves out too much; 'user', yuk; 'involved service user' just sounds pretentious; 'advocate' is good but too many do not understand its usage in this context; 'consumer' is the term widely used in cancer research, and given some kind of 'official' status by its use in NCRI – but some baulk – it is too passive perhaps and sounds as if you are on the receiving end, not actively engaged in trying to change things, develop new things.

'Patient representative', although widely used in the NHS, is a title many shy away from, arguing that they cannot and do not claim to be representative of all other patients. The perception is that if that is what it says on your badge, you risk being seen as claiming a universal knowledge that you cannot possibly have. 'Expert patient' is sometimes used in involvement but has a different connotation for health professionals and is not widely liked by patients. I have indeed heard it used as a derogatory label, by one patient of another.

'People affected by cancer' has an attractive neutrality but does nothing to indicate active involvement. It does, however, offer the virtue of inclusiveness: embracing patients, carers, friends and family. I've seen myself referred to as a cancer activist (in a grant application), which I quite liked, but it seems too overtly political for many. 'CancerVoices' is the term Macmillan Cancer Support use to describe their bank of people affected by cancer who wish to be involved in service improvement and in influencing research. It works brilliantly in that context – I can introduce myself as a CancerVoice and not feel embarrassed, and people 'get it' straight away. It has, however, become very much a Macmillan 'brand'. 'Lay person' offers neutrality about the individual, but with no suggestion as to role. All are used – often interchangeably. Ardron and Kendall (2010) use at least five of these descriptors in their account of PPI in UK cancer research. Each of the various terms used to represent us, or that we choose to use about ourselves, makes a claim of some kind about the knowledge we are bringing to the table.

In an extreme example, the term 'the usual suspects' may be seen in different ways: as an acknowledgement that it is often the same small group of people active in, say, a hospital cancer user group; as a sign of respect for the commitment and work put in; as a grim acceptance that efforts to find more people have foundered but we are grateful for the input. It does not come over that way if it is about you. It is perceived as suspicious, dismissive of the knowledge you bring and as a label that disrespects your type of knowledge. The inference is that your knowledge is merely anecdotal, not evidence based.

The type of knowledge that service users are seen to bring is reflected in their title, which accounts perhaps for the dislike many hold for 'patient representative' as a title. Many users feel that it stakes too high a claim, a claim to knowledge they can not possibly have; while professionals often challenge just how representative you can be. Ethnic, cultural and class diversity issues highlight this – attempts to make involvement more reflective of the population at large have so far had only partial success. Whatever experiential knowledge I offer it is neither that of a teenage cancer patient nor that of a minority ethnic woman unable to discuss her proposed mastectomy at home. It has been highlighted, however, that members of the national CLG involved in high-level strategy meetings about cancer research also have extensive local links with everyday patients in hospital wards 'and with people living with their cancers on a day to day basis' (Ardron and Kendall, 2010, p 161). These links, they conclude, 'ensure that the voice of everyday people is heard consistently, coherently and democratically in the high offices of the land' (2010, p 161).

This argument works to support the credibility of the experiential knowledge that those CLG members bring to their discussions. In my own case, when I have been a member of national policy groups, it has seemed very important to me that I was rooted in my local cancer network and hospital groups. I needed confidence that the experiential knowledge I offered in discussion was not only mine, but also reflected the experiences and feelings of others. Often people want 'the patient view' and I have to say, there isn't one: there are several. Cancer Partnership groups strengthen *their* knowledge of current patient experience by having access to regular surveys of local patients' recent experience of treatment, surveys that are increasingly shaped by our involvement in the design.

If our lack of representativeness is one challenge thrown out to cancer advocates, another is being out of touch: out of touch with current treatments and clinical conditions, out of touch with our own feelings about it all. Our experiential knowledge is seen as being out of date. There is a real difficulty for advocates here, as many cancer involvement groups stipulate an interval of two years since first cancer diagnosis before you can become a member, precisely so that members are able to distance themselves and not be 'too emotional'. The authenticity of our experiential knowledge is subject to challenge for being too recent on the one hand, and too much in the past on the other.

Hinterlands

Other forms of experiential knowledge at play in involvement in cancer services and research are seen in the non-cancer experiences and skills we users bring to our involvements. Life skills, community and trades union activism, working backgrounds in training, engineering and social work inter alia figured in a study of the impact on individuals of their involvements in cancer and palliative care (Cotterell et al, 2011). The skills and knowledge these experiences contribute are rich and varied, often more varied and less middle class than is the perception. A reported frustration is that these forms of experiential knowledge too often go unrecognised by the professionals who service users work alongside (Cotterell et al, 2011).

Other ways in which experiential knowledge is brought into play in cancer services are via patient and carer membership of Cancer Network tumour site-specific and so-called cross-cutting (for example research, chemotherapy) groups. The Cancer Quality Measures require at least two lay members on each of these groups. In practice this means that a Network group for head and neck cancer, for example, charged with coordinating care and research, is able to draw directly on the experiential knowledge of two patient/carer members, and through them, indirectly on the perspectives of other people affected by head and neck cancers with whom they are in touch via local support and involvement work. The extent to which groups comply with these measures is scrutinised in the quality assurance Cancer Peer Review Programme where patients and carers are part of the multidisciplinary review teams, alongside healthcare professionals, and sometimes chair reviews: evidence that at least some of the time the range of experience we bring *is* acknowledged.

Putting experience more centre stage

A number of recent initiatives have been designed to ensure that the experiential knowledge of people affected by cancer has more influence than heretofore in cancer research. The 'Listening Study', a UK-wide cancer research prioritisation exercise, described patient and carer priorities, and demonstrated that they were different from those of researchers and clinicians (Macmillan Cancer Support, 2006). Those priorities had emerged from the experiential knowledge of study participants. One outcome of these findings has been the introduction of Macmillan's User Led Research scheme, introduced in 2006, which has enabled many people affected by cancer to work alongside 'professional' researchers and in some cases to design and lead their own studies. As a beneficiary of this scheme, one of my [CM] challenges has been to live with the pace of publication and dissemination. I want the knowledge we have gained to be shared and shared widely: with academic researchers, yes, but also with those involved, or those who might become involved if they learned about some of the benefits others experience.

Challenging issues

Research illustrates the central role that experiential knowledge plays in personal understandings about cancer and in personal cancer care decision making (d'Agincourt-Canning, 2005; Carlsson and Nilbert, 2007; Etchegary et al, 2008). There is also evidence that involvement in cancer services and research is something that people affected by cancer are keen to pursue and that they want that involvement to be effective and to make a difference – something not always achieved (Cotterell et al, 2011). Professional and service user knowledge differences can lead to misunderstandings and, for service users, frustration. Some occur when professional knowledge is expressed, in ignorance of the possible impact.

Some examples may help illuminate these knowledge differences: 'I go to (name of clinical trial group) once a month ... I thought breast cancer was curable but it turns out not to be the case ... I thought ... I should be clear (from cancer) and then I found out that is not the case' (Cotterell et al, 2011). This is powerful and distressing knowledge if it is new to you and heard in a context where there is no support framework. Another participant in the same study reported: 'I have been made more aware of the depressing levels of achievement and gaps in the British experience in diagnosing, treating and preventing cancers' (Cotterell et al, 2011). Another challenging impact can be when service user knowledge appears to have limited influence on professional decision making: 'There is definitely some resistance to certain things that have been brought up ... I think sometimes there is still a huge element of staff paying lip service ... there are still too many staff, the management, who it's a token gesture' (Cotterell et al, 2011).

There are also examples of professional wariness when personal experiences have been disclosed within meetings with co-productive aims (Sitzia et al, 2006; Attree et al, 2009). The following cancer professional, speaking about service user group members raising personal experiences, illustrates this point: 'It is very difficult dealing with that, because obviously you don't want to minimise the problems that somebody is having but, you know, the group is about looking at things on a wider basis' (Sitzia et al, 2006, p 69).

Some professionals see experiential knowledge as useful only if service users also have scientific knowledge, as the following cancer professional indicated in a study of Consumer Research Panels:

> I personally think they can achieve very little unless the actual consumer has got some scientific grounding or some scientific background ... for actually formulating the scientific question or designing what best treatment to look for, or being able to tease out the literature issues that push you to ask a question or not, I think they are irrelevant really, just an extra tier of ticking a box to just get on with your trial. (Brown et al, 2006, p 118)

Differences in knowledge are clearly seen as a problem, then, with limited understanding or recognition of the nature and use of experiential knowledge. The evidence in this setting clearly indicates that many health professionals 'do not do partnership working', and that the idea of professionals and service users pooling knowledge to improve services is a problematic concept (Sitzia et al, 2006; Attree et al, 2009). In cancer care there appears to be a contradiction in that while the involvement of service users, of people affected by cancer, is rooted in policy and also now in practice, there are limits placed on the experiential knowledge that is permissible. The input of service users is seen as important within cancer services and research as a way to ensure that services and research are grounded in the personal first-hand experience and concerns of those who have been in receipt of these services and research. However, covert assumptions made by some professionals mean that specific direct personal experiences are considered unacceptable. This can lead to a disparity between the knowledge that service users wish to utilise and the knowledge that professionals wish to access.

One example of service users' knowledge becoming accepted as valid and acted upon can be seen in recent national policy initiatives designed to address the lack of care after cancer treatment ends. Service users had long spoken of feelings of abandonment at this stage, of difficulties they experienced in managing their lives beyond cancer. The Cancer Reform Strategy (DH, 2007a) made a commitment to improve patients' experience of living with and beyond cancer. As a result, the National Cancer Survivorship Initiative (NCSI) was established to consider a range of approaches to survivorship care. This initiative was formally launched on 11 September 2008; it takes account of and builds on the knowledge that people affected by cancer have of the emotional (living with uncertainty), practical (getting back to work) and financial (the costs of cancer) impacts brought about by a cancer diagnosis.

There are other complexities concerning differences in knowledge; there is anecdotal evidence that service users themselves, in this setting of cancer services, can add to the professional wariness about sharing experiential knowledge. Service user members of cancer service and research groups identify a tension between drawing on one's own experience and being stuck in it. To be authentic and hence valuable to others, we need to be rooted in our own experience but not bound by it. For some, it is about being able to turn their experiential knowledge into something else; a translation process where their knowledge is transformed, in their own mind, and in discussion with others (who may be fellow service users, professionals or a person such as a service user facilitator), into something generalisable; something that can be acted upon.

An example from current practice can be seen in my own local cancer network where service users have been trained in interviewing so that they can explore current chemotherapy patients' experiences of services and how they would like to see those services develop in future. Not recounting or imposing one's own views, but drawing out the views of others, requires a disciplined and dispassionate approach. It is hoped that this produces greater readiness to participate and richer and more subtly shaded data. A further example of experiential knowledge differing from that of professionals can be seen in the outcome of a recent patients' reference panel to support commissioning of future services in another part of the network. Contrary to many professional expectations, patients' preferred location for delivery of chemotherapy was in the clinical setting, and not at home.

Conclusion

Service user involvement within cancer services and research has developed a great deal over a decade or so. However, as involvement becomes embedded in commissioning and service specifications, for example, it arguably becomes increasingly professionalised, as its very status places pressure on those involved to operate in ways that diminish the very experiential knowledge that often led to their involvement in the first place. There may be an expectation that direct personal experience has to be 'translated' in order to become accepted as an 'involvement' contribution, that is to say, a piece of experiential knowledge that is valued. An important challenge for the future in this setting is to value this experience and find ways to accommodate service needs with those who have first-hand experience of cancer, its impact and the impact of services on them. Involved service users in the context of cancer care would do well to note the possibilities as highlighted from wider user movements in terms of collectively championing knowledge production (see the Introduction to this book, for example). One key aspect of user movements may be their ability to 'own' their distinct knowledge and to convey this externally.

While much progress has been made to develop and embed service user involvement in cancer service improvement and research, there are clear tensions and 'blocks' that inhibit such involvement having the highest impact and that inhibits productive co-working between service users and health professionals in this setting. We hope that this chapter has illustrated that experiential knowledge is a central element of involvement and one that is ignored or sidelined to the detriment of the organisations and individuals concerned.

Part One

User movements

Questions for reflection

The contributions in Part One have explored different ways in which service users have come together in their own organisations and sought to make changes in policy, services and the way in which issues relating to disability, mental health problems and illness are understood. Rather than offer any conclusions, we suggest that the contributions in Part One raise the following questions, which could usefully be a focus for discussion among students and activists, and which might be used to guide further research into collective action among service users. These questions are not exhaustive and may be approached in different ways. For example, they may be used to assist the study of user involvement and/or they may be used as a way of critically interrogating the collection gathered in Part One.

- How are accounts of user movements produced by activists themselves different from the accounts that researchers produce as a result of research and theoretical analysis? What are the benefits and disadvantages of each type of account?
- The growth of user movements can be related to experiences of discrimination and of lack of voice within services. Oppositional action based in shared experiences of disadvantage also contributed to the development of alternative analyses of, for example, the meaning of disability and mental illness. User involvement is now official policy, and service delivery models emphasise individual choice and use of mainstream services. What impact is this likely to have on autonomous collective action among service users and carers and the further development of a collective voice for those who are marginalised?
- Collective action has been built around shared identities and experiences, but it has also been argued that it is strongest when there are broad alliances between diverse groups of service users. What are the advantages and disadvantages of enabling diversity in collective action compared to topic- or condition-specific action?
- Early action within the disability movement was directed against voluntary organisations *for* rather than *of* disabled people. Is that distinction still sustainable? Can we understand voluntary organisations as part of 'the user movement' and, conversely, are user-led organisations any different from other third sector organisations?

- What are the advantages and disadvantages to service providers of working with autonomous user organisations, and what are the advantages and disadvantages to user-led organisations of entering into partnerships with service providers?

Part Two

User involvement in services

Marian Barnes and Phil Cotterell

Introduction

Part Two is concerned with user involvement in the context of service delivery. The development of user involvement within the United Kingdom (UK) was briefly described in the Introduction to this book and specific examples of user involvement in practice are explored in the chapters that follow. Here we discuss some of the key issues affecting the way in which this has developed. As a starting point we need to recognise that user involvement, as both a concept and as a practice, can have multiple meanings. As we have already seen, what user involvement is, what it aims to achieve and the term 'user' itself can be contested notions. In this book, the term 'user' is employed to refer to a person who receives or who is eligible to receive health and social care services and to carers of such people, who may be family or close friends. We acknowledge the limitations of the term, but adopt it as the most generic and least ideologically charged of the various alternatives.

The benefits and challenges of user involvement have received wide-ranging attention from researchers, service users and practitioners committed to developing more participatory practices. From one perspective, the development of such practices can be understood to reflect broader shifts in the relationship between government and people. For example, Suzy Braye has linked user involvement with: 'the participatory rights and responsibilities of citizenship and participatory democracy, which aspires to put government in touch with the people, and promotes the social inclusion of those traditionally marginalised within the power structures of society' (Braye, 2000, p 9).

From this perspective, the intended consequences of user involvement include heightening people's level of independence, promoting human and civil rights, and strengthening democracy (Beresford and Croft, 1993; Harrison and Mort, 1998). The promotion of user involvement in service decision making is also seen as a means of ensuring accountability and balancing managerial and professional power (Barnes, 1997a). These perspectives suggest that participation is an overtly political process, with objectives of enabling greater equality and more democratic decision making as well as securing improved services. While participation and user involvement are now embedded within official discourse, this is a comparatively recent phenomenon and community groups and user movements have campaigned for greater inclusion and participation (Beresford and Croft, 1993; Barnes et al, 2007). Morris (1994, p 1) notes the 'insistence by historically powerless groups that they want to be involved in decisions which determine the quality of their lives' and that they want 'their voices heard, to be part of their community rather than set apart from it'. As we saw in Part One, this user-led drive for involvement may be seen in the proliferation of support groups, self-help groups, more politically focused user groups, information networks, social groups and, more recently, internet chat rooms, blogs and websites dedicated to the sharing of experiences and support. But it has also had an impact on the nature and extent of initiatives within health and social care services through which service users have been able to have a voice in service decision making and, more fundamentally, on the way in which services are now accessed and provided.

From a professional perspective within health and social care, enhancing practice to account for the views and wishes of users is seen as one measure of 'best practice'. Nearly 20 years ago, Marsh and Fisher (1992) developed an approach to 'partnership practice' that identified 'good intentions' on the part of social workers in terms of service user involvement in decision making about the care and support they received, but which also identified substantial barriers to achieving this. In a health services context, the concept of 'shared decision making' between clinicians and patients (eg Charles et al, 1997) was advanced to promote practices by which treatment decisions would be made as a result of discussion and information sharing between doctor and patient.

On the face of it, such developments suggest that practitioners have been seeking to enable service users to have a say about services for many years. But Lindow and Morris (1995) among others have argued that unequal power relationships between community care organisations and service users have remained, and Carr (2004) has suggested that social care services struggle to meaningfully embed user involvement as part of organisation and practice. Duffy and McKeever (Chapter Eight) offer what might be considered an extreme example of what this can look like in practice, although they argue that this reflects what encounters with service managers can feel like to users. In areas where it is considered more difficult to 'do' effective involvement due to issues of marginalisation, Oliviere (2001) highlights how professionals may present difficulties for user involvement by declaring that patients need protecting, and by not recognising the relevance of involvement for patients, while a study by Gott et al (2000), which aimed to establish the extent of user involvement in cancer care, found many inconsistencies among health care managers in their commitment and effort in applying principles of user involvement in practice. This has been endorsed by evaluated user initiatives specifically within the 34 cancer networks in England (Sitzia et al, 2006).

Because of the barriers to changing the way in which health and social care practitioners work, practices such as advocacy have been developed to strengthen service users' voices in their individual encounters with service providers. Advocacy is designed to enable service users to have their voice represented in service decision making, even in situations where they are unable to speak directly for themselves or need help to do so. As we saw in Part One, advocacy may be provided by user organisations, but it is also provided by specialist advocacy organisations that may not be user led.

But it is the campaign for direct payments by the disabled people's movement that has resulted in the model of service delivery that is now being promoted as the most effective means by which service users can have their say about the care and support they receive. The barriers to equalising relationships between service users and providers through the development of new forms of practice, even in the context of support from advocates, underpin the arguments for direct payments, personalised budgets and self-directed support (Leadbeater et al, 2008). Thus, while some practitioners and organisations have been defensive in relation to user involvement, government policy has continued to promote this. The 2010 coalition government claims to want to 'put patients at the heart of the NHS' and states its aim to 'champion patient and carer involvement' (DH, 2010a, pp 3, 13). In its 'Vision for Adult Social Care' (DH, 2010b), the coalition government confirmed its commitment to the personalisation agenda, claiming: 'People, not service providers or systems, should hold the choice and control about their care. Personal budgets and direct payments are a powerful way to give people control' (DH, 2010b, p 15).

The mechanisms for user involvement introduced within the personalisation agenda emphasise individual decision making about services to meet individual needs. Power or control over such decisions is exerted by means of choices about the use of individual budgets or direct payments. However, as Evans and Jones (Chapter Seven)demonstrate, user involvement in service decision making can go well beyond the individual level and many of the initiatives that developed from the late 1980s within both health and social care were based on opportunities for service users to come together to take part in the planning, development and evaluation of services, and to shape purchasing or commissioning decisions through the development of user-defined quality criteria (eg Barnes and Wistow, 1994; Raynes et al, 2001). Kelson (1997, p 6) highlights the importance of the user perspective with regard to the planning, delivery and monitoring of services and specifically argues that this can lead to a better understanding of user needs and priorities, better relationships between healthcare organisations and their users, and the existence of a sense of ownership, partnership and collaboration. In an example of innovative practice in the context of services for people with dementia, Aveyard and Davies (2006) anticipate the type of 'co-production' initiative that Farr (Chapter Six) describes. They discuss how residents and relatives worked with staff to improve the experiences of living and working in a residential home. In these types of examples, the focus is less on individual control of services, and more on collaboration and collective action to improve service quality for all.

Summarising the different contexts for user involvement, Kemshall and Littlechild (2000, p 10) identified four areas in which users' participation has developed: their own use of a service, strategic planning, the development of user-led services, and in research (see Part Three). Different methods and models of involvement have different objectives and can deliver different outcomes, although this has not always been well articulated. As strategies for involving users started to develop it became clear that organisations needed to be clear about their level of commitment and the degree of user involvement they were looking for, otherwise an unhelpful, unclear attempt at involvement was likely to result. As Staniszewska and colleagues (Chapter Ten) demonstrate, poorly designed involvement initiatives without a good understanding between public officials and service users can generate negative outcomes. On the other hand, McKinley and Yiannoullou (Chapter Nine) show that training and support for participation can in themselves generate positive outcomes – although they may result in service users deciding that they wish to use their skills in contexts other than improving staff awareness.

Underpinning the different models of involvement that have been developed have been differences in philosophy and ideology (eg Barnes and Walker, 1996). A distinction drawn early in the development of such initiatives was that between 'consumerist' and 'democratic' versions of involvement. It was argued that the consumerist approach is broadly concerned with improving services, ensuring that the 'customers' or 'consumers' are satisfied with what is available to them. In contrast, a democratic approach embodies ideals of participatory democracy, and is concerned with enabling people to have more control and influence over issues that affect their lives. This goes further than enabling people to make decisions about their personal care, although this is important to people, and extends to enhancing the way people can collectively make changes to improve their situation. Beresford and Croft (1993) argued that democratic approaches to user involvement are the most challenging to implement as they necessitate changes to traditional ways of working at the level of policy, practice and ideology. This can threaten the power of providers, but it can also be a way of building different types of relationships between service providers and users, as in examples cited above.

An important issue is where control lies. For genuine democratic participation to exist, there needs to be a commitment on behalf of those in positions of power to make participation work for the right reasons.

Shaping a service or initiative to be acceptable to the people who need it will involve making real and lasting changes to how the organisation is structured and managed. It has been argued that without these structural changes, effective participation is unlikely to be maintained and an effective challenge to people's exclusion and oppression is unlikely to occur. It is too early to see whether the 'transformation' heralded by personalisation fulfils the aspirations of those who see this as the participative approach that will turn public service delivery on its head (Leadbeater et al, 2008, p 10). If this does deliver in the way that service users want, then this suggests that consumerist rather than democratic models of involvement have won out, as the mechanism through which users are to exercise control is by making individual purchasing or commissioning decisions, not through the exercise of collective voice in participative decision-making forums.

But alongside the strongly individual focus of personalisation, more collective models of involvement continue to be evident in the context of co-production (Hunter and Ritchie, 2007; Needham and Carr, 2009). The 'co' in co-production refers both to collaboration among service users and to cooperation between users and providers of services. As Needham and Carr (2009, p 3) note, the idea that service users have expertise to contribute to producing effective public services is not new. As we review the way in which user involvement has changed and developed over the past 20-30 years, we can see the way in which the same 'type' of activity can come to be described in new ways as well as the way in which competing ideologies and discourses structure the range of opportunities on offer.

six

Collaboration in public services: can service users and staff participate together?

Michelle Farr

Introduction

Developing alliances between service users and workers can be an important way to advance liberatory reform within social welfare services (Beresford and Croft, 2004). External to public service institutions, campaigns have sometimes brought together service users, workers and trades unions where there are shared interests, illustrated through recent examples of protests against public service cuts (BBC, 2010). Organisations such as the Social Work Action Network (SWAN) draw together practitioners, social welfare users, academics and students, united through addressing social and structural inequalities. SWAN's manifesto states that 'progressive change must involve users and all front line workers' (Jones et al, 2004). Campaigns and networks such as these are independent of particular public service organisations, so can these partnerships operate within specific institutional boundaries as well? This chapter analyses organisational processes that explicitly involve both people who deliver services and people who receive services within joint partnerships in co-design and co-production projects. These participative mechanisms promote and value the experience, skills and knowledge of people who use services, developing partnerships with staff to shape and redesign services. I first examine the definitions and processes of co-design and co-production, drawing on academic literature and evaluations of co-design and co-production projects. Then, I describe research I have conducted into the practices of co-design and co-production in the National Health Service (NHS) and local government. I consider the benefits and difficulties of involving both staff and service users within these processes, exploring how they sit within a public sector institutional context.

Co-design and co-production: definitions and processes

Co-design can be defined broadly as a collaborative activity that involves different stakeholders in a design process 'designing with people, not merely for people' (Bradwell and Marr, 2008, p 17). Within experience-based co-design (EBCD) in the health service, users become co-designers, where they are 'integrally bound up in the whole improvement and innovation process.... The "co" in co-design is a significant and powerful prefix, suggesting more of a partnership and shared leadership, with NHS staff continuing to play a key role in leading service design but alongside patients and users' (Bate and Robert, 2007, pp 9-10).

There are many definitions of co-production. At the core of these is the understanding that public service users take an active part in producing services and their outcomes. Co-production highlights the importance of 'involving citizens in collaborative relationships with more empowered frontline staff' (Needham and Carr, 2009, p 1). It has been promoted as a means of service users sharing power with professionals where all team members are equal, all members trade their assets, power is shared with the recognition of expertise and talents, and outcomes ensure that human rights are embedded over political and economic concerns (Hurst, 2009). Practically, there are overlaps between co-production and co-design and they share key theoretical assumptions (Farr and Cressey, 2010). Both can be used to model how active citizens who use services and public service staff can come together within a collaborative partnership, through which they contribute and share tacit and situated forms of knowledge, experiences and skills, to develop more person-centred public services.

Service user involvement

Co-design and co-production processes often begin by understanding users' situated experiences:'you start from the people themselves and find out what they think works well and what needs to be addressed' (Brand, 2009, p 4). Young (2000) has argued that practices based in deliberative democracy have exclusionary implications through privileging reasoned and dispassionate argument. In contrast to this, co-design and co-production processes extend these accepted rational deliberative styles and aim to create new spaces that promote the importance of narrative, experiences, emotion, skills and knowledge of people who use services. Hodge (2005, p 177) critiques how most of the discourse within user involvement 'is action-oriented and instrumentalised, in the process objectifying the lived experiences of service users'. Conversely, co-design projects often use 'touch points', moments where people experience services and engage with them, which can induce different emotions and memories (Parker and Heapy, 2006). By using touch points, emotions in co-design are neither relegated nor rationalised but form a catalyst for further action to change services.

Staff involvement

Some co-production literature has highlighted the potential of staff resistances to more collaborative ways of working (Bovaird, 2007). In contrast, co-design and co-production projects that engage staff and ask them about their own experiences and feelings about service provision, have supported collaborative working (Bate and Robert, 2007; Needham, 2008). Involving staff can create a more equal process, enabling insights and reflections on working practices. This follows Carr's (2007, p 273) advocacy of supporting frontline staff 'to express their ideas, feelings and experiences, rather than defending systems and management practices with which they may actually disagree or find restrictive'. Within co-design and co-production processes, diverse staff groups who all contribute to a particular service are sometimes brought together to discuss the particular concerns that they face before going on to discuss issues in forums with service users (for example, Bate and Robert, 2007; Needham, 2007).

Involving staff and service users together

The bringing together of staff and service user perspectives in co-design and co-production projects can facilitate a greater understanding of particular service issues. For example, a co-production event in housing illustrated how 'tenants were surprised to see the concerns of the officers overlapping so closely with their own' (Needham, 2007, p 228). In health services, EBCD (Bate and Robert, 2007) is a process that draws together staff and service users. Initially, narratives about service users' experiences are collected and in some services, such as cancer (Bate and Robert, 2007), Alzheimer's disease (Tan and Szebeko, 2009) and emergency departments (Iedema et al, 2008), service users have been filmed sharing their personal and emotional experiences of particular services. Once service users have reviewed and consented to the showing of these films, they can be shared through events with staff that provide the particular service, providing a catalyst for conversation with users to review services and prioritise improvements (Bate and Robert, 2007). Barnes (2008b) provides examples of how staff have sometimes rejected user narratives within deliberative forums where they were unable to take on board the emotional impact of the experiences of services. In contrast to this, these films of service users' experiences have engaged staff and enabled reflection and connection to people who use services (Bate and Robert, 2007). They can strengthen the ability of staff 'to reflect on their own practice' and provide 'a means to validate staff understandings of patients' experiences' (Iedema et al, 2008, pp 33-4). This can galvanise action, using emotional experiences and responses in a way that Mouffe (2002, p 9) advocates, 'mobilising them for democratic ends ... creating collective forms of identification'. The extent of organisational change that can be sparked from these processes may depend on levels of staff autonomy and decision-making power (Needham, 2007). Iedema et al (2008, p 35) illustrate within EBCD processes in health services how staff can 'carry the burden of competing responsibilities ... [which] strained the resources and patience of some members of the project teams'. However, staff still spoke 'enthusiastically about their positive experiences'. A wider review of both co-production and co-design literature (Farr and Cressey, 2010) does illustrate a vast range of outcomes where different projects have developed new forms of social capital, extended social networks, provided value for money, made specific service improvements and raised people's self-esteem, wellbeing, confidence, dignity and quality of life.

Research and case studies

I conducted research to explore the processes and outcomes of various co-design and co-production projects, using critical realism as a theoretical framework. My methodology and analysis were informed by both a morphogenetic approach (Archer, 1995) and realistic evaluation (Pawson and Tilley, 1997). Initially, I interviewed eight facilitators and service improvement specialists (labelled as 'expert interviews' within this chapter) who have been involved in a number of EBCD, co-design or co-production projects to explore common themes across different services including local government, and a variety of health services including accident and emergency, community health facilities, cancer services and other hospital-based services. This was followed by two longitudinal case studies within the NHS and local government, using an ethnographic approach. My own role within both of these cases was as an independent researcher and evaluator, observing the process through meetings and events and interviewing different people about their involvement in the projects. The local government case focused on a small-scale innovation programme that developed projects using co-design and co-production practices to inform strategic policy making and create more person-centred public services. They engaged staff and citizens in collaborative projects and worked in policy and service areas such as housing, public health and social services, working with local communities, families on a low income and people who have been in prison. One particular project mentioned here, focused on the experiences and needs of low-income families living within areas of deprivation that have been the subject of numerous regeneration initiatives. Case study data included participant observation at three events and 16 interviews.

The NHS case focused on a project that aimed to develop person-centred services, using EBCD within cancer services in two large hospitals, closely following the methodology set out in Bate and Robert (2007). This service improvement process explored the whole of the patient pathway, initially asking both staff and service users individually about their experiences of providing and receiving services (users were also filmed). Responses were then collated to provide material for reflection at separate staff and user events where priorities for improvement were identified. At the user event, an edited film was shown, which had been made from the separate individual films. A co-design event was then held where service users and staff came together to share their experiences and staff were shown the user film, following users' consent to this. Staff and user priorities for improvement were shared and voted on, with the most popular areas forming the focus of further work. Staff and service users then developed and redesigned services together through individual co-design groups who met over a period of time to implement improvements. Data from this case used here consists of participant observation at the staff, user and co-design events, with 71 feedback questionnaires from participants (25 service users and 46 staff) completed after the events. Findings from this ongoing research are now explored, addressing the strengths and tensions within these projects, the impact of the institutional context that these projects are situated within and whether underlying power relations can be challenged through this work.

Benefits and challenges

Benefits

Interviews highlighted the importance of emotions in catalysing change within services. Particularly within health co-design and co-production work, the lived experiences of service users reconnected staff with people emotionally:

> 'Empathy has a half life, I've discovered this, one of the things that really works is allowing clinicians to empathise. They do empathise, they are in it for the right reasons, most of them. But they lose the desire to empathise because of the stresses of the job. And I think sometimes what you have to do is create situations in which they can refresh that empathy.' (Expert interview, health co-production facilitator)

Within EBCD the use of film to convey the experiences of service users seemed to have a powerful effect:

'When I have seen a key "aha" moment is when people hear the stories.... Particularly if people have got film....They see the film and they say "oh my goodness, that's a patient from my organisation," they often recognise the patient, the patient being under their care, that makes a difference, and hearing and seeing them talking about their experiences. I have watched a number of people hearing stuff for the first time and they just sit and their heads are shaking and they are going "oh, how could it be like that." They also recognise what the patients are saying.' (Expert interview, NHS service improvement specialist)

Similarly, service users who took part in the film felt that it could have a big impact:

'My feelings were that if anything was going to make a difference, this film would – it came from the heart.' (EBCD case, service user comment on film)

In the EBCD case study, I observed an event where staff and service users came together to share their different experiences. Within this event I felt that staff showed a deep level of recognition and respect for the openness with which users shared their experiences and emotions, which enabled honest and respectful discussions between staff and users. Through sharing experiences, staff found that user views could sometimes validate their own concerns about the provision of the service, service users commenting on the same phenomenon:

'I thought the staff were very aware of the issues we talked about and that it was a mutually supportive experience.' (EBCD case, service user comment)

Within both the local government and the EBCD cases, the involvement of both staff and service users enabled people to reflect on their own experiences and understand the perspectives of others outside of an everyday pressurised service environment. A 'space to think' enabled staff to reflect on their working practices:

'If a frontline worker is able to almost take a step back and look at the process in which they work ... they actually can start to reflect on what they know that would be helpful to improve the system. And often they are not given that opportunity ... they are working so hard that they don't have the opportunity to reflect on it.' (Local government case, project manager)

Equalising the impact of organisational hierarchy within this space was important:

> 'If part of the team may be excluded from [the] process ... I just don't think [that] inspires creativity or maybe even innovation within the team.... Ideas come from the bottom up but if the manager excludes maybe that bottom layer from the strategic planning of their team, maybe they're not going to get the right kind of ideas and issues coming through....' (Local government case, frontline staff)

Through facilitating reflexivity with both staff and service users, these spaces can enable the development of relationships and trust. Intersubjectivity is a key mechanism to these processes, where both staff and service users begin to see issues from other people's perspectives, building understanding to catalyse change within a localised context:

> 'The most powerful part of the process is the co-design session where people come together and they see what the challenges are from the different stakeholders and actually have a chance then to discuss why they are a challenge and where they fit within their context.... I would say that out of all of the projects that we have done we have always seen the biggest mindset shift happen there and you then start to get the cynics become like the champions.' (Expert interview, co-design facilitator)

In EBCD where both staff and service users were involved in improvement processes, this enabled different people with diverse skills to influence service development:

> 'It's about bringing people with different perspectives and we talk about patients and we tend to forget that they are full-time mothers who have fantastic planning, they're lawyers, they're film makers, we forget that they bring a valuable perspective from their industry to help us shape our services.' (Expert interview, NHS service improvement specialist)

Challenges

There are possible tensions in attempting to engage both service users and frontline staff in the same service improvement process. Careful negotiation and facilitation is essential:

'By setting up a workshop where you are going to have service providers and service users and not do any of that preparatory experience sharing and familiarisation, you are going to set yourself up for failure because the providers will make assumptions about the users and the users will make assumptions about the providers through experiences that they have all had.' (Local government case, manager)

In EBCD, users and staff came together in co-design groups after initial separate events. Different processes were used in the local government case and in some projects it was not felt appropriate to involve staff and service users together at the same time. Here, staff were involved in separate parts of the process from people who had experienced services:

'[W]ith the families' work we actually decided not to involve users and providers in the same groups.... We had a sense that these families would not talk as honestly or openly if there were representatives of the state there.... We were very clear that in doing that we then had to find ways of involving staff further on in the process.' (Local government case, coordinator)

The balance of involving staff and service users and addressing different people's concerns, interests and issues was clearly an art and thoughtful planning and facilitation skills were vital. Where this was achieved it could have a powerful impact:

'[The families' workshop] managed to maintain an extraordinary discipline and be very constructive and creative as well.... It was a very, very positive and creative and supportive way of doing things, which I found ... well, an inspiration to me.... Are there arguments? Yeah, hundreds of arguments and I think that's fantastic that it's done in such a way that your views are respected and appreciated.' (Local government case, manager)

When prioritising improvements within case studies, where staff and user priorities diverged, the continued focus on both staff and user experiences could be difficult to sustain in the long term and projects tended to focus on user priorities. Within interviews, some project managers, when asked about both staff and user participation, spoke solely of user involvement.

Institutional context

Public sector structures, cultures, official procedures and resources could constrain collaborative working. Negotiating and promoting co-production and co-design projects within complex, organisational political systems can be a major task:

> '[H]alf of my time was basically spent constantly creating and recreating the permissions for us to do this in the first place. The dynamics of the organisation, the politics and all of that was so important and had I not been doing that I'm sure that it would have been squashed.... It is threatening, it does challenge the way that things get done....' (Expert interview, co-production facilitator)

Service managers played a vital role to "create the conditions, create the space" (expert interview, co-production/co-design facilitator): without their authority and backing, projects could easily stall. Staff working within these projects could feel that they were working around organisational systems rather than being supported by them. Restrictions from existing policies and procedures could arise through the implementation of improvements. The scope and agenda of co-design projects could sometimes be limited, some tending to focus on service design and delivery issues within institutional boundaries:

> '[W]hat we were trying to do was redesign our model of emergency care from when the person hit our front door to when they left our front door....' (Expert interview, NHS service improvement lead)

Other projects attempted to widen their scope, looking beyond current service provision. The local government case fed in specifically to corporate policy, attempting to build a bridge between the realities of citizens' lives and future policy; however, embedding this work within policy took time and tenacity. Diffusing the approach through the organisation tended to happen through more organic means, using existing networks of practitioners keen to promote more participative ways of working. Influencing a wide range of leaders and senior managers to adopt these methods through the organisation could be a challenge. Both users' and staff's enthusiasm often drove these projects, yet resources and broader, structured organisational support may be needed to ensure the embedding of this work through the wider institution.

Conclusions

This chapter has illustrated how co-production and co-design projects engage with service users' experiences, emotions and skills and promote collective dialogue to catalyse reflection and action, involving both staff and users in improvement processes. However, organisational politics, cultures, policies and procedures may restrict impact and influence. While some literature suggests that practitioners can resist sharing power with users (Bovaird, 2007, p 857), the context and organisational structures within which staff work may affect their own autonomy to respond to service users. Indeed, within developing case study research there are many examples where service user priorities have taken precedence over staff concerns and interests. Change within these projects can remain localised and they usually focus on service delivery and design issues. Although projects draw on some social movement processes, they are not independent from organisations and thus do not provide a vehicle for independent campaigning, unlike autonomous user-controlled organisations. This lack of independence may compromise the ability to tackle wider issues beyond service delivery, delimiting influence in wider political and structural areas. The concepts of co-design and co-production do not have the same political or ideological roots that either worker participation (through worker movements and trades unions) or service user participation (through welfare service user movements and user-controlled organisations) have and as such may be less attached to wider political concerns (Beresford, 2009a; Farr and Cressey, 2010). While Hurst (2009) highlights that co-production means that outcomes ensure that human rights are embedded over political and economic concerns, policy discourse on co-production is becoming increasingly associated with ways of making public service savings. Important changes have been made within organisations through EBCD, co-design and co-production projects; however, underlying institutional power relations remain less affected. Thus, while service user and worker collaborations can have an impact within organisational boundaries, independent and autonomous campaigning groups may have greater freedom to tackle wider structural inequalities and challenge current public sector cuts.

Acknowledgements

Many thanks to all the people who have given time and support to enable this ongoing research. Organisations and participants have been anonymised to maintain confidentiality. The funding of the Economic and Social Research Council through a +3 Quota Award is gratefully acknowledged.

seven

Changing patterns of service user involvement, 1990-2010

Clare Evans and Ray Jones

This chapter tracks the changing pattern of service user involvement in social policy development between 1990 and 2010. Social policy has itself developed in line with current societal and political priorities of personal choice and control and in response to learning from service users. Drawing on our experience locally and nationally, at times shared and at others separate, we seek to demonstrate these developments and the interaction between them. We speak from our very different perspectives – one as a director of social services, and the other as both a director of a county user-controlled organisation, Wiltshire and Swindon Users' Network (WSUN), and a user contributor nationally to service user involvement in social policy making.

This chapter primarily traces the journey in one area, Wiltshire, of increasing service user engagement, initially in influencing and then in substantially shaping, controlling and managing services to assist disabled people. For the most part this user engagement was through the formation and development of Wiltshire and Swindon Users Network, an innovative network controlled by service users. The model of user involvement developed by WSUN is based on democratic citizenship and disability equality principles in the period 1991 to 2011 (and still continuing). WSUN's membership were all disabled and older people with physical and sensory impairments, learning difficulties and mental health difficulties who were long-term users or potential users of social care who sought to have collective influence and impact through their involvement based on the expertise of their 'lived experience'. In total, in 1996, over 700 people were registered as voting members of WSUN, participating in activities focused on collective advocacy to achieve influence and impact by disabled people.

As WSUN negotiated different kinds of user involvement in different aspects of health and social care, what was most valued were those possibilities where greatest immediate impact could be achieved. These included the co-production of policies and services, with disabled people involved from the start through WSUN. This contrasted with council- and National Health Service (NHS)-dominated formal consultation exercises where disabled people had little influence on setting agendas or on the outcomes. WSUN also sought to deliver services on independent living, information provision and advocacy, where peer support among service users was key to service delivery design and acceptability.

In a review of user involvement nationally, Carr (2004) noted that service users identified user involvement in general terms as having little influence. Yet at the same time, WSUN, as a well-resourced, focused and integrated generic user-controlled organisation, identified different users who were involved in over 60 different opportunities for involvement at any one time. Locally, it was described as 'riddling the system'. While no formal research evaluation was carried out, the perception of relevant stakeholders at that time of such levels of user involvement was that it was achieving a long-term shift in culture within social services, and indeed in health, housing and public transport services, to being more user focused and responsive.

Crucial to the success and impact of user involvement to achieve influence was the face-to-face dialogue between members of WSUN, policy makers and paid professionals. Through WSUN, service users had opportunities for peer support and training as they engaged with policy makers and practitioners in local services and had an important opportunity to network with service users more widely to check out the perspectives held by others. For example, a programme was developed to bring older people together in each of the four district council areas that nestled within the boundary of Wiltshire County Council. There were often over a hundred older people attending each meeting. There was also a well-established programme, 'Our Time to Talk', for people with mental health difficulties to come together regularly at local meetings across the county. In addition, outreach programmes to engage with disabled people from minority ethnic communities (leading to the development by local agencies of specialist and more culturally sensitive services) and with isolated disabled people in sparsely populated rural areas were also organised.

To understand the timeline of this journey, it may be helpful to map developments in Wiltshire alongside developments nationally (see Figure 7.1). What this shows is that disabled people in Wiltshire, as with disabled people nationally and in other local areas, were often initiating and driving national policy and practice changes rather than primarily being the passive recipients of these changes.

The NHS and Community Care Act 1990, following on from the Griffiths Report (1988), was the trigger for the consciousness-raising moment for service users in Wiltshire to organise to influence. The self-organisation of service users began with the formation in 1991 of a user steering group, generated and initiated by Clare Evans, and seeking the involvement of other disabled individuals and small self-help groups. The initial aims were to influence the local Community Care Plan and to set up an infrastructure for disabled people to support each other and to seek continuing influence.

Figure 7.1: The national and Wiltshire timelines

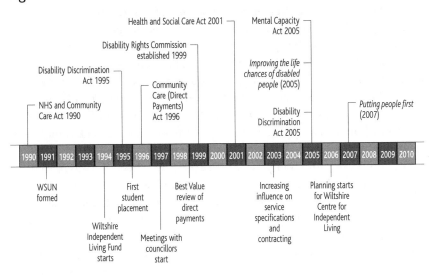

Service users and social services education and training

In 1992, service users embraced the new community care philosophy and the structures to implement it – care management, assessment of need and individual care plans, for example (see Means et al, 2003; Jones, 2007). A seemingly appropriate next step, in this climate, was to have service users participate in professional care management training. The challenge for professionals was to learn not to fit those requiring services into existing patterns of service delivery, but to look at individuals' needs assessments as a starting point. At the same time, service users were learning of a new opportunity to have their individual needs identified. The two groups complemented each other, and joint training enabled them to learn together.

It was important to plan the involvement on good practice lines. Few disabled people locally had an understanding of disability equality and the social model of disability (Oliver and Barnes, 1998; Oliver, 2004; Barnes and Mercer, 2004) so training was provided for service users through WSUN. There was also a need to avoid service users being token visual aids in paid professional-led training. However, with service users as equal participants in twos and threes together with prospective care managers, service users could support each other and bring their individual perspectives to small group exercises within the training days.

Another important aspect of this work was that payment was agreed with social services in recognition that user participants brought expertise to the training. This payment of £30 a day in 1992 for user participants was negotiated between the director of social services and director of WSUN and smoothly implemented because of the shared vision of the negotiators, which valued the experience and expertise of service users (Evans and Hughes, 1993). It was also assisted at the time by the government making available to local councils specific development funding for community care.

The involvement of disabled people in training professionals in social care and in health and other services is an example of local action initiated and led by disabled people within WSUN. It has been repeated and replicated elsewhere, with a lasting and wider influence and impact. This is evident in national policy and practice, with the General Social Care Council now requiring the direct participation of service users in all social work degree programmes (see, for example, GSCC, 2006). What was a local innovative initiative by disabled people has been mainstreamed nationally (SCIE, 2009).

From 1994, WSUN also provided practice placements for social work students from the local universities and further education college, giving a rich experience for students who may have had little exposure to or contact with disabled people. The WSUN director was herself a qualified social worker and practice teacher so students on placement were also supervised directly by a disabled person. (More recently within WSUN, other disabled people have acted as workplace supervisors.) This experience was powerful with, in particular, the student working alongside disabled people who were in control and in charge, not the social work student. The impact on building recognition for the students of disabled people's competence, contribution and capacity was considerable. WSUN also itself benefited from the additional income from the payments received for the placements and from the additional capacity provided by the students by, for example, a specific student-resourced outreach programme to bring together blind and visually impaired service users.

Further impact was achieved by disabled people being extensively involved, through WSUN, in local social work courses (as well as within in-house agency training programmes), including student selection, course design, course delivery and teaching, and student assessment. It was not only, therefore, the local service agencies who were 'riddled' with the experience and expertise of service users but also the local universities and colleges.

Service users and quality standards and assessment

As community care became established and the purchaser/provider split was developed, the subject of 'quality of service' and how it could be measured in contracts with providers became an issue. For service users, this required a change in patterns of user involvement from, for example, working with home care staff to develop the monitoring of in-house services to sharing thinking on quality standards and service specifications for contracted services. Results of this included, among many others, service users significantly shaping the specification and the awarding of contracts for the NHS wheelchair service, the countywide community equipment service, a new respite care service and Supporting People (a government programme to fund and improve housing-related support services).

There was no clear understanding in social services of how service users' perspectives on quality were to be incorporated into contracts since, by definition, they were individual perspectives and had not been collated or aggregated. From this, thinking developed by users in WSUN about the need for consideration of user-defined outcomes led to links with Tessa Harding of the National Institute for Social Work and Peter Beresford of Brunel University. Consequently, in 1997, Community Care Development funding was obtained nationally for Shaping Our Lives, a user-controlled research programme on user-defined outcomes (Beresford et al, 1997). This in turn led to the establishment of the Shaping Our Lives network of user groups, which has become the national voice of service user groups widely involved in research and consultation.

Over 10 years later, outcomes identified by service users were pivotal in the introduction of the new policy of 'personalisation' (DH, 2007b). From being a marginalised perspective, considered difficult to measure and raising professional concerns that needs and wishes may be confused, service users' desired outcomes became a mainstream consideration and a keystone of social care policy development.

User-controlled research

Formal research was another area that service users within WSUN chose to develop to demonstrate the value and importance of their perspective and to influence change. In 1994-95, WSUN had the opportunity of exploring the issues involved in user-controlled research in collaboration with an academic ally, Mike Fisher, then at the University of Bristol. Funding was obtained and a working group of service users established to identify research agendas that were seen as a priority by service users, and to design all the processes needed for service users to be in control of research to the point of production of the research findings (WSUN, 1996; Evans and Fisher, 1999). Subsequent research into the views of users of the Wiltshire Independent Living Fund added to the body of knowledge informing the legalisation of direct payments to enable service users to purchase their own care.

Later, service users in WSUN obtained funding from the Joseph Rowntree Foundation to carry out a user-controlled 'Best Value review' of direct payments in Wiltshire County Council (Evans et al, 2002; Evans and Jones, 2005; Jones and Evans, 2006). While in 1994 the idea of service users carrying out their own research was rare, and any such research was not necessarily considered valid, by 2010 it had become more mainstream. Involving service users in designing research is now a requirement of many research funders, including the new School for Social Care Research (NIHR, 2010).

Service user involvement in shaping research agendas makes the research more relevant to, and informed by, the experience and expertise of service users. Service user engagement in research fieldwork may also make the research experience more sensitive and appropriate for respondents. Service user involvement in the interpretation of the research findings is likely to make the conclusions more realistic and grounded.

Service users and direct payments

It was no coincidence that the subject chosen for user-controlled research on the first two occasions by WSUN was the provision of cash by the local authority to enable disabled people to purchase their own support, and the provision of such support services by disabled people's organisations. This is the area of social policy in which service users have had most influence through their direct participation and co-production, and through establishing alternative models of user-controlled service delivery. This reflected the development of the disabled people-led independent living agenda (Morris, 1993) and more recently the government's 'personalisation' agenda (DH, 2007b).

Following on from the development of the independent living movement in the 1970s and 1980s (Campbell and Oliver, 1996), small numbers of disabled people in the late 1980s and early 1990s campaigned for the opportunity to organise and purchase their own support and assistance by employing personal assistants through third-party funding schemes set up by local authorities. These enabled local authorities, for whom it was illegal at that time to make cash payments direct to service users, to give funding to voluntary sector organisations, who then paid cash to disabled people in line with their social services assessment.

In Wiltshire, the opportunity of government-allocated Community Care infrastructure funding gave professional allies in the social services department and service users the opportunity of working together to set up Wiltshire Independent Living Fund (WILF) in 1994 (Evans, 1995). The proposal for WILF came from the director of social services, who specified that his development staff should work jointly with WSUN members and allies to establish a service to transfer control of cash to disabled people. Right from the beginning, reflecting WSUN's commitment to the social model of disability, WILF was available not only for people with physical or sensory impairments, but also for people with learning disabilities and mental health difficulties. Nationally, their inclusion was initially very limited (Jones, 2000). Within two years of WILF being established in 1994, over £1 million was being transferred as cash payments to disabled people.

The WILF scheme differed from those in other local authorities because the assessment of need was based on self-assessment external to social services. Disabled people defined their own needs and the assistance they might require, with support if necessary to undertake this self-assessment. Cash payments were based on this assessment and agreed by a WILF panel of disabled people, advised but not controlled by workers from the social services department. There were inevitable tensions because of the local authority requirement to ration resources, but the principles involved were very similar to those that emerged nationally 15 years later with the introduction of self-directed support and the In Control project (Poll et al, 2006).

Nationally, the campaigning of disabled people and their allies among directors of social services led to legislation (Community Care [Direct Payments] Act, 1996) to legalise direct cash payments to disabled people. In preparation for this, as Department of Health officials sought to prepare guidelines for local authorities on implementing the direct payment legislation, they visited Wiltshire to learn about the kinds of support service that disabled people had designed and used to meet their own needs when using cash from third-party schemes to purchase their own care.

With the change in legislation and the opportunity to transfer social care funding direct to disabled people, WSUN initiated a partnership with the University of Bath. Funding was obtained from the Joseph Rowntree Foundation for a user-created and -run Best Value review of direct payments in Wiltshire (at that time, and may be since, this was the only fully user-controlled Best Value review nationally). This substantially informed local learning about and the reshaping of the direct payment policies and processes (Evans et al, 2002). Subsequently, Wiltshire's nationally reported performance indicator on progress and numbers in promoting direct payments was one of the best in the country (SSI and Audit Commission, 2000). It was only through the Health and Social Care Act in 2001 that the provision of direct payments by local authorities was made mandatory.

Service users and service user controlled services

WSUN also designed, hosted and directly managed the Wiltshire Independent Living Support Service (initially the WILF Support Service), which was established locally to support and assist people considering or already receiving direct payments. This service was largely staffed by disabled people with personal experience and expertise in using direct payments. It provided information and advice to those considering a direct payment and, if requested and required, assisted disabled people to apply for direct payments and to arrange and manage assistance. This was an optional service for direct payment users in Wiltshire, but its availability was a major resource in containing the stress and time that could be experienced by disabled people in managing their direct payments and personal assistance. This issue was explored in the national research on direct payments within individual budgets (Glendinning et al, 2008).

Designing and delivering user-led advocacy services to meet the needs of a variety of users, was another area of user-controlled service provision that WSUN was able to develop. Drawing initially on NHS-managed joint finance, it included advocacy for service users with learning difficulties, which grew into a self-advocacy group and eventually Wiltshire People First; a mental health crisis advocacy service designed and developed by users of mental health services; and a care management advocacy service for older people developed by a group of older people in WSUN, supported by staff. When provision of information services for disabled people with physical impairments was a Joint Finance priority in 1994, users in WSUN were able to secure funding and develop a one-stop information centre in Salisbury and lead an Information Federation across Wiltshire.

All of these user-led developments and achievements were assisted by having an independent user-controlled organisation that had built both competence and credibility over the years in shaping and delivering services and which was inclusive for all disabled people. It was recognised and welcomed by statutory social services and health agencies as a resource and platform for engaging with service users, without the costly and complex requirement to separately identify communities of service users to involve in each and every policy or service development.

Service users and councillors

A further development with and by service users, and initially proposed by the director of social services within the local authority, sought to create opportunities for service users to influence councillors in their policy decisions about budgets and funding. A process was established whereby, alongside the election of councillors every four years, service users through WSUN would also elect two physically impaired service users, two service users with learning disabilities, two users of mental health services and two older service users. Several days prior to each Social Services Committee meeting, the elected service users met together with the lead social services spokespersons for each political group, gave their views about the decisions to be made by the Committee and raised other issues with councillors.

Service users themselves decided that they did not want to take a formal part in voting at committee meetings on decisions, potentially being compromised in having to restrain expenditure, for example (see Scherer and Sexton, 2010). But they did develop a model where two service users would attend each committee meeting and would have a right to speak in public on the issues being considered. This had the impact of councillors being confronted with the real-life implications of decisions they were taking, and demonstrable changes were achieved in relation, for example, to charging policies. The service user voice had a credibility different from that of the council's senior managers at committee meetings, and sometimes was in opposition to the views of the social services managers, but the service user independence and experience was valued and respected.

Speaking out about cuts

A consequence of local service users having created a strong collective voice was that WSUN was well informed about the experiences and views of service users, had credibility when sharing these views, and had confidence and access in getting these views heard, whether directly to councillors and managers, or through the media.

One of the strengths was that when senior managers were constrained from being able to speak in public as strongly and as forcefully as they might like about the impact of decisions taken nationally and locally by politicians, especially about financial cuts, the information that was available through the managers to WSUN allowed service users themselves to make the comments that needed to be made (Jones, 2009). On many occasions this received coverage in the local, regional and national press, local and national radio, and regional television, and was no doubt a consideration in the minds of those decision makers locally who had to recommend, decide on and implement cuts in budgets and services that would have a real impact on the lives of service users.

Service users, community development and competitive tendering

However, interaction between local and national policy makers and service users' influence is not always straightforward. At times the national policy agenda, as worked out at local authority level, can work, perhaps unintentionally, to destroy initiatives by local user groups as well as support them. This is particularly true of Centres for Independent Living (CILs), which had grown up to support all aspects of independent living and in particular cash payments schemes. As the local authority contracting process developed in line with strict European Union legal requirements to competitively tender contracts, cash-strapped local authorities found reasons to award contracts to support direct payment schemes to the lowest-cost providers who were likely to be private commercial providers or national charities not led by disabled people. This ignored the learning from CILs about the value of peer support and the role that local organisations of disabled people could play in delivering direct payment support services. Many CILs were derailed by this process and reduced to a shadow of their former selves in relation to funding, structure and local influence. The impact of this for WSUN came in 2002 when WSUN lost the contract for the Direct Payments Support Service to a provider external to Wiltshire (compare the experience of the Nottingham Advocacy Group, Chapter Two).

Tensions and conflicts were also experienced within local authorities. Social services managers and practitioners who were close to service users and communities, and committed to services locally created and controlled by service users and community organisations, were confronted by a market economy philosophy. It was a philosophy encapsulated in Thatcherism's 'compulsory competitive tendering' and Blairite 'Best Value' with its emphasis on comparing and competing. These processes were often championed by local council departments more versed in managing contracts for roads, rubbish and recycling, and the outcome was an undermining of local relationships, commitment and trust. The focus was on price rather than people, and cash rather than community. However, the social services director negotiated within Wiltshire that funding for service user groups was exempt from the general contract regulations of the council, so it was only the loss of the contract for the Direct Payments Support Service that affected WSUN. Nevertheless, this was still an income loss for WSUN and a loss of local user influence, sensitivity, knowledge and control.

Service users and Centres for Independent Living

Significant in arresting this development was the user-led government report (PMSU, 2005) that was developed by disabled people working with national government policy makers, through a process of co-production. A main focus of this report was independent living, with the recommendation that every local authority area should have by 2010 a local organisation controlled by disabled people to support independent living. The Department of Health worked with disabled people in a development programme to achieve this goal, which was translated into a local authority target for the use of Personalisation Transition Funding.

This example clearly demonstrates the move of professionals to a service user-created and -led agenda, albeit repackaged in the professional language of 'personalisation', 'Resource Allocation Systems', 'individual budgets' and 'self-directed support'. It also shows the role of the state in learning to work as an ally of service users and service user-led and -controlled organisations, since by definition the state could not itself set these organisations up. This work has been accompanied by jointly led regional initiatives related to all aspects of self-directed support with capacity-building funding available for the development of user-led organisations in each local authority area.

We have thus arrived at a new stage of service user-controlled activity in Wiltshire, another step on the journey of disabled people empowering themselves and influencing others. Disabled people are once again engaged in Wiltshire in dialogue with Wiltshire County Council in a partnership relationship and in establishing the provision of services of a CIL to support all self-directed support users. The journey continues!

eight

Looking out from the middle: influencing policy change through user involvement

Joe Duffy and Brendan McKeever

Background

This chapter discusses how policy changes and practices occurred as a result of a research study in Northern Ireland where service user and carer researchers worked collaboratively with academic researchers to recommend strategic and operational ways in which larger health and social care organisations could more meaningfully engage with service users and carers. The study, 'Looking out from the Middle' (Duffy, 2008), was commissioned by the Social Care Institute for Excellence (SCIE) in partnership with the Northern Ireland Social Care Council (NISCC)[1] and the Regulation and Quality Improvement Authority (RQIA).[2] The key objectives of this research were as follows:

- to provide a short summary of the history and principles of user involvement;
- to describe the current situation in Northern Ireland;
- to discuss a range of options for the further inclusion and participation of users and carers in the work of NISCC, RQIA and SCIE.

This chapter demonstrates how the views of health and social care service users and carers helped shape and ground the recommendations of the 2008 study report. These are now embodied in a SCIE-published Action Plan agreed by and for the three organisations. The chapter therefore involves critical discussion on the following key themes:

- service users, carers and academics as co-researchers: the challenges and opportunities;
- how to overcome service user/carer scepticism in research through sensitive preparations;

- consulting with marginalised/seldom-heard groups: challenges and opportunities;
- the nature of unproductive consultations, as identified by users/carers.

Furthermore, the chapter concludes with two case study scenarios, which were used at a number of recent workshops in Northern Ireland and Bristol. These demonstrate examples of both productive and unproductive consultations with service users. In the analysis of these scenarios, the themes from the research 'Looking out from the Middle' are referred to as a context for embedding good practice in meaningful partnership working with service users and carers.

Introduction

> 'We need to see what we are being consulted about is making a difference ... we have to be in the middle looking out.' (Service user)

This research, its title captured by the service user quote mentioned above, is about *the middle*. In this way, it captures the real-life experiences of service users and carers in Northern Ireland, many of whom had expressed genuine scepticism towards being involved in the study. Having said that, the research report (Duffy, 2008) did see the light of day, its findings were acted on and policy was changed! However, this publication was not just about users and carers, it also proactively engaged with those who plan and deliver services. It was therefore refreshing to find that, among managers of services, there was also an acknowledgement of the expertise of users: "Users of services are in the best position to highlight what is good and poor about the services they receive" (senior manager).

What therefore emerged in response to this research was a commitment by three major health and social care organisations to continue to develop their own work in relation to user involvement within and across all aspects of their working practices. This is a very tangible result that challenges perceptions and negative attitudes, which argue that nothing has changed and that user involvement makes no real difference.

Meaningful involvement

There have been many experiences where the approach and processes used in consultations have been tokenistic. Indeed, some of the user and carer researchers involved in this research have had first-hand experience of this themselves. In 'Looking out from the Middle', the process was equally as important as the report outcome. Informed by Lathlean et al's (2006) continuum of participation, service users and carers were collaborators in the research. By involving users, carers and academics together in this way in the research process, it was hoped that those responding would have more confidence in agreeing to take part in the study. As a result, what are often described as 'seldom-heard' groups in Northern Ireland agreed to get involved, for example Traveller women, relatives of people affected by cancer, young carers and a group representing gay and bisexual men's health issues (please see Beresford and Branfield, Chapter Three). Time was invested in engaging these groups, far beyond what is usually anticipated. In these ways it was hoped to address many of the negative issues associated with consultation and to demonstrate an inclusive approach to this study.

The most important ingredient in this preparation was trust. In this context, trust meant reassuring the groups consulted that this was a serious study which would have pragmatic outcomes and impact. The advance planning was user focused, sensitive to their issues, but crucially informed by users and carers as co-researchers. With user/carer researchers and academics working together in preparing the interview schedules, interview questions, consent forms and other relevant information about the commissioning organisations prior to the commencement of fieldwork, the research team was confident that this would go a long way to reassuring the research respondents that this was a genuine and well-intentioned piece of research.

With NISCC, RQIA and SCIE subsequently agreeing to take the research recommendations forward in a planned way, those involved could see for themselves a real outcome from all they had contributed to the process. This was enhanced by inviting all of the groups consulted to the research launch in March 2008, writing the report in accessible language and directly attributing the title of the report to comments from one of the groups consulted.

Service users, carers and academics as co-researchers: the challenges and opportunities

It was clear in this study that the team was expected to produce a high-quality, evidence-informed publication that would set out a clear roadmap for the three organisations. Within this expectation lay the first of our fundamental challenges in a team comprising academics and user/carer researchers with various skills and experiences. Mindful of the potential for oppressive perceptions that could exist towards service users and carers as researchers and the need to avoid tokenistically pleasing the research commissioners (McLaughlin, 2009a, p 1), the team very openly discussed and agreed to undertake tasks that were within the skills and expertise of its members. Developing the capacity and skills of each other in particular ways in which members could learn new skills and reflect on different ways of approaching research was also valued. In this way we felt that there was a true spirit of collaboration in how we approached the research (Lathlean, et al, 2006), thereby cultivating 'equal research relationships' (Postle et al, 2008, p 251; Barnes and Mercer, 1997). On a similar point, these sensitivities echo the thoughts of Beresford and Rose (2009, p 12): 'Because of the emphasis on research as a systematic means of producing knowledge, a particularly high value is frequently placed on it ... this can cause problems for people who are not highly valued, since their accounts may command less respect than those of the researchers who research them.'

As a reflection of this commitment towards true partnership working, the team openly acknowledged the respective contributions everyone could make and accordingly various tasks were then delegated. What very quickly became apparent was how much we could learn from each other. Beresford (2003) again helpfully indicates the unique contribution that service user researchers can bring to the research process by their ability to identify and empathise with research participants given the proximity of their own life experiences. He goes on to suggest that this type of identification will ultimately lead to better-quality research and outcomes. We found this to be true from the very early point of designing the interview schedule and the template for use in analysing our findings. The latter exemplifies what Sweeney (2009, p 22) describes as user researchers developing 'a variety of methodological approaches in developing their own particular approach'.

Addressing scepticism, tokenism and consultation fatigue

> There are concerns that service user researchers are invited to participate simply to 'tick the box' for user involvement, rather than to make a meaningful contribution. (Sweeney, 2009, p 33)

Service user/carer researchers are understandably wary and sceptical about research involvement that claims to be truly collaborative and democratic in nature when many come from backgrounds and histories dominated by oppression and power inequalities (Turner and Beresford, 2005, cited in Sweeney et al, 2009). Within this research we therefore agreed that user/carer researchers and university researchers would collaboratively work together in all aspects of the research process. This sense of partnership working is reflected within existing continuums around user involvement in research such as those by Lathlean et al (2006). As Sweeney's (2009, p 33) quote above suggests, and as Rose (2003) also reminds us, service users are aware of involvement in research that is purely for 'window dressing'. Such 'involvement' therefore raises suspicions about 'tokenism' (Campbell, 1996), which the research team dealt with directly by being transparent about the skills, experience and capabilities that everybody could collectively offer. The importance of giving close attention to preparation was one key issue that emanated from these discussions and more importantly was a way of addressing issues that many research respondents would ultimately express in terms of 'consultation fatigue'.

Doing the research

A total of 34 interviews with 148 group respondents and individuals were conducted over the six months of the study. Many of these groups had prior experience of involvement in research, however for several this was their first such experience. Each interview required about three weeks to plan, involving the lead researcher making the first contact with a group representative or nominated third party by telephone, followed by a confirmation email giving more detailed written and accessible information about the research study. Attention to detail at this preparation stage, which came on the advice of user/carer researchers, would subsequently yield dividends in the willingness of the research respondents to engage with us. Nevertheless, all of the researchers had to then commit considerable time in the interviews to addressing deep sentiments of suspicion and hurt that many respondents expressed as a result of previous negative experiences in research, and deep-seated concerns that nothing would come from their involvement in terms of outcomes. One of the key recommendations in our research report addressed the issue of communication:

> 'Organisations don't always give you the information you need to influence them.' (Disability Advocacy Group)

> '… there is no substitute to reaching out to users/carers in person.' (Staff member, residential unit for older people)

> '… senior managers need to come out to see young people in the community.' (Support group for young people)

These quotes from three user and staff groups portray a call for health and social care organisations to improve their communication with the public. In terms of impact and in seriously responding to the report's recommendations to address this issue, the three commissioning organisations now host an annual user involvement conference in Northern Ireland, which at the time of writing is in its third year. At one level this is an opportunity for the organisations to feed back progress on user involvement initiatives, however what we witnessed from the conference in March 2010 was how far the organisations have travelled in seriously embracing the research findings. This conference demonstrated, in a very positive way, that our research findings have not sat on the shelves gathering dust (as some people feared). What was even more significant was the developmental approach to the planning of the conference itself, in which users and carers were centrally involved. As a tangible outcome and directly as a result of user and carer input, the information presented at the conference was more accessible to all of the participants' needs, technology was kept to a minimum, more users and carers presented, physical access issues were fully addressed and all presentations were time limited. There was a distinct sense that the conference belonged to the participants, which included users and carers as well as voluntary and statutory staff representatives.

From all of this it would appear that partnership working has now become an established way of working. Or has it? In their response to the recommendations coming from *Looking out from the middle* (Duffy, 2008), the organisations published an Action Plan detailing the actions they would implement. 'The commissioning organisations see this research as a continuation of a process of participation, engagement and partnership with users and carers in our work in health and social care in Northern Ireland' (SCIE, 2008, p 2).

In the public feedback coming from the conference, equally it was emphasised that we have come a distance, but there is still a journey to go. Feedback has indicated that we are making progress in highlighting the value base of user involvement and its potential positive impact. This is a process we are still working on so as to reach the final goal where it is universally accepted.

Those who perceive that the journey involving partnership working is now over, that we have reached our goal, would best listen to the participants at that conference. The target audience in 'Looking out from the Middle' was distinctly different from the 'norm'. The research team felt that if there could be engagement with marginalised groups, with seldom-heard people, then this would prove that real engagement was possible. What was inspiring and even more encouraging for the research team was the willingness expressed by these groups and individuals not just to engage with our research but also to show a willingness to further engage after the research was completed. Marginalised groups therefore did engage and researchers from a user and academic background were critically important in this occurring.

Since the publication of this research, the authors have further reflected on advancing additional ways to increase the impact of the findings. One strategy they have developed for this is through the enactment of role play by using drama. To help illustrate a number of key issues highlighted in the original report and to draw attention to ways in which meaningful partnership working can be achieved, the following scenarios have been created. To date, the authors have presented these as part of disseminating the findings from the research in an accessible way at conferences and on post-qualifying courses where students have been facilitated in critically engaging with key issues relevant to user involvement.

How not to engage

There are no easy answers about how to engage, although it is a critical exercise in developing partnership working. What follows is an illustration, based on fictitious role play, which raises some key issues in relation to user engagement.

The scene

Set in a headquarters office of a health and social care organisation, the dialogue occurs between an individual user and a manager with responsibility for planning services. There are two separate sessions: the first emphasises negative points in relation to engagement; the second attempts to highlight positive points.

The characters

The role play has two characters. Mr Roger Overthetop represents the statutory agencies, those who plan and provide services. In this case, he is a manager working in the headquarters of a health and social care organisation. The other character, Mr John Margin, is a service user.

Scene 1 – the negative

Mr Overthetop: 'You are very welcome, Mr Margin, thank you for coming, I hope you found your way OK.'

Mr Margin: 'Thanks, I finally found the right direction but the bus was very expensive. By the way, just call me John.'

Mr Overthetop: 'Apologies, Mr Margin, but you know with budgets and cuts, bus fares are just not a priority. All sounds good in User Involvement procedures but whoever thought up those guidelines must have been from another planet.'

Mr Margin: 'User Involvement, what does that mean?'

Mr Overthetop: 'Oh you do not have to worry about that, we have experts here at the department who are well qualified, many with postgraduate certificates, worked for years with users who know all there is to know about you lot. Sure my secretary sent you a leaflet.'

Mr Margin: 'I could not understand the leaflet, it was full of big words and things I knew nothing about.'

Mr Overthetop: 'Mr Margin, that is our everyday language here, maybe if you got some training, you might be able to fit in more and understand what all this is about, or really just the bits you need to understand. Maybe we could set up a training course for you, run by my department, my colleagues might help you.'

Mr Margin: 'But what about your training?'

Mr Overthetop: [angrily] 'How dare you. I have a PhD in Communication Studies, a Masters in Social Care Studies and a Degree in Business Management. And you dare to suggest training!'

Mr Margin: 'I meant maybe users doing the training.'

Mr Overthetop: 'Training sessions based on people moaning and complaining about services they never got and were not even entitled to, trying to tell us experts what we should be doing. Then do-gooders from a certain university trying to make all this respectable. Training, they call it, they would be better at home.'

At this point, Mr Margin gets up uncomfortably and Mr Overthetop seems very embarrassed.

Mr Margin: 'I think I will go now.'

Mr Overthetop: 'Why, what is wrong?'

Mr Margin: 'Since I have arrived, you have shown me no respect, have dismissed any ideas that I have had a chance to put to you, have insulted my intelligence and have made no effort to make me feel comfortable. You imply I know nothing and you and your colleagues are the experts. You could not even reimburse my bus fares, send me out directions or even offer a cup of tea.'

Mr Overthetop: 'I must apologise, I did not think you people were so sensitive. But bear with me, these User Involvement guidelines mean I have a few boxes to tick and then you can be on your way. People expect so much about consultation and engagement, whereas nothing has changed. These tick boxes will be more than enough and then we can decide how things will proceed.'

Mr Margin: 'But….'

Mr Overthetop: 'Look just let me finish this since I went to the bother of inviting you in.'

Mr Margin: 'Nothing has changed. I have wasted my time and money. All the talk, all the hype – nothing. Bye!'

Mr Margin walks out abruptly.

Mr Overthetop: 'I have never met such an ignorant, disrespectful person in my life. I knew this User Involvement was a total waste of time. Maybe if they trained that lot up, taught them some manners, maybe then we could start but really what do they know about planning and delivering services? Let's get real.'

THE END

Reflections on Scene 1

Almost everything in this scene is negative, which is quite deliberate to make a point. The point simply is that the small things can create barriers to engagement. No one would claim that this role play is based on reality; however, there are many users who could identify with at least parts of this.

Unfortunately, Mr Overthetop sees nothing wrong with the way he is behaving. It is as if he comes from a 'culture' where users are treated like this and where professionals are the experts and know everything. Mr Overthetop did not invite Mr Margin into his office because he wanted to hear his views. He invited him in because the policy of his department made him do so. In other words, there was no real commitment to user involvement and no feeling for what it was about.

At times, Mr Overthetop was very critical of the whole policy on user involvement. He was just ticking the box, showing that he did what he was supposed to do, but without any commitment whatsoever and with no effort to engage Mr Margin.

At the heart of this scene is how Mr Overthetop treated Mr Margin. He was totally disrespectful of Mr Margin and ignored his wishes. The expertise, the information, the power, all were held by the department (or so Mr Overthetop thought). There was no engagement, no participation, no consultation, a waste of time.

Scene 2 – the positive

Mr Overthetop: 'Good morning, Mr Margin.'

Mr Margin: 'Good morning, just call me John.'

Mr Overthetop: 'Well John, did you get here OK? By the way, just call me Roger; we keep things very informal here even though the building could put you off.'

Mr Margin: 'Thanks, the directions you sent out were very clear and the return taxi fare was very helpful. Having someone meet me at reception and a cup of tea when I arrived at your department, all made a difference.'

Mr Overthetop: 'I think it is the least we can do in return for you coming in today. You have an idea what this is about?'

Mr Margin: 'I am not saying I fully understand it all, but that information you sent was very clear, in plain language and all those abbreviations were explained, which was a great help.'

Mr Overthetop: 'Tell me a little about yourself, if you don't mind?'

Mr Margin: 'Well, I have been what you call a service user for over 20 years and I think have built up a certain knowledge of services, at least as they affect me.'

Mr Overthetop: 'I am sure you have, that is why I want to listen to you today. I know some people here still think they know everything. I would not like to think I am one of those. I have a disabled son myself and although I have not as many years' experience as you, at least I have some idea.'

Mr Margin: 'That is good to know, I feel people in your position who have direct experience, often have a different attitude.'

Mr Overthetop: 'Will we get down to business then? First what does PPI mean to you?'

Mr Margin: 'That summary you sent was useful but I know there is more to it than just that. But to me it seems to be about health and social care staff getting more involved with users and carers.'

Mr Overthetop: 'I wish you had written the document, what you have said is really what we are trying to do, to involve people more. I have to add as well that we all need training, including myself, to help make this happen and most of all there has to be mutual respect. Here's me going on.'

Mr Margin: 'I am so glad to hear that training is for all. For years it just seemed that service users should be trained so we could fit in. Also you hit a sore point, mutual respect. I'll not go into the many times that meetings like this in the past left me feeling small, less than human at times or just so angry that I was misunderstood.'

Mr Overthetop: 'Look, I have a form here and I could simply tick all the boxes and for some that would be fine. I feel I have taken up enough of your time today and I know you have been invited to meet a few of my colleagues over lunch today. Would you mind coming back and chatting with me again and I will give you some questions to think about as well as giving you an opportunity to discuss your own ideas and thoughts?'

Mr Margin: 'No problem, I would like that.'

Mr Overthetop: 'Thank you.'

Mr Margin: 'I am sure some of your colleagues feel you go over the top with all this.'

Mr Overthetop: 'I do not think I go far enough but we will discuss this further another time. Thank you for today.'

THE END

Reflections on Scene 2

From the beginning it is clear that barriers have been addressed in advance to make Mr Margin feel at ease and to reduce any stress associated with the visit. This shows a real appreciation of the user situation, an empathy and understanding of user issues and a willingness to address them. Things such as being met at reception, being given a cup of tea, a map in advance and a refund of travel fares, addressing Mr Margin by his first name and providing accessible information are all significant to this process. These are not major costly items but simple things that show that users are valued and appreciated. This sets a positive scene for engagement.

By comparing these two scenes, many lessons can be learnt. Within them is the key to engagement or tokenism. Making sure that all of the practical things are seen to will help in this but it cannot be a tick-box exercise. It must be real, a real engagement between John and Roger, not a stand-off between Mr Overthetop and Mr Margin!

Concluding thoughts

In these two scenarios, many of the issues raised through the research 'Looking out from the Middle' are demonstrated. The contrast between the two quite different situations illustrates a number of themes central to the research. Two such themes are the importance of communication and the necessity of attentiveness to practical arrangements. The absence of either could be very problematic.

The role play is a tool. It is a tool that highlights both the negative and positive experiences that users have had. Furthermore, it questions behaviour that leaves users tired, confused and lost in the wake of poor communication and disrespectful treatment. To our surprise and dismay, when we have acted out these scenes on several occasions, many participants have concurred that the negative scene 1 is fairly commonplace! This, in turn, however, has facilitated discussion about how to seriously approach user involvement and the pitfalls that need to be avoided. Through such discussion, the role play has acted as a catalyst for bringing our research recommendations to life by highlighting the importance of feedback and outcomes, values, practicalities and communication as core themes central to engaging service users.

The three organisations funding this research have shown commitment to responding to and acting on the findings. For its part, SCIE, which has had a long tradition of engagement on user issues, has positively endorsed this work as evidenced by the following comments from its participation manager:

> SCIE was delighted to be involved in the partnership work which led firstly to the publication of Looking out from the Middle and then to the establishment of annual conferences which aim to strengthen user and carer involvement in health and social care in NI [Northern Ireland]. The publication of this research was a key moment in the systematic and strategic development of user

and carer involvement in NI. It was both symbolic and practical; symbolic in that RQIA, NISCC and SCIE jointly made a public commitment to user involvement and practical in that this was combined with a focused and specific Action Plan. The annual conferences embody this commitment and are an opportunity for users and carers to hold RQIA, NISCC and SCIE to account, reflect on progress and share learning.[3]

NISCC has also embraced the research recommendations. Although already having a proven track record on promoting user issues since its formation in 2001, the launch of the research report (Duffy, 2008) generated a review and rethink of its approach to user involvement. Very soon after the report's publication, NISCC launched a new Participation Group:

> The NISCC Participation Group is taking the work of these reference groups to a new level; taking forward and further developing the Council's user and carer agenda and addressing the recommendations of the 'Looking out from the Middle' research into effective user involvement which was undertaken by the Queen's University Belfast in 2008. The Participation Group will assess how the NISCC engages with users and carers and then it will develop principles and standards to encourage the development of best practice. (www.niscc.info)

This group now works actively in advising the council on user involvement issues at both strategic and operational levels and its activities essentially straddle the core themes from the research.

In order to ensure that the recommendations of the research are implemented in a sustainable and robust fashion, RQIA has also taken a strategic approach, which integrates user and carer involvement throughout its work. A significant level of commitment and leadership has been shown within the organisation, demonstrated in the RQIA Corporate Strategy for 2009-12, which states: 'We recognise that by engaging effectively with the public and our stakeholders through all aspects of our work, we will achieve improvements in quality in health and social care services in Northern Ireland' (RQIA, 2009:4).

A Public Participation Strategy has been developed by RQIA, adopting a user-focused approach. This included the establishment of a Public Participation Steering and Advisory Group, which involves membership from a wide range of stakeholders. The progress of the action plan is overseen and supervised by the Public Participation Implementation and Monitoring Group, which includes two RQIA board members and a range of RQIA staff. Public participation progress is also reported at RQIA board meetings on a regular basis. A wide range of practical initiatives have been undertaken using the principles identified in *Looking out from the middle* (Duffy, 2008). RQIA embraces the learning from the research and hopes to continue to develop in this area. RQIA's public participation manager said:

'The research has given us confidence to engage with and create positive relationships with service users and carers. This in turn has enabled us to devise innovative and successful methods of engagement. One of the most rewarding, and at times challenging, activities has been the process of organizing the 2010 Conference 'Is Partnership Working?' with service users and carers. It is clear that truly listening to and engaging with service users and carers can add value and an extra dimension to activities that in the past we would have organised with no external involvement. The research has also strengthened our working relationships with NISCC and SCIE and created the opportunity to involve the Patient Client Council in the planning of our annual user and carer conference in 2011.'[4]

We believe that service user and carer researchers have made a difference through their engagement in research that has produced real outcomes in terms of policy change. By publishing a joint Action Plan, the three commissioning organisations sent out a strong message about the impact of the findings and recommendations and how seriously these were being viewed and, more importantly, acted upon. By responding in such a way, we believe that such commitment sends out a positive message to service users and carers about the contribution they can make to research when they are truly at the heart of the process.

Notes

[1] The regulatory body for social work and social care workers in Northern Ireland.

[2] The independent body responsible for monitoring and inspecting the availability and quality of health and social care services in Northern Ireland.

[3] Information provided by Pete Fleischmann, Participation Manager, SCIE.

[4] Information provided by Roisin Kelly, Participation Manager, RQIA.

nine

Changing minds: unleashing the potential of mental health service users – a critical perspective on current models of service user involvement and their impact on wellbeing and 'recovery'

Stephanie McKinley and Sarah Yiannoullou

In this chapter we describe and critique a leadership programme to develop and equip people who use mental health services to deliver mental health awareness training. The programme was called Changing Minds. Initially, however, we briefly review the context for the development of the programme.

Over the past 10 years, service user involvement has finally become enshrined in policy. The government has made it a requirement that people who use mental health services should be at the heart of them in terms of design, delivery, commissioning and operations. It is a *'must do'* for the mental health system and an *'opportunity to do'* for those using mental health services.

Service user involvement is now considered to be commonplace within all types of health and social care structures. Recent health policy states that it is there to 'strengthen the way the public and patients are involved in the way the NHS works' – Health and Social Care Act 2001. The NHS Reform and Healthcare Professionals Act 2002 and the Health and Social Care (Community Health and Standards) Act 2003 are just some of the policies that help to champion user involvement in healthcare.

Service user involvement has traditionally been built on Arnstein's (1969) 'ladder of citizen participation'. It has been useful to use this model as a way of considering the different ways in which user involvement is undertaken and perceived by organisations. We have seen a number of diagrammatical versions of Arnstein's ladder (Figure 9.1) used to conceptualise the idea of levels of participation and conflicting power agendas.

More recent debates have argued the limitations of such a model. Tritter and McCallum (2006, p 165) point out:

Figure 9.1: Arnstein's ladder of citizen participation

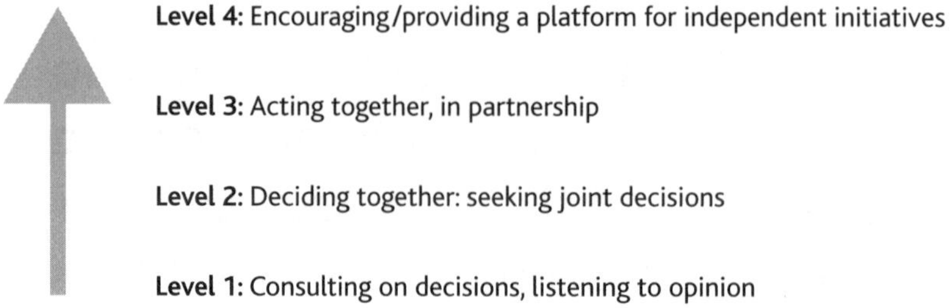

Level 4: Encouraging/providing a platform for independent initiatives

Level 3: Acting together, in partnership

Level 2: Deciding together: seeking joint decisions

Level 1: Consulting on decisions, listening to opinion

Source: Arnstein (1969)

A linear, hierarchical model of involvement (Arnstein's ladder) fails to capture the dynamic and evolutionary nature of user involvement. Nor does it recognise the agency of users who may seek different methods of involvement in relation to different issues and at different times. Similarly, Arnstein's model does not acknowledge the fact that some users may not wish to be involved.

Arnstein's model relates to moving up the 'ladder' towards claiming or even seizing control in terms of real power and involvement. In healthcare, types of involvement will traditionally range from manipulation; information giving (often one way); consultation that offers options and invites feedback; partnership that facilitates the sharing of ideas and shared decision making; acting together to implement ideas and decisions; to supporting independent initiatives so that others can do what they want, thus having full control.

It is the authors' experience that making user involvement a reality at these upper rungs, is where skills, knowledge and confidence are currently lacking. When engaging and/or employing people who have used mental health services as consultants or facilitators to undertake recruitment of staff, training, service monitoring and evaluation or user-led research, the usual professional considerations and policies should be applied. There should also be additional respect for and sensitivity to the experiences that have led to their service use and involvement activity.

Faulkner (2009) sets out the Purpose, Presence, Process, Impact (PPPI) approach, which describes a way of monitoring involvement and its complexities in an accessible way:

• *Purpose.* Having a clear purpose for involvement enables everyone to understand their role and avoids the risk of tokenism and involvement for its own sake.

- *Presence.* This relates the number of service users and carers involved and their characteristics in relation to the project/programme (eg age, gender, ethnicity, specific (service/diagnosis/treatment) experience and so on).
- *Process.* At what level in the project/programme are service users and carers involved? What role(s) are they occupying? How is the process of involvement experienced by all? What support do they have access to? Is the programme or work stream engaging good practice guidelines to involve people?
- *Impact.* What impact – if any – are service users or carers having on the programme or work stream? What impact is the involvement having on them?

Being 'involved' should have a positive impact on how the service is used, perceived and experienced by the stakeholders in receipt of them and should enhance their wellbeing. They are obviously the people best placed to know what they need and what works. The impact of involvement is influenced by the purpose, presence and process, and measuring the wellbeing impact of any type of service user involvement is critical to its success (see Purtell et al, Chapter Seventeen and Barber et al, Chapter Eighteen).

There is much knowledge and experience suggesting that service user involvement programmes can promote recovery through opportunities that improve mental wellbeing. Unfortunately, recorded outcomes are usually focused on quantitative data relating to the throughput of people (who go on to be involved in the activity of the organisation in question), with a lack of attention to the qualitative evidence of the positive impact on participants.

The underlying ethos of the Changing Minds programme was that it was important to understand the impact of involvement on the wellbeing of participants. The paternalistic structures and systems within which many programmes operate often undermine integrity and potential for meaningful involvement. The values underpinning involving people must incorporate empowerment and an enhancement of wellbeing, while giving participants a sense of ownership over processes that can now be done 'with' rather than 'to' them. Opportunities for growth and development must be part of all involvement processes.

From running the Changing Minds programme, clinical outcomes have improved as people have learned how to work with others, develop new skills and feel heard and valued. Participants from the Changing Minds programme said the following:

> 'I've learnt that mental illness doesn't have to be something to be ashamed of all the time. It doesn't always have to have negative connotations with it.'

'I'm proud to be a service user and I wouldn't have said that before this experience.'

'You become less equal when you use services, (on the course) you learn your experience is really valuable.'

Decision making involvement can occur at individual, service and strategic levels or at individual, group and organisational levels. The aims and methods of involvement and the diversity of participants must be considered throughout. We are aware at policy level that most 'involvement' is indirect and often exclusive. For instance, there are many examples of training that supports board and committee involvement, but all too often the business of these types of boards does not allow for the diversity and views of people to be truly engaged and does not provide the necessary support and information to involve people in an effective, confident and equal way.

For those seeking to be involved, a variety of disadvantages such as a lack of trust and/or a resistance to sharing or relinquishing power from those in powerful positions, and poor organisational structures in this area of work, will continue to keep involvement and engagement activity at a non-participatory level.

Staff in the wider service also have to challenge their own preconceptions about what individuals are capable of, as do the service users themselves. The service's 'paternalistic' approach to those in its care (that people are too unwell to be able to do much), as well as the punitive and disempowering way that some people experience their use of secondary services, does not help with confronting this issue. If these perceptions can be shifted then it is possible that user involvement can quite literally transform lives.

True involvement is about people having some kind of control and say over what happens to them and how they are treated. It involves choice and we would argue that it is a chance to challenge and to develop the people who are being involved.

Clear objectives, attention to people's rights, a supported process, quality and outcome evaluation (including measuring wellbeing), developing trust and individual capacity to participate, building consensus around agenda and goals, sharing knowledge and experience, providing the resources, means and conditions for sustainability and support to do so, are all aspects of meaningful involvement that cannot be underestimated.

It is much easier to involve people in ways where skills and knowledge are not necessary as part of the process and to call that 'involvement', for example asking people as part of their care plan what services they want to access. However, if service users are to be at the heart of the service they receive then services need to be more creative in terms of how involvement is approached. There should not be a 'one-size-fits-all' approach, but one that is tailored to the individual's needs and desires and not those of the organisation.

If involvement is to happen effectively, we need to give healthcare organisations and their staff the skills, support and knowledge to enable this to happen. The extra considerations that come with genuine user involvement, such as ongoing support and development, supervision, communication costs, payment for travel expenses and payment for training delivered, are often overlooked. All this needs to be factored in when implementing service user initiatives if they are to be supported and sustained appropriately.

Having clear role descriptions for staff who are responsible for involvement and awareness of the developing stages of involvement is a key part of making service user involvement a positive experience for all involved. Piecemeal resources and systemic and cultural barriers prevent people from achieving their potential. Lack of strategic thinking and cross-departmental working has implications for the effectiveness of systems and structures that are essential to successful involvement.

We continually see service user involvement being implemented in isolation from the rest of the structure instead of it being embedded in all ways of working across all departments. If there is no structure or system in place that takes account of, for example, meeting structures, good practice guidance and payment for involvement, or if policies on involvement are vague and/or not adhered to, this leads to work being chaotic and inconsistent. Setting things up from scratch takes time and all too often there is no clear indication of who is responsible for what. In public organisations, the context within which user involvement is expected to happen, for instance the inflexibility of the different systems/departments that are designed around the organisation rather than service users' needs is a reoccurring problem. This inflexibility has an impact on the wellbeing of the people being involved.

If organisations are serious about involving service users, they need to be less short-sighted when testing out new initiatives and make sure that they plan resource allocation to ensure that the work can continue and be built upon. If involvement happens because it has to and not because it is genuinely valued, the barriers to involvement become almost impenetrable. Services miss out on an important chance to have a positive rather than negative impact on individual health, wellbeing and empowerment, which can impact enormously on recovery and/or clinical outcomes, and of course on service improvement.

In our experience, involvement is often seen as time consuming and of limited value, commonly the responsibility of one or a few workers and with scarce dedicated resources. Of course, involvement is happening across different services locally but it varies dramatically in quality and is even patchier at a national level.

Wallcraft (2003, p 5) stated in the report *On Our Own Terms* that: 'There is a need for national standards on user involvement and for much stronger commitment at all levels to the implementation of the outcomes of involvement.'

In the next section we explore the initiative Changing Minds, a training as trainers co-facilitation course, which is an example of a structured progressive development programme. We outline the processes and challenges experienced in making this a reality for all those involved.

The Changing Minds programme

Many people who use secondary mental health services feel excluded from mainstream life due to the stigma and discrimination that surrounds mental ill-health. This has an impact on wellbeing, self-esteem, levels of confidence and also perceived ability to become involved in meaningful ways. Work and employment possibilities can also be affected due to contact with the services. Research has shown that *equitable social* face-to-face contact (Thornicroft, 2006) is one of the best ways of challenging stigma and discrimination about mental ill-health.

Training requires a level of expertise that develops many transferable work skills. It is an excellent way for people with mental ill-health to become involved in shaping the services they receive and to be role models for others experiencing distress. Having awareness raised by people with direct experience of stigma and discrimination has a powerful impact within services and the community in general. It can support a possible route back into having a valued social role in community life, employment or even a new identity: from a recipient of services to a provider. It could, therefore, improve recovery/clinical outcomes. It is also an excellent opportunity for people to use their 'expert' mental health experience in a positive way.

In reality, persuading mental health and primary care trusts to recognise this as a possible route to involving people effectively was very challenging. This was due to the limited ways in which and internalised stigma regarding how user involvement is viewed in organisations such as these.

In 2004, the South London and Maudsley Foundation NHS Trust (SLaM) made the radical proposal to design with other partner organisations a training as co-trainers course – Changing Minds (formerly SUTO – Service User Training Opportunities). Changing Minds aimed to develop and equip participants to design and co-deliver mental health awareness training courses to challenge stigma and discrimination within staff groups and their local communities.

The Trust was able to fund a post to design the course, but unable to provide a supported budget to deliver the course in practice. Regardless of where the money comes from, funding a post in isolation will lead to further frustrations, for the staff who are delivering the service and particularly for the service users in receipt of the service.

The additional funding necessary came from one of the partners who originally designed the course – Lewisham Social Care and Health. Subsequent funding for courses from 2005 to 2010 was obtained from Lewisham Social Care and Health, Jobcentre Plus, Croydon Enterprise and a Big Lottery-funded project called Well London. The first challenge was working with five funders who had different expectations and requirements.

In terms of resources, it is interesting to note that apart from the first two courses, all funding for this type of work has come from outside of the health sector. This is despite the sector having a remit to involve people in shaping the services they receive and to give them support to do so. This is a damning indictment of how some mental health and primary care trusts are lagging behind.

Changing Minds is a therapeutic intervention that involves social learning and skill building in order to challenge the status quo. People undertake a nine-month part-time training course (consisting of 14-19 sessions) that equips them with the skills to co-design and co-deliver training from their own perspective and to be paid for this.

The Changing Minds vision was to develop a 'pool' of trainers who would deliver training using their direct mental ill-health experience to inform and enrich the experience of (in the first instance) the staff participants. The emphasis was on the 'pool' of trainers being trainers who happened to have a mental health diagnosis – not 'mental health service users who are doing a bit of training' as had been the case with previous schemes. It was proposed that an experienced trainer would offer support and development as and when needed. The pool would deliver different types of mental health awareness training according to preference and expertise, for example substance abuse, self-harm, wellbeing, coping with bipolar disorders and what carers need to know, and be paid for this work.

Participants could then transform their identity from being unemployed and a receiver of services to a provider who was a trainer. They could use their sometimes quite harrowing experiences to inform and educate others so that things could improve for everyone. The author (and programme lead) Stephanie McKinley, herself a user of mental health services, wanted to prove that a structured development programme that enabled people to be heard and involved properly in a different role, would improve wellbeing and sense of self. It was hoped that between three and four trainers would graduate to form the initial pool and with each successive course more graduates would increase the number. Figure 9.2 outlines the underlying integrity of the programme and the way it was run.

The course has run nine times since 2004, with 63 out of 105 participants graduating (60%). The reasons why 40% of participants did not complete

Figure 9.2: Programme integrity

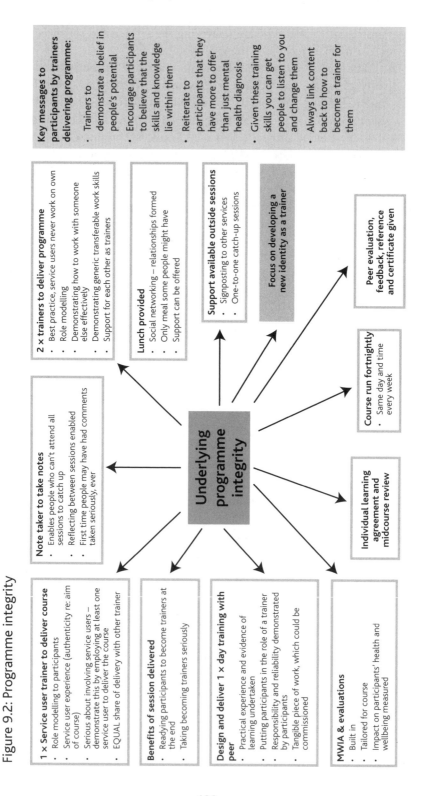

the programme ranged from 'became unwell' to 'gained employment' or simply feeling that the course was not right for them at that time. Sessions ran for three hours every other week. It covered a range of topics such as aims and objectives, group dynamics, facilitation skills, presenting information, structuring a training course, how adults learn, and equal opportunities. Particular attention was paid to the uniqueness of the client group, so sessions on answering difficult questions and impact on benefits were also included.

Monitoring of wellbeing was built into the entire course so that participants' experience of the programme could be evaluated throughout and support and guidance offered if necessary. These measurements were gathered from participants on the pilot course using the Mental Wellbeing Impact Assessment (MWIA) tool (CSIP and DH, 2007). The MWIA enables stakeholders to assess the impact of a project against the four key determinants the research evidence suggests promote mental wellbeing: control, resilience, participation and inclusion. Each factor has up to 10 components. For example, within the determinant of participation, having a valued role is a component.

The measures identified were used as regular measurements throughout the subsequent courses. They were taken anonymously at three different points: prior to the participant starting, in the middle and at the end of the course. This enabled regular monitoring of participants' mental health and wellbeing. We argue that measurements of this kind should be built into *all* types of user involvement so that we can make sure that we are having a positive and not a negative effect. In the case of Changing Minds, it was acknowledged that the monitoring supported engagement and completion levels.

MWIAs were conducted with participants from all of the courses from 2004 to 2010. Results from five of the nine courses show a high degree of consistency between participants across all courses on the determinants of mental wellbeing that Changing Minds has the greatest impact on.

The course was found to have had the greatest impact on:

- having a valued role – through going into voluntary work, paid employment and training delivery;
- ability to make decision and choices;
- self-esteem;
- increased confidence;
- development of supportive social networks;
- optimism;
- challenging discrimination.

Qualitative feedback during the course and subsequent follow-up sessions provided evidence that strongly suggests that the programme has improved people's quality of life and wellbeing.

'I now feel I am more than just a diagnosis and label.'

'Being on the course has been about moving on with my life.'

'I was asked to be a godfather and have looked after my godson, something that would not have happened before [the Changing Minds programme].'

'It opened doors we didn't know were there.'

'Better than any therapy.'

Each session included gathering feedback about how participants were experiencing the course, together with any changes they wanted to see. Participants chose the times and days when the course took place, careful monitoring of participants progress was undertaken during debriefing sessions, one-to-one sessions were offered to participants, open workshops sessions were held to explore and enhance training skills further and a reference was given at the end of the course, along with a certificate.

Participants were encouraged to form support networks both within and outside of the course. Lunch was provided as well as a graduation ceremony where participants chose the venue, food, guests and music. All these things were discussed in a further follow-up session to inform future courses and improve on the weaknesses that had been identified. Graduates were offered opportunities to co-facilitate the next course with the eventual idea that they would run their own Changing Minds programme with another graduate. The long-term aim was to set up a training social enterprise that would be user led and independent of SLaM. Subsequent programmes from 2008 to 2010 were delivered by commissioning local organisations across 16 London boroughs.

Expectations and outcomes

It is interesting in retrospect to look at the original outcomes/targets of the different stakeholders. These included funders' expectations of the numbers completing the programme, the number of programmes run, graduates from specific communities, the number of sessions delivered by graduates, and learning networks developed.

The programme lead was keen to see and evidence the positive impact on wellbeing, internalised stigma around ability challenged, increased confidence and self-esteem, transformation of recipient to provider, the development of transferable work skills, increased employment opportunities for all participants and a pool of trainers to support the mental health promotion work.

SLaM wanted a pool of trainers who could be called on to deliver training to their workforce and to increase levels of involvement across the organisation.

The participants' expectations included wanting to be purposefully engaged, developing existing and/or new skills, widening knowledge and experience, testing out abilities in a safe and supportive environment, forming relationships, reducing isolation, working towards an identified goal, having social contact, having their voice heard and influencing staff, being with peers, being employed and receiving a certificate of achievement.

The commissioned organisations (delivering the programmes) wanted targets for participants recruited to and completing the programme, positive health and wellbeing outcomes for participants, graduates delivering training sessions as part of follow-up contracts and capacity building their own service user involvement activity.

What in fact happened was that graduates had such a positive experience that they exceeded *anticipated* outcomes and expectations. Some people are now either in full- or part-time work and back to feeling able to be socially included again. Research shows that after six months' absence from work there is only a 50% chance of a return to work, after 12 months this decreases to 25% (Sainsbury Centre for Mental Health, 2007, Briefing 27 Benefits and work for people with mental health problems: A briefing for mental health workers (British Society of Rehabilitation Medicine, 2003) and after two years it is practically nil (Sainsbury Centre for Mental Health, 2007, Briefing 34 Work and wellbeing: Developing primary mental health care services (Waddell & Burton (2006)). Most of the graduates had an average unemployment rate of four years.

Of the 63 graduates (from the nine courses), we were able to obtain data from 39 of them. According to the data, 23 (59%) graduates were involved in delivering training at the 12-month follow-ups for each for the years.

Thirty-eight (60%) of the graduates have been delivering, are currently delivering or are actively planning to deliver mental health awareness training sessions through the commissioned organisations and 25 (39%) of the graduates have been involved in delivering mental health awareness training within SLaM. At the time of writing there were only seven (11%) available to deliver training in SLaM.

Twenty-four (38%) graduates have either gone back into full- or part-time work (including the delivery of the training) and 10 (43%) have gone onto further education opportunities. We suggest that this particular programme is extremely successful at fulfilling SLaM's mission:

> ... a focus on recovery, which helps everyone who uses our services to maximise their potential. This includes: helping people access employment and education opportunities; not providing services that encourage institutionalisation within the community; and regularly reviewing packages of care to ensure that they are not creating dependence. We need to work with service users and their carers and social networks to support people in their lives. (SLaM Strategy 2009–13)

But interestingly, in terms of the expectation that the Changing Minds programme would provide a 'pool of trainers', results were perceived to be poor by SLaM (see Table 9.1).

However, it must be borne in mind that the course was set up to provide trainers for SLaM to use to challenge stigma and discrimination in its own services and surrounding communities, not necessarily to supply an employment route back into society. Through their involvement, project participants were enabled to transform their lives and identities from recipient to provider after being made helpless and dependent by the very system that was designed to support and empower them. The course has been so successful that the graduates are no longer just using their skills in the health and social care arena, but in some cases are now working part or full time.

We would argue that what is termed 'success' by an organisation needs to be reframed. Having confidence, skills and self-esteem so improved in a short space of time (to the point where individuals feel able to carry on with their lives and make choices about what is important for them and act on them) is something to be celebrated and applauded. But this aspect of success is often undervalued. Organisations will look at the resources invested and the 'perceived' minimal return or achievement of the set targets/outcomes. We would argue that what is not the organisation's gain is society's. If service user involvement is being done properly we should be seeing more of this type of thing happening for those who are ready and want to go back to their mainstream lives. Secondary service trusts and primary care trusts need to invest more in programmes like Changing Minds that have the ability to transform identities and sense of self if we want to improve public health outcomes in the long term.

Who is service user involvement really for? The government says that it is for the patients to feel more empowered and be able to say more clearly what they want from the services they receive. As we have demonstrated, if you do it too successfully you may decrease your chances of having any

Table 9.1: Targeted outcomes versus actual outcomes from each funder

Jobcentre Plus		Croydon Business		Well London	
Targeted outcomes	Actual outcomes	Targeted outcomes	Actual outcomes	Targeted outcomes	Actual outcomes
10-15 black and minority ethnic (BME) clients to be trained	9 BME clients identified. Target not met – 4 BME clients finished course	3 courses to be run	Only 2 run due to late funding	5 training courses to be run to train 30 people	4 training courses run – due to lack of take-up in West – 33 people trained
Clients who complete training to be considered for employment under Supported Permitted Work (SPW) Scheme if not employed by other providers	All offered employment under SPW rules	30 people to start	27 people started (90% target completed)	3 learning networks to be run	4 learning networks were run
		20 people to complete	14 people competed (70% target completed)	240 mental health awareness (MHA) training sessions to be run across 20 boroughs. Now 216 training sessions across 18 boroughs – due to 2 boroughs not running project	
		22 training sessions to be delivered involving graduates	31 training sessions delivered (150% target completed)	12 MHA events to be run in 4 boroughs	

real involvement at all as people move out of the system and go back to their mainstream lives.

There are other excellent examples of service user/survivor Training as Trainers/Leadership programmes across the country, different in name but similar in that they are mostly service user led and/or designed. Service user-led organisations and groups are starting to come together at a national level through the National Survivor User Network (NSUN) and other regional groupings and networks in an attempt not only to influence the mental health agenda but also to lead it. Despite the struggle for funding, people are organising themselves and looking at user-led training, research and service delivery rather than just picking up 'service user involvement contracts' that are often short term and under-resourced. Peer-led services, which have been developing in countries such as New Zealand and the United States, are now becoming a reality in the United Kingdom.

Perhaps leadership rather than citizen control is more realistic when talking about involvement in health and social care. Leadership is about people setting the agenda and implementing their own solutions to problems rather than attempting to seize control of what exists.

The Changing Minds programme is a good example of people contributing to the public health agenda by becoming equipped to lead the way and widening their influence beyond health and social care settings. Social learning refers to collective engagement in which goals and knowledge are shared through interactions; problems and solutions are identified as a result of greater insight; and actions are taken that transform and change a situation. Working at this higher level of complexity and participation has enabled individuals to move a much greater distance than was originally anticipated.

Those who provide mental health services not only have a duty of care, they also have a responsibility to assist people to become self-reliant to the point where they are back in the community and have no need of them. Involvement as demonstrated by Changing Minds can bring that kind of opportunity if they let it.

ten

Moving forward: understanding the negative experiences and impacts of patient and public involvement in health service planning, development and evaluation

Sophie Staniszewska, Carole Mockford, Andy Gibson,
Sandy Herron-Marx and Rebecca Putz

Introduction

Health and social care services across the United Kingdom (UK) are now committed to involving users in the planning, development and evaluation of their services, reinforced by policy and legislation (Staniszewska et al, 2008). The importance of patient and public involvement (PPI) has also been emphasised in the coalition government's White Paper, *Equity and excellence: Liberating the NHS* (DH, 2010a). However, the translation of these policy commitments into practice and the impact that they have remain open to question, for example a paper from the Local Government Information Unit (LGIU, 2008) highlights the top-down nature of many of these initiatives. PPI can take various forms, from inviting lay members onto committees such as in primary care trusts (PCTs), to setting up independent groups of people (patients, carers, general public), to service users conducting or leading their own projects. The terminology describing involvement can vary. For the purposes of this chapter, we have used patient and public involvement (PPI) as it is a broad term and can include a wide constituency of individuals. We will also use 'service users' to refer to individuals involved in studies, reflecting INVOLVE terminology.

The success of involvement depends on many factors, including how well planned and conducted the involvement is, how inclusive the process is, time constraints and budgetary resources, skills, encouragement and motivation. The rich and complex involvement activity in health and social care is reflected in the many and varied studies that have been published (Mockford et al, 2009). PPI could be regarded as a complex intervention with a specific aim and focus, and with the potential for both positive and negative impacts, as any other type of intervention may have. Of those studies that have considered the impact of PPI, most have focused on the positive impacts, with relatively few considering more negative impacts and how these can be mitigated. Poorly designed and conducted PPI has the potential for significant negative impact, as we describe in this chapter. The term 'negative impact' used in this context refers to inadvertent or adverse effects that can arise from PPI. The negative impact of involvement is not well defined and is not underpinned by an agreed conceptual or theoretical model (Brett et al, 2009; Mockford et al, 2009). With this in mind, we have adopted a broad approach and have considered any type of negative impact or experience, or effect, at any level, as being potentially relevant. Studies do not often highlight negative impacts and it can be difficult to identify these and separate them from broader negative experiences. As the evidence base underpinning PPI develops, our understanding of the nature of negative impact is likely to become clearer, with better insights into the different types of negative impact that occur at different levels and in different areas.

In this chapter we offer some steps towards developing this understanding, drawing on research undertaken at the National Centre for Involvement between 2006 and 2009, in particular a systematic review of the literature focusing on the impact of user involvement on National Health Service (NHS) healthcare services (Mockford et al, 2009), a study of PPI in PCT commissioning (NCI 2009 a,b) and information provided about practice by health professionals who completed the annual survey of involvement activity across NHS trusts over three years (Herron-Marx et al, 2009). The literature review was undertaken to better understand the current evidence underpinning PPI, identify key challenges, and make recommendations to enable the area to develop a coherent evidence base that is conceptually clear and methodologically robust (Mockford et al, 2009). A systematic review is a very thorough literature review that has a clear audit trail so its quality can be assessed and others can assess its adequacy. The annual survey examined the state of PPI from 2006 to 2009. It captured data from PPI leads in NHS trusts about what PPI looks like in practice and its impact (Herron-Marx et al, 2009). The PPI lead is the nominated person or persons in a trust responsible for PPI activities – these can be stand-alone roles or integrated into other job descriptions. The research into PPI in PCT commissioning drew on case studies based in three PCTs, drawing on documentary analysis, interviews and observations of meetings.

While we are able to report a range of negative impacts, it is important to recognise that the evidence underpinning PPI is limited, mainly because of inadequate reporting, particularly in relation to impact, although it should be acknowledged that some studies did not necessarily intend to evaluate impact as a primary or secondary outcome. However, of those papers that included impact, the poor detail of reporting, the unclear content validity and the lack of standardised ways to capture, report or measure impact are all important limitations (Brett et al, 2009; Staniszewska et al, 2011). As a result, our knowledge of negative impacts is relatively sparse and our findings could be described as representing the visible part of potentially a much larger 'iceberg' of impact requiring exploration. We would encourage all those reporting on impact in more depth to allow further illumination of the concept of both positive and negative impact.

We recognise that some researchers and service users may view the reporting of negative impact as a sensitive topic and suggest that discussion about involvement should focus on the positive aspects of involvement, as there is often enough difficulty convincing sceptics about its merits. However, we argue that it is vital to understand what does not work well and what types of PPI can have negative impacts. Such evidence can help researchers and service users to mitigate or manage these impacts, and to develop better ways of working that may avoid them. Interestingly, while the systematic review included all relevant papers from 1997 to 2009, most discussion about negative impacts occurred in earlier papers. It is not clear why a reduction has occurred at a time when interest in impact has expanded. It could also be argued that there is a moral obligation to understand the negative impact that any activity can have on all the individuals involved, with the aim of managing and minimising it.

Overall, the systematic review found that PPI had impacts at all levels of health services with varying influence on outcomes, from designing patient literature (eg Carney et al, 2006) to inputting into the design of new healthcare buildings and environment (Perkins et al, 2004). Service users appeared to gain personally with new social contacts (Fudge et al, 2008), feeling valued and listened to (Ripley et al, 2007) and being personally rewarded (Cotterell et al, 2004). They were able to develop various skills, such as presentation and representation skills (Dearden-Phillips and Fountain, 2005) and they learned how to influence change in the NHS (Taylor et al, 2004). Local communities were reported to benefit from an increased knowledge of services and improved dialogue with service providers. There seemed to be a sense that positive changes were taking place, with reported change in NHS culture and a greater awareness of patient and community interests by NHS staff and management. Such positive benefits form the main part of the impact evidence base (Mockford et al, 2009). A much smaller number of studies reported on the more negative impact on NHS staff, service users and community. These will be discussed later in the chapter. Findings from the survey are included in the next section. The survey was the final one of a series of three annual surveys of PPI within NHS trusts across England between 2006 and 2009.

PPI impact on NHS staff

NHS staff emerged as an important group in relation to both positive and negative impacts. There was evidence that PPI had had an impact on changes in NHS staff, including their professional attitudes, values and beliefs, improved awareness of service user perspectives, and improved relationships with voluntary organisations. However, there were also some less favourable descriptions of impact, such as the tensions and conflict that sometimes resulted from the emergence of differing expectations between users and staff (Peck et al, 2002). In other situations, some individuals saw PPI as a less important priority, which had to be put on the 'back burner' (South, 2004) as there were time restraints, workload restrictions and a lack of experience of service user involvement. One study (Peck et al, 2002) was generally positive about involvement, but reported on the differing expectations of service users compared to professional members of a joint commissioning board (JCB). Comments by JCB members included that some of the matters raised were not appropriate to this forum, feelings that lay members brought a lot of preconceptions and prejudice with them, and that the lay members had not achieved what the board wanted them to. One senior member of the board was quoted as saying: 'we've enabled them, we've helped them financially, we've put training in for them to help them find their own direction, and they've failed to do that' (Peck et al, 2002, p 447).

However, these comments reflect only one perspective and do not tell us how service users, carers or members of the public felt about the quality of the opportunities they were offered, the level of support they were offered or the scope to interact with professionals on their own terms or to set their own agenda. Furthermore, studies reporting the difficulties of implementing the involvement of service users in PCTs sometimes described less tolerance by PCT members of individuals who lacked experience in this environment. The response from some lay members of PCTs seemed to be that they were overwhelmed by the experience, and problems occurred from their lack knowledge of the PCT structures, processes and purpose (Peck et al, 2002). Alborz et al (2002) found that lay members of PCTs were less likely to contribute to clinical governance, prescribing or commissioning matters. Only a small number reported that they wanted to be involved in such activities although it is not clear why. In one study that examined six projects from a mental health collaborative, one patient was quoted as saying: "A lot of it goes over my head because I'm not familiar with everything they are talking about. I was a patient and I've never heard about this side of things" (Robert et al, 2003, p 67). A community psychiatric nurse from the same study found: 'of all the service users we approached, they all wanted a low key position – they weren't very happy about being part of meetings and talking in front of so many people' (Robert et al, 2003, p 67). Lay members also found it difficult to define a clear role for themselves and a clear mechanism in which to work (Mountford and Anderson, 2001).

Two further studies mentioned the difficulties that general practice surgeries had with user involvement. In one study, staff in one surgery were not confident that patients were enthusiastic and felt that general practitioners (GPs) lacked the time to be involved. The GPs were not convinced that their PPI group had changed the way things were done and felt that they needed more confidence to make suggestions for change. There was a feeling that there were difficulties getting 'appropriate' people involved and that there were unrealistic expectations expressed by service users (Mountford and Anderson, 2001). In the other study, support for PPI seemed less obvious at the general practice level, with little awareness of PPI and a feeling that it was not a priority (South, 2004).

While helpful in providing a flavour of the more negative experiences and impacts on staff, these studies only offer a partial perspective, possibly because such impacts did not form their main focus. Detailed accounts of negative impacts on NHS staff are relatively rare and so difficult to use in detailed planning of their mitigation. The examples recounted also reflect the difficulties of the notion of partnership (Barnes and Cotterell, Introduction, this volume), as they highlight tensions between user-led and officially determined participation initiatives.

More detailed experiences were collected by the annual surveys of PPI in NHS trusts (Herron-Marx et al, 2009). These surveys found that PPI can have a positive impact on staff (including staff retention, satisfaction, rewarding experiences, career progression and status) but also found evidence of the negative impacts of involvement. These included increased levels of stress, 'burn out', increased sickness rates and fatigue. Staff respondents recognised that these were the 'unexpected and unwanted side effects' of involvement and the negative impact of PPI was more frequently reported in the 2009 survey than in the previous two annual surveys. There are a few possible reasons for this. The expectation for widespread involvement in the NHS has increased across healthcare. This has placed increased pressure on PPI leads to deliver quickly and created difficulties as building capacity and capability for PPI takes time. Often there were insufficient resources, including time, money, people and facilities, important factors for successful PPI.

In addition to the survey, the commissioning study also found evidence of negative impacts of resource constraints (National Centre for Involvement, 2009a, p 14): '"One of the questions we were asked was how are you going to deliver all of this with two staff. And it was … yes, two whole time equivalent, how can you deliver this with two whole time equivalent staff?" (Member of PCT PPI Team).'

Lack of clarity and inconsistency over 'payment for time' of patients, carers and the public caused additional stresses in the commissioning study.

A variety of approaches were adopted (often within the same trust) and this made some uncomfortable. As one PCT commissioner describes:

> So at each stage what kind of level of involvement do you need? What does that look like? And what does best practice look like? And I mean there will be bits that are applicable to some projects that aren't to others, but just some kind of process and some kind of templates that we can work towards. So we've got a steer as to what we should be doing. (National Centre for Involvement, 2009a, p 13)

Lack of consistency over language used and lack of clear criteria from which to assess PPI practice added to the challenges faced by PPI leads. Many felt despondent and ineffectual in pushing forward this agenda. Frequently, respondents felt that PPI was not a mechanism for change but rather a mechanism to ratify existing or predetermined high-level decisions and there was a lot of 'hearing' but not a lot of 'real listening' happening. For example, one PCT procurement manager in the commissioning study reported that PPI had added little to their work:

> What we got from the public didn't make a great deal of change to what we were already going forward with anyway and when we had something … like we were firing about 88 questions at the bidders, at the potential providers, we've perhaps added three or four bullets to selected questions and answers so we've probably amended 3 out of the 88 questions. (National Centre for Involvement, 2009b, p 15)

The 'emotional labour of PPI' often had a profound impact on NHS staff and this appears to be a growing trend – an important issue that requires further attention. Staff sometimes felt drained by their efforts to push forward PPI. A detailed account of the negative impact of involvement in relation to the survey data collected by the National Centre for Involvement is provided by Herron-Marx et al (2009).

PPI impact on service users

In addition to NHS staff, service users reported a range of PPI impacts. The systematic review found a range of studies that documented the positive impacts that involvement can have on service users, often described in terms of personal gains or developing skills. A smaller number of studies reported more negative impacts, which could lead to users experiencing feelings of disappointment, lack of worth or being dissatisfied with their contribution (Mockford et al, 2009). Lay board members rated their influence as fairly limited on key decision-making boards (Pickard and Smith, 2001; Alborz,

2002; Peck et al, 2002). A small number felt that their skills were under-used (Alborz, 2002). In addition, some felt ineffective due to a lack of technical knowledge (Pickard and Smith, 2001). In one study, the workload of the subgroup of a primary care group (PCG – precursor to PCT) was so significant that PPI was very low on the agenda and pursued largely without a user input (Anderson and Florin, 2001a). In another study (PPI forums working with the PCG), projects remained unfinished due to service users leaving the forum for reasons including limited funding and not enough 'manpower' (Berry, 2008). The descriptions of these studies also indicate the difficulty of examining PPI activity longitudinally when NHS structures are liable to change fairly regularly. As with studies describing impact on staff, many of the studies reporting negative impacts leave the reader with many questions about the detail of the process, the reasons for particular actions and the specific impact. This underlines the need for future reporting of negative impact in papers and reports to be much more detailed and comprehensive, to enable a fuller understanding of how, why and where negative impacts are occurring.

From the systematic review data it became apparent that users appeared more likely to be involved in certain activities, such as primary care development, and less likely to contribute to clinical governance, prescribing or commissioning (Alborz, 2002). There is some evidence from the commissioning study that NHS commissioners are resistant to involving patients, carers and the public directly in this process because of concerns about commercial confidentiality, legal liability and the complexity of the process involved, as one procurement manager explains: 'Even the names of the business are commercially sensitive, who's bidding and who's not bidding. We would need to ensure that patients … participants appreciated that and agreed to be bound by the terms and conditions of disclosure and so on' (National Centre for Involvement, 2009b, p 12). Similarly, the potentially complex nature of the procurement process was seen as a barrier to involvement in another project:

> We didn't think it would be a good use of her time (patient representative) to read through all seven tenders, which are over 100 page documents. We also had interview sessions with the providers. Now we did consider inviting her along, the patient rep along to those sessions, but again they were quite detailed sessions and it would have taken two whole days of her time, and again we didn't think that that was going to be appropriate. (Commissioner) (National Centre for Involvement, 2009a, p 15)

The success of service users' involvement depended on a range of factors. Often there was too much work for too few people. One user representative felt that sometimes expectations of what service users were capable of were too high:'to expect one person to carry that burden single handed is expecting far too much, and you're in danger of injuring that very person' (Peck et al, 2002 p 447). Sometimes individuals or groups were given too many tasks, for example one trust was in touch with only one user group that had 12 active members out of a total of 70 members (Crawford et al, 2003).

Feeling isolated as the only user, being unfamiliar with NHS structures and policy and having difficulties speaking in front of many people were areas in which some users struggled (Robert et al, 2003). Success seemed to be linked to positive support and could be offered in the form of training to help everyone understand their role in broader context. Where there was a lack of support, this could lead to difficulties. For example, lay members struggled to be heard or were ignored due to little support or commitment towards PPI from other board members (Anderson and Florin, 2001b). 'The chairman stopped the meeting at two minutes to four (when it was due to finish at 4pm) and said "we'd better stop to let M give his report." I had to ask him if he was being facetious' (lay member) (Milewa et al, 2002a p 43). This illustrates some of the difficulties that emerged when partnerships were viewed as predominantly adopting existing ways of working within healthcare organisations, rather than being discussed and agreed by all participants, including NHS staff and PPI representatives.

In another study, the joint executive team were viewed as controlling the agenda of the JCB including the content of the discussion, which was seen to exclude the user and carer participants who felt they had no say (Peck et al, 2002). Another study found less priority given to PPI:'it hasn't been a priority over the first 8 or 9 months ... clinical governance, telling people who we are, prescriptions, or prescribing – we've had to address those first. So public participation is only just getting onto the agenda' (lay member) (Milewa et al, 2002b p 43). In other situations, service users lacked the correct information to enable them to participate because of the sheer volume of information they received and professional communication styles (Pickard and Smith, 2001). In other cases, users found difficulty finding a clear role and mechanism in which to work (Mountford and Anderson, 2001). These findings highlight the negative experiences users can have when appropriate support, training and commitment are lacking. They also indicate that the impacts of involvement are linked to the context and process of involvement, and ultimately the overall outcomes of any involvement activity (Brett et al, 2009).

PPI impact on the community

Apart from the community benefits resulting from the addition of new or improved services, the systematic review found that local communities benefited from increased knowledge, improved dialogue and an improved awareness of others. The term 'community' was interpreted broadly in the systematic review to include studies that examined local residential or geographical groups, hospital communities of patients or groups of people who shared the same ethnicity, sexuality or medical condition (Mockford et al, 2009).

While most impacts reported were positive, again there was a range of more negative experiences or impacts identified in studies, and broader contextual issues including concerns around representation, low awareness of boards and trusts by the community, low priority for PPI, reliance on involving existing user groups by trusts rather than service users from the wider community, and a lack of evidence of community influence. While some studies reflected times when healthcare was organised differently, their messages still have relevance in today's NHS. Many of the studies described the difficulties that service users and local communities had experienced, which may have impeded wider PPI. Some older studies of PCGs, which were differently structured from the PCTs, which superseded them in 2000-01, found concerns around a lack of representation of the local community and patients (Alborz, 2002), especially black and minority ethnic groups on PCG boards (Crawford et al, 2003). There was also low awareness of the existence of PCGs by the general public (Alborz, 2002). Such contextual issues are important to consider as part of the potential for PPI to have an impact. There was also a lack of interest in the community aspect of PPI within the PCG, with more emphasis on individual health, choice and behaviour (Anderson and Florin, 2001c). One community participation subgroup of a PCG failed as no clear roles were defined (Anderson and Florin, 2001d). Some PCGs tended to rely on existing groups such as community health councils, the Council for Voluntary Services (CVS), patient participation groups who worked within GP surgeries and voluntary groups. PPI had primarily included the provision of information in the form of newsletters or public meetings to organisations and groups, households and patients, rather than inviting them to participate in decision making (Pickard and Smith, 2001). In a separate study of one PCG (Anderson and Florin, 2001c), it was found that the PPI subgroup operated in a fairly opportunistic way by buying into existing local initiatives such as the borough's citizens' panel and the health authority's diabetic focus groups. This latter study found that the PPI subgroup lacked confidence, knowledge and a clear focus on what it was trying to achieve.

The commissioning study also found evidence that carrying out PPI, if done in a superficial way, may cause longlasting damage particularly among groups who are socially marginalised and experience the most severe health consequences of social and economic deprivation:

And I think some of it is because patients have felt, because they haven't been listened to in the past, what's the point? And there's a bit of apathy that we have to acknowledge and sometimes with our tight timeframes and our workload, I can only work with the people that want to be worked with, I'd like to encourage and support the people that don't because they actually know, but you don't get the time to do that sort of thing and go out there. (Member of PCT PPI team) (National Centre for Involvement, 2009b, p 14)

These studies indicated that the potential for negative impacts of PPI seemed to relate to the context and process in which PPI was operating. As with impacts on staff and users, it was difficult to separate negative experiences from more specific impacts, often because the detail of reporting was relatively limited. It was also unclear whether studies had content validity, that is, they reported all the relevant aspects of impact they had identified. Thus, we only have partial information, which does not provide a full understanding of the negative impacts for communities.

Summary

This chapter draws together some of the negative, unforeseen or iatrogenic impacts identified in the systematic review (Mockford et al, 2009), the annual survey (Herron-Marx et al, 2009) and the commissioning study (National Centre for Involvement 2009a,b). There were many reports of the problems and difficulties encountered by service users, staff and management, and the wider community. The potential for one person's positive impact to be another person's negative impact needs to be acknowledged. From the perspective of the systematic review, both the user and the health professional 'voice' appeared to be present. The experiences of users were often written about in an empathic way, while health professionals' experiences could sometimes sound as though individuals were less tolerant of what seemed to be a different way of working, with little acknowledgement of their already high workload. However, the outcomes of involvement seemed to be predominantly defined by the organisations involved rather than service users so we know relatively little about the outcomes that service users wanted to achieve. Such difficulties challenge the notion of true partnership as certain groups dominate the ways in which methods, context or process are decided. Such elements require discussion and agreement before the focus of the PPI activity is discussed.

The negative experiences and impacts on service users included users not feeling able to contribute as they wanted because they felt they lacked the knowledge or experience required, some felt uncomfortable speaking out at meetings and others felt that their personal skills were under-used. Successful involvement seemed to be underpinned by support and commitment from professionals, training in their role, and being able to see how they had made a difference. Problems were also experienced by professionals, who reported feeling that service users often had their own agenda, which did not fit into the process of decision making and this could lead to conflict. Some studies also highlighted the lack of a clear mechanism through which service users could feed into the decision-making system. These negative experiences or impacts may have been due to the complexities of NHS organisation, the pace of change that sometimes reduced the priority given to PPI, or a lack of time and resources of local services and management boards to spend on PPI. Local communities were also reported to have a low awareness of the existence of NHS structures. Consequently, they lacked the opportunity to become involved, particularly if there was a reliance on using existing groups in PPI, and a low priority was placed on their involvement. This may explain why there was little evidence of how the community had been influencing service planning and development.

The most helpful review studies reported both positive and negative factors arising from PPI. It is important that future studies continue to ensure a full understanding of the difference that PPI makes. There are sometimes assumptions made about the positive impacts with relatively little consideration of negative impacts. These types of impacts came through much more clearly in the survey and strongly support the need for researchers to explore them more thoroughly.

The nature of negative impact

While it has been possible to identify a range of negative impacts, such impacts remain poorly conceptualised and poorly reported. It is clear that negative impact is sometimes difficult to draw out, is included in descriptions of experiences, can take different forms and is likely to be multidimensional, with different impacts relevant for different groups and different situations. Some descriptions of negative impact are also closely tied in with the context and process of involvement, making it hard to separate out these elements. Future researchers need to enhance the conceptual and theoretical understanding of both negative and positive impacts. Future work may be enriched by building on sociological theory and empirical research on the link between knowledge and power and how they operate within social relationships of care.

Interestingly, older studies tended to comment more on negative impacts, which poses a challenge for current studies and a question of why this debate has not been developed when interest in impact has increased more generally. This trend needs to be reversed with new studies significantly enhancing the detail with which they report negative impact. The complexity of negative impact also needs to be considered, so that better understanding can lead to effective mitigation.

Our argument is that identifying and understanding negative impact is vital in developing, monitoring and evaluating PPI strategies and in deciding how to minimise such impact. Our analysis suggests that there are a number of conditions that can mitigate against negative impacts and promote positive impact (see Box 10.1).

Negative impacts can only be mitigated if they are identified and action taken. Such mitigation could also be important in ensuring the potential for positive impacts to be fully realised. It is possible that, in some situations, negative impacts may override any possibility for a project to impact positively. It is also important that such negative impacts are considered positively. While this may seem a slight contradiction, we argue that the

---

Box 10.1: Mitigating against negative impacts

- An understanding or knowledge about PPI and methods.
- Ensuring that the context and process for PPI are appropriate.
- Good facilitation of PPI into practice.
- An agreed form of partnership working.
- Being prepared to experiment with alternative meeting formats, venues and approaches.
- Being prepared to give up some element of control in order to allow a genuine and creative dialogue to develop.
- Being willing to put the resources of the organisation at the service of users as well as expecting users to support organisational objectives.
- Recognising that PPI is about a whole systems implementation, which means team working and integration of key ideas across the whole organisation.
- Good support for everyone in the process.
- Appropriate information.
- Clarity in roles.
- Openness.
- Transparency.
- Clarity in expectations and what PPI might achieve.
- Valuing the potential for PPI to have an impact.
- Monitoring the process and remedying negative impacts when identified.
- Clearly identifying the impacts of PPI and collaboratively feeding these back to staff, users and the community to encourage a positive cycle of involvement.

---

identification, management and mitigation of negative impacts would benefit from the adoption of the type of approach adopted in appreciative inquiry. This is a particular way of asking questions and envisioning the future that fosters positive relationships and builds on the basic goodness in a person, a situation or an organisation. This enhances a system's capacity for collaboration and change. In this way, there would be potential for embedding PPI in a way that ensures that the negative impacts are identified and through their recognition strengthens the potential for PPI to have a positive impact.

Conclusion

This chapter has highlighted the need for negative impacts of PPI to be recognised, in order to mitigate their effects. Some of the negative impacts identified in this chapter appear to be associated with factors such as poor planning and lack of resources. These are important to recognise and can be mitigated to some extent. However, this chapter has also identified negative experiences and impacts that are harder to mitigate and question the notion of partnership working in healthcare. These negative experiences and impact seem to be related to the predominantly top-down nature of PPI initiatives where users and communities are involved in particular ways, to fit in with existing systems and practices. There are few accounts of users working collaboratively with healthcare professionals to establish ways of working and agree the context and process of PPI. In many ways, current PPI practice in healthcare still reflects a 'glass ceiling', which users cannot break through. To some extent, this glass ceiling is imposed by legislation and NHS structures. However, more fundamental change may be necessary if the policy commitment to PPI is to be fulfilled and the idea of the 'Big Society' truly implemented. Possible ways of developing more equal forms of partnership in healthcare could be developed by drawing on practice in health and social care research where user-led and collaborative forms of involvement have evolved. Continuing to develop our understanding of the negative impacts of all types of PPI will be vital in the future, to enable an understanding of what works, for whom and in what circumstances.

Part Two

User involvement in services

Questions for reflection

Contributions in Part Two focused on issues that emerge from initiatives that aim to enable service users to work with service providers in achieving change. Again, we offer the following questions to stimulate further reflection and research:

- Can collaborative working between service users and professionals ever be understood as a partnership? Is co-production effectively the same as partnership?
- How well embedded is user involvement in service-providing organisations, and what are the factors that support effective mainstreaming of user involvement initiatives?
- Why might service users decide not to continue to devote their energies to involvement activities that are embedded within services? What are the advantages and disadvantages to users of focusing their efforts in this context?
- How effective can user involvement be in achieving significant change in practice and service delivery? What are the comparative benefits of strategies based in education, training and awareness raising in comparison with direct input to service decision making?
- What are the advantages to service providers of user input to decision making – at individual and collective levels? Should their resistance to such involvement always be understood as professional defensiveness?
- The distinction between 'choice'-based and 'voice'-based mechanisms for user influence was drawn early on in the development of user involvement as a mechanism for change. Can personalisation be understood as the triumph of choice over voice? If so, what are likely to be the consequences of this? What are the different roles played by individual and collective involvement in service design, delivery and evaluation?

Part Three

User involvement in research

Marian Barnes and Phil Cotterell

Introduction

Alongside demands for greater involvement of service users in policy making, planning and delivery of services, service users have also sought greater involvement in research that affects their lives. Many of the papers submitted to the conference that this collection is based on were orientated towards user involvement in research. This suggests that this is now a significant site for user involvement and user-led activity and that the co-production of knowledge is seen as an important way of achieving change. The concept of 'co-production' can be applied both to service delivery (Bovaird, 2007; Needham, 2007) and to the production of new knowledge. Involvement in research can be conceptualised not only in terms of enabling reciprocal and more equal relationships to be formed between professionals and users, but also as an approach to collectivising knowledge production.

Since the 1990s, there has been increasing mainstream acceptance and promotion of user involvement in research (DH, 2005, 2006), but the origins of this have a much longer history, located in the campaigning of the disability movement over control of the process of research production. A widely acknowledged influential 'moment' in this history concerns research conducted in the 1960s and the subsequent response of disabled activists to this. Paul Hunt, a wheelchair user with muscular dystrophy, lived at 'Le Court', a Leonard Cheshire Home, and while he was there he led an important struggle by disabled residents to have control over their lives (Hunt, 2001). A study commissioned by the then Ministry of Health into the participation of residents in 22 of these Leonard Cheshire 'homes' was conducted between 1966 and 1969 by Eric Miller and Geraldine Gwynne of the Tavistock Institute for Human Relations. This has become a landmark within disability research mainly due to Hunt's critique of it. The residents anticipated that the researchers would have some sympathy for their situation and aspirations. The report of the research, *A life apart* (Miller and Gwynne, 1972), concluded that the segregated system was oppressive to the residents. However, it only recommended operational improvements in the institutions rather than the elimination of the system itself, and significantly for residents like Hunt, avoided the recommendation that residents should be more involved in the management of their homes. The residents felt that they had been 'conned' (Hunt, 1981).

As Hunt's (1981) paper 'Settling accounts with the parasite people' described, there were reasonable grounds for expecting that the researchers would highlight residents' lack of power and control over their everyday lives due to the institution the researchers came from. However, Hunt argued that the research was 'profoundly biased and committed *against* the resident's interests' (Hunt, 1981, emphasis in original). His critique was not only scathing but also visionary. Although the social model of disability and emancipatory research had not then been articulated with the clarity and force with which subsequent disability activists have promoted these ideas, Hunt had a clear vision that became one strand of influence on the development of the social model and of emancipatory research.

In developing arguments for emancipatory research, disabled people were focusing on who controls research: who decides what research should be done, how it is done and how it should be used? They argued that research needs to raise consciousness and be an empowering process that is clearly focused on challenging the status quo and promoting change for those who are the focus of the research (Oliver, 1992; Zarb, 1992). Epistemologically, such research is rooted in the social model of disability with its foci on oppressive structural factors. Thus, it also needs to be understood as part of a political project, which is about power as well as knowledge.

Mental health service users and survivors have also pursued radical approaches to research in which they and their organisations seek to shape the research agenda and process (eg Faulkner and Layzell, 1999). This model of research has often been referred to as 'user-led' research within mental health and more widely (Beresford and Evans, 1999; Nicholls et al, 2003; Williams, 2003). In many cases, mental health service users have worked with allies among academic researchers to develop participatory research practices. The Service User Research Enterprise (SURE) based at the Institute of Psychiatry is an example of how collaborations between service user researchers and academics can be operationalised. Service users are employed as researchers and this initiative has an emphasis on users' priorities for research topics. Similarly, Suresearch is a group of mental health service users who have been working with allies at the University of Birmingham since 2000. This group 'aims to influence the quality, ethics and values of mental health research by linking with other local, regional and national partnerships in the mental health arena' (www.suresearch.org.uk/index.html). Another indication of the development of user involvement in research is the publication of a book entitled *This is survivor research* (Sweeney et al, 2009), which brings together reports of mental health user/survivor research that has been undertaken by doctoral research students who have mental health problems, as well as those employed as service user researchers.

Involvement in mental health research is discussed in several chapters within the present book, and in Chapter Fifteen, Turner and Gillard reflect on the continuing challenges for users in retaining a distinctive voice within collaborative research enterprises.

It is significant that the development of user-led research is linked to areas in which service users have come together around shared experiences and have campaigned not only for changes in service delivery, but also for changes in the ways in which disability and mental illness are understood. In other contexts it is often researchers who have taken the lead in promoting participatory research and the motivations of service users and others who become involved may be rather different from the political motivations of disabled people who have promoted emancipatory research (see also Cotterell and Morris, Chapter Five). For example, while there are now many examples of good practice in older people's involvement in research (Barnes and Taylor, 2007), as Ward and Gahagan demonstrate (Chapter Fourteen), such initiatives are often led by academic researchers and the older people who become involved may not start out seeing this as a route to empowerment.

User-led and emancipatory research has developed rather separately from participatory action research (PAR), although they have many similarities with it. PAR has its origins in community development and in particular the role of community inquiry in challenging Western 'experts' in development contexts in the global South (Leach et al, 2005). But such methods have also been adopted by communities wanting to challenge professional expertise and the assumptions underpinning technological development in the developed world (Fischer, 2000). In these contexts, the concept of 'local knowledge' is used in very similar ways to that of 'experiential knowledge' in relation to users of health and social care services.

Just as user involvement in services is now official policy, so too is user involvement in research. The Department of Health set up an advisory group to support 'patient and public involvement' in research in 1996. Now known as INVOLVE, this group has been instrumental in the advancement of active involvement in health service, public health and social care research. Applicants for National Institute for Health Research funding have to demonstrate how they have involved patients and/or the public in developing their proposal and what their continuing involvement will be. Different factors have brought about this shift. One is the concern about the honesty, ethics and general conduct of health research brought about by high-profile scandals such as that at Alder Hey Children's Hospital, where children's body parts were used for research without their parents' consent (Redfern et al, 2001), and that of the Bristol Royal Infirmary, where experimental treatments and innovations were conducted with no consent or ethical approval (DH, 2001c). Another factor relates to increasing critical discussion arguing that active involvement produces better research, research that is more relevant to people's needs, is more reliable and collects more useful information, as well as being more ethical (Hanley, 1999; Fisher, 2002).

In the context of health and social care today, it is clear that user involvement in research occupies a prominent position, with all major research funding organisations in the United Kingdom expecting studies they fund to have evidence of user involvement in all or some research activities. However, despite official acceptance and promotion of user involvement in research, resistance towards it is ongoing among some researchers. This resistance can originate from the perception that there is no proof that such involvement makes a positive difference to research, that involvement is unrepresentative, too costly, time consuming or simply too difficult. Boote et al (2002) outline these objections, contending that they are not easily dismissed, and go on to call for 'measures' and 'evaluations' that enable the effect of involvement on research to be developed. A consensus study contributed to understandings of what it is to successfully involve users in research (Telford et al, 2004). Eight principles and indicators of successful user involvement in research were agreed. Efforts to tease out what constitutes effective involvement or how to measure the impact of involvement continue, as outlined in Barber et al's contribution in this Part (Chapter Eighteen). However, such endeavours are not seen uncritically in all quarters, as Purtell and colleagues illustrate (Chapter Seventeen). Staddon's contribution to this Part (Chapter Sixteen), which discusses experiences of researching with women with alcohol issues, highlights another aspect of the 'impact' question. Users may be supported to carry out research, but they can also face considerable difficulty in getting results published and being taken seriously.

Despite this note of caution regarding the measurement of impact, research funders and researchers themselves remain focused on this issue. Key challenges with regard to establishing the impact of involvement include issues with assessment itself (involvement is usually a complex process), with the difficulty of predicting where involvement is likely to have the greatest impact (benefits of involvement may vary depending on context), and the challenge of identifying the added value of involvement (what benefit exactly does involvement bring to research and under what circumstances?) (Staley, 2009). A recent systematic review of involvement in research highlighted the need to report on a wide range of impact factors, both process and context (Brett et al, 2009). Uncertainties as to the efficacy of user involvement in research may be partly responsible for the low numbers of researchers who actively work with users in studies: 17% out of over 500 health researchers surveyed by Barber et al (2007) involved users, for example. More recently it has been shown that health researchers remain 'uncomfortable' about involving members of the public in research (Thompson et al, 2009).

Three chapters in this collection discuss examples of projects where researchers have worked with young people: young mothers (Brady and colleagues, Chapter Eleven); young people working with researchers in relation to public health issues (Brady and colleagues, Chapter Twelve); and young people with hearing loss (Kirkwood, Chapter Thirteen). These examples highlight the different dynamics that there can be between researchers and 'users' (not always a helpful term) when power relationships also embody an age dimension. The young mothers project raises important questions about differences *between* 'users' and Kirkwood also highlights the way in which context can impact on relationships and dynamics. One helpful insight that comes from considering the range of contributions in Part Three is the importance of assuming neither that all users will share the same type of motivation for taking part in research, nor that the preferred relationship between users and researchers will be the same in all cases.

There is now a body of research in which users have played an active part in most health and social care contexts. It is important to reflect on what this may mean to those users, and their constituencies, who become involved in research, what it means for those who regard themselves as 'professional' researchers and what it means for research itself. For example, the National Health Service is now adept at including users in processes such as research commissioning bodies, but does this necessarily equate to any substantial change to the lives of users or to the nature of the research that is commissioned? There is now a well-developed infrastructure of Patient and Public Involvement (PPI) in health and social care research but is the subsequent research, in terms of both process and outcomes, radically different to conventional research? How easy is it for user researchers to secure funds for research that might challenge either dominant methodological or policy assumptions? While the acceptance of the value of user input in research can be seen as an indicator of the success of action by service users, such success can also bring its own challenges of retaining and developing a distinctive voice.

eleven

Young mothers' experiential knowledge and the research process

Geraldine Brady, Geraldine Brown and Corinne Wilson

Introduction

As a research team, and over a number of years, we have undertaken a range of research studies that have explored experiences of teenage pregnancy and young parenthood. Our experience of undertaking research in this area has uncovered inherent tensions when thinking about service user involvement and participatory methods. Academic researchers can be reluctant to reveal such tensions or limitations in their research, but we believe that a focus on the *process* of research with service users, as well as on any findings or recommendations, is essential to gaining a clearer understanding of what is meant when referring to service user inclusion, involvement or participation. Or, to re-emphasise this point, what we do and the way we do it is as important as the final outcome or output. Our actions as researchers not only have impact in terms of how our findings may be used or interpreted, but also impact on the service users with whom we are directly engaged.

Attempts to include the voices of service users have become a common feature of health and social care service commissioning. The participation of people who may be in receipt of services in the development of policy or practice is often regarded as being beneficial by both commissioners and users of services. For example, health and social care commissioning often advocates including the voices and experiences of those who may be defined as being 'socially excluded', 'marginalised', 'vulnerable', 'hard to reach' and 'at risk'. It is often assumed that issues associated with inequality are being addressed from the 'bottom up' (Ferguson, 2008). Unequal power relations and the ways in which the grounded or bottom-up knowledge is produced, received and valued attracts less critical reflection from commissioners, the research community and service users (see Cotterell and Morris, Chapter Five). This is our focus here.

In this chapter we highlight the way in which research around teenage pregnancy has been commissioned in relation to a specific political agenda. We suggest that the United Kingdom (UK) teenage pregnancy policy framework serves to limit the possibility for pregnant teenagers and young mothers' views and experiences to challenge the dominant discourse. This pervasive verbal and written discourse authoritatively places their experiences outside of the norm, constructing teenage pregnancy as negative for young women, their children and wider society. We suggest that the case of teenage pregnancy demonstrates how inclusion of service users does not necessarily lead to participatory research or to services that meet needs. In this chapter we are particularly talking about 'young mothers', rather than 'young parents'; as Alldred and David (2009) note, the discourse of 'parents' can mask inequalities and difficulties that are compounded by gender. Our contribution is a discussion of participation in relation to teenage mothers; our final reflections, however, relate to what this may tell us about 'service user' participation more widely.

Teenage pregnancy: policy context

Throughout this book, contributing authors have defined what they understand to be the meaning of service user involvement, and explanations are many and varied. The term is contested and, as the editors of this book note, language is not neutral and is used in order to define people, sometimes in a rather limited way. As authors writing in this field have observed (Beresford and Branfield, 2006), people who become involved in shaping health and social care agendas may be led and encouraged by services themselves to do so, or, may be self-organised activists who have come together and united around a common cause, issue or group identity. The experiential knowledge of service users has been acknowledged as a form of expertise that can benefit the development of practice, policy and research (DH, 2001d).

Teenage mothers are not generally in a position to influence practice or policy. They cannot be said to have mounted any kind of collective challenge or collective action in relation to their treatment by services or by wider society. This may set them apart from other service user groups. Having said this, there is recognition within policy that learning can be gained from the experiences of young mothers, but the way in which this has taken place has been influenced by the parameters of the policy framework.

As Wilson (2007) has argued elsewhere, young mothers' status is ambiguous, they are perceived as both unable to make a successful transition to adulthood and as unsuccessful children. Public discourse identifies young mothers as 'socially excluded', 'vulnerable' and 'at risk' (SEU, 1999). Responses from the media and the wider public to the 'problem' of teenage pregnancy continually sanction their difference and these young women are perceived to be inappropriately pregnant. At the time of writing this chapter, government policy continued to provide the backdrop to the way in which the lives of teenage mothers are viewed:

For a variety of reasons – lack of knowledge, lack of confidence to resist pressure, poor access to advice and support, low aspirations – around 40,000 young women become pregnant each year.... For conceptions that end in a birth, there are often costs too – poorer child health outcomes, poor maternal emotional health and well-being, and increased chances of both teenage parents and their children living in poverty. (DCSF, 2010, ministerial foreword)

Teenage parenthood has become amplified as a social problem, capturing significant political and social dynamics and anxieties (MacVarish, 2010). Despite the existence of a growing body of research that challenges the inevitability of poor outcomes related to parental age (Arai, 2009; Duncan et al, 2010), the over-riding political priority remains the reduction in rates of teenage pregnancy. Dominant negative discourses are realised not just in the reactions of individual practitioners, but in institutional and organisational responses to young women's pregnancies and their status as a mother. Young women internalise some of the dominant negative discourses (Wilson et al, 2002; Bailey et al, 2004) and communication between them and service providers is often complicated by unspoken misunderstandings on both sides. Teenage mothers are a socially silenced group whose opinions are not heard in the public sphere. They are not a group who has organised to represent themselves and neither are they a group that commands much public sympathy.

Inclusion and involvement of young mothers

As we have argued elsewhere (Brown et al, 2009) certain themes have been central to the political response to addressing teenage pregnancy, and such themes have led to an overwhelming emphasis being placed on the promotion of measures to prevent teenage pregnancy. Defining teenage pregnancy as a 'social problem' has effectively limited capacity to understand the complexity and meaning that young people ascribe to parenting. Overall, there has been a failure to acknowledge that, for some young women, teenage pregnancy can be positive and a means of social inclusion (Cater and Coleman, 2006; Arai, 2009; Duncan et al, 2010). As far back as the 1980s, Phoenix (1988, 1991) recognised that the overwhelmingly negative focus referred to previously is produced by people who are not themselves young mothers but rather outsiders, and that the views and experiences of teenage parents need to be part of the solution to the 'problem' of teenage pregnancy. Throughout our own research we have argued for an insider–outsider continuum, recognising that a supportive family member (for example) is not an outsider in the way that someone who is ill-informed may be (Letherby et al, 2002). More recently, alongside the increased recognition of the role that service users can play in service development more generally, commissioners now aim to include young mothers when developing services or carrying out research; experiential knowledge plays an important part when identifying barriers to accessing services and the support needs of teenage parents.

Consultation with teenage mothers has become a common feature of service commissioning (Meyrick, 2002), but it can be argued that interest in the views and perspectives of 'insiders' has been co-opted in support of the wider agenda, which associates teenage pregnancy with multiple risk factors and social exclusion (Kidger, 2005). The inclusion of teenage mothers in service development or delivery is underpinned by assumptions that their experience is largely negative. This can then lead to young mothers being deployed as moral guardians, relaying a moral message about their experience of becoming pregnant at an early age and of the hardship associated with young motherhood. For example, in a study of a school sex education programme, which engaged young mothers to deliver part of the Sex and Relationships Education (SRE) programme, Kidger (2005) found that young mothers often colluded with the dominant negative messages relating to teenage sexual behaviour, pregnancy and motherhood; the stories that they told of their lives were shaped in order to fit in with such messages and served to improve their own moral positioning. Yet often there exists a disjuncture between the reality of the experience of being a teenage mother and that of the image portrayed in government strategy and policy, the media and wider society. In summary, a positive portrayal of teenage mothering goes against the dominant 'story' of teenage pregnancy and motherhood.

Research approach

In undertaking research that explores the experience of teenage pregnancy and young parenthood, much of our work has been commissioned by local authorities and primary care trusts – Teenage Pregnancy Partnerships. We have been concerned to challenge the stigma, prejudice, inequality and oppression that pregnant teenagers and young mothers face. We have adopted an inclusive approach, drawing on traditional methods (semi-structured interviews, focus groups) and participatory methods, including youth club activities, storyboards, story booklets and filmmaking. We have worked with young mothers to develop training materials and resources that reflect their own experiences and bring to life individual biographical stories, serving as a challenge to the stereotypical view of 'the teenage mother'. Young mothers have also trained as trainers, to deliver training alongside the research team to multi-agency groups of practitioners. Our aim is to make research count by shifting the focus of research from outputs and outcomes to include active engagement with the impact of research (Letherby and Bywaters, 2007) on commissioners, service providers, service users and researchers, thereby extending traditional research approaches and agendas. We adopt a grounded 'insider' approach to data collection and analysis, informed by feminist principles and principles of social justice.

In 2008, we were commissioned by a Teenage Pregnancy Partnership to develop a training programme for health, social care, housing and youth practitioners who had a remit for working with young parents. The call for tenders identified the inclusion of young mothers in the development of the training programme as key. Following the success of our proposal to undertake the work, we visited young parent groups, run by the Youth Service, and consulted with 26 young mothers about their experiences of pregnancy and parenting and of encounters with a range of services. The findings of this consultation shaped the issues that became the focus of the training programme. Six young mothers (aged 17-19 years) expressed an interest in involvement in the project and were recruited to participate in workshops and to be trained as trainers. One young mother was unable to complete the project.

The workshops were held at Coventry University; this provided a new learning experience for the young women. Our approach to facilitating the workshops gave the young women an opportunity to shape the content and delivery of the training. Issues raised during the wider consultation were explored and the young women suggested ways to deliver the training and the types of resources to be included. The research design included five workshops, the first four being development sessions while the final workshop was a train-the-trainer session. The workshops started at 10am and ended at 3pm and an on-site crèche was provided (in the form of a mobile crèche bus) for the young women's babies and children.

Drawing on text and personal photographs, the young women chose to develop individual story booklets in order to provide practitioners with an insight into their lives, and to present a more holistic view of the lives of young families. The young women decided on the design, layout, text and images to be included and the individuality of each story served to challenge the overwhelmingly negative image of 'the teenage mum'. Workshop activities focused on writing about their experiences of being young mothers, developing individual story booklets and designing the final training pack. Personal conversation among the young women and the research team was ongoing throughout and when asked what had been the motivation for taking part, one young mother said "As a teen mum, I wanted to challenge the stereotypes people have."

The young women expressed an interest in making a film about their experiences. It was agreed that this would be an excellent resource to reach a wider audience than those who would attend the training sessions. The young women felt that it was their opportunity for their voices to be heard. One young mother said "[It's] very important as issues are raised that would not normally be raised, as a teen mum is able to offer information based on personal experience," and another said "It is important to get our point across rather than people assuming what we are like." The remainder of this chapter will discuss issues that arose following the recording of the DVD.

Issues and challenges: participatory methods and service user involvement

Each of the young women felt that it was important for young mothers to be involved in delivering training to practitioners who have a remit for working with young mothers and the young women were fully committed to participating in the workshops. However, at the train-the-trainer session, less than two weeks before we were scheduled to begin delivery of the training to practitioner groups, a significant difference of opinion was expressed. The aim of the session was to review the materials that had been developed, to plan the training delivery and to ensure that everyone felt comfortable with their role. The young women watched their filmed discussion and in response to being asked by one of the research team how they would feel if their child became a teenage parent, one young woman said that she would not like her daughter, who was five years old, to come to her when she was a teenager and tell her that she was pregnant. She strongly felt that this would be a disappointment to her, although she would still love her and not ostracise her, as her own mother had (albeit temporarily). One of the other young women asked how she could say that, after she had been through the experience of being pregnant as a school-aged teenager herself. It became clear that two or three of the young women felt that in expressing that view she was undermining the work that they were doing in promoting a more positive view of young mothering. They did not want the comment to appear in the DVD and asked for it to be edited out.

What emerged from this incident was that there were inherent tensions between our concern for the wellbeing of the young women and the need to meet the objectives of the project commissioner. More time and a skilful approach were needed to attempt to reach a resolution – both on that day and before delivering the training programme to practitioners. Time was constrained as within less than an hour of the outbreak of the disagreement a minibus was arriving to take the young women and their children home. Furthermore, the training programme had been widely advertised, practitioners had booked their place on the course and it was to be delivered in less than two weeks.

Up until this point, the group had been working productively together over a number of weeks and, encouraged by us, had shared their personal experiences within the space that we had created. This was a space where we had assured them that all of their opinions would be valued and that their contribution was of importance. The conflict that arose may have left some of the young women feeling disempowered. We felt, to varying degrees, that the integrity of our approach became compromised as delivery of the training was neither cancelled nor postponed and the pressure to produce an output had an impact on our attempt to resolve the situation. Ultimately, the practitioners were shown only the parts of the DVD that were approved by all of the young women. This decision was not unanimous and caused unease among the research team, raising issues of power differentials – between researchers and researched, between the group of young women and between the research team – in terms of whose views were included and whose views were silenced.

Irrespective of what had happened during the process of developing the training materials, all of the young women remained committed and were keen to deliver the training, to contribute to discussions about the lives of young parents and (at a later date) to present the evaluation of the training programme to the commissioners. The project was well received and positively endorsed by the practitioners who attended and by the commissioning body.

Group identity, individual experience

This experience of including service users in research and training raises a number of questions, particularly in relation to the interplay of identity and stigma. In terms of group identity, there often exists a misapprehension that people who share the same group identity or label are an homogeneous group. But just as there are differences *between* insiders and outsiders, so there are differences *among* insiders. Young mothers are often determined that their own child will not experience the difficulties and challenges that they have experienced. It is understandable that a young mother would want life to be easier for her child, yet it is the circumstances surrounding early motherhood that lead to such difficulties, rather than early motherhood per se. Importantly, although identity as a teenage mother may be shared, there are also differences in terms of social background, educational experience, experience of employment, access to resources, ethnicity and age at which each becomes a parent (in this case, ranging from 13 to 17 years). Therefore, young mothers' experiences of stigma, discrimination and oppression may differ significantly or be interpreted variously.

However, as we have argued elsewhere, young mothers' own experiences of being marginalised makes challenging this all the more difficult. The stigma of being a young mother has been likened to a 'social death' (Whitehead, 2001) and this sense of stigmatisation endures, often into grandparenthood (Formby et al, 2010). As demonstrated before, what was shared among these young women was an identity as part of a demonised group who are constantly looked down on and criticised by wider society. Aware that they are perceived to lack aspiration and to have low expectations, young mothers strive to distance themselves from the stereotype of 'the teenage mum' by engaging with young parent groups or parenting classes and by making plans around education, employment or training. Many young mothers also try to establish and maintain traditional family structures, even when such relationships have the potential to be abusive. The 'hierarchy of motherhood' (DiLapi, 1989) coupled with the negative framing of teenage pregnancy ensures that the dominant messages are reproduced by young mothers, who *feel* the sense of failure that they are expected to feel. They know that others judge them and find their mothering skills wanting. The way in which this feeling plays out can be in the 'othering' of young women who are also teenage parents, but are thought to be not at all like the person themselves. In short, although young mothers resist aspects of the dominant negative discourse, they accept and aspire to other aspects, thus the insider perspective is not a simple rejection of the outsider view but a complex mixture of acceptance and resistance (Bailey et al, 2002). This draws our attention to an important issue: while service user involvement has the potential to open up opportunities for people, it also has the potential to reinforce certain ideas, which can potentially be disempowering, and this is not often talked about openly.

Political drivers towards inclusion of service users

The involvement of the young mothers in the development and delivery of the training programme was not only governed by practical pressures and deadlines, but was also framed within broader political drivers. The Teenage Pregnancy Partnership's commissioning of this training project was influenced by a concern to meet NEET to EET targets, that is, move young mothers who were NEET (not in education, employment or training) into EET (in education employment and training), in line with the political conceptualisation of 'support' for young mothers. Throughout the consultation phase of this project and the developmental workshops, young mothers identified a number of challenges to simplistic understandings of the transition from NEET to EET. During delivery of the training programme to practitioners some young mothers spoke about their desire to take time to establish themselves in their new role as a mother before thinking about EET.

Many young mothers equate being a 'good' mother with staying home with their child/ren until they go to school (Graham and McDermott, 2005) and concern about more pressing matters such as appropriate housing, inadequate income or violence is likely to place EET further down their list of priorities. In addition, there are often a number of barriers that may prevent engagement, such as lack of childcare, poor access to transport, lack of information and a lack of flexible provision in the education sector. Graham and McDermott (2005, p 26) suggest that young parents recognise 'the importance of education for future employment but do not anchor their future identities in the labour market ... futures are built, instead, around motherhood, where the opportunities for self esteem and social respect appear more certain'. This view serves to challenge the implication that young mothers are reluctant to engage in education, employment and training yet allowing a young mother time to be a mother was at odds with the (at the time of writing) target-driven strategy of achieving 60% EET by 2010.

As Purtell et al (Chapter Seventeen, this volume) note, the motivation to get involved with a project is usually driven by people's experience outside of the project, rather than the project itself. The young mothers who worked with us reflected on their involvement in developing the training programme and said that it was "[c]hallenging, it brought difficult emotions and issues," and that "[i]t seemed quite rushed at the end," but they also said "I really enjoyed being a part of this, as we were involved right from the beginning."

Lessons learnt

Our experience raises questions about the meaning of inclusion and involvement of young parents in research, training and service development. This account is an initial exploration of some of the issues from our perspective; each of the young women will have their own recollection.

Our approach involves locating individual experiences of injustice or marginalisation within wider social, political and economic structures. We take a relational, inclusive approach to research and development and introduce young mothers to thinking about their lives from an alternative perspective. This disruption of dominant ideas needs to be undertaken sensitively. The importance of this process is that the legacy of the project might be that young mothers draw something positive from their encounter with us. Knowledge can be powerful, but can just as readily be disempowering if time and care are not taken to ensure that involvement is a positive experience. Given the opportunity to tell their story, a story that challenged accepted ideas about teenage pregnancy being hard, depressing and unfulfilling, anything that threatened this more positive alternative was found to be reproducing the message of wider society.

When using participatory methods to engage and include service users, time needs to be taken to understand the diverse needs, experiences and views of young people, yet the short-term nature of funding often militates against the effectiveness of young people's participation (Cavet and Sloper, 2004). Time to talk and to listen was often limited and this sometimes led to a tension between pressure to meet the aim of the sessions and responding appropriately to needs. As well as being involved in this training programme, young women's lives were embedded in personal relationships; some were experiencing difficult life events and others were making plans for marriage – all wanted to share their experiences with us.

The inclusion of young mothers in developing and delivering training to practitioners can lead and has led to service improvement (Mickel, 2008). But, as this account has shown, participatory methods are not inherently more inclusive. Gallacher and Gallacher (2005) note that the use of participatory methods is often equated with enabling the exercise of agency as children/ young people become involved in the construction of knowledge about themselves. Most crucial to a just endeavour is the way in which researchers engage with service users; being honest and open about what they aim to achieve and prioritising a discussion of 'the messy contingencies of research encounters' (Gallacher and Gallacher, 2005, p 8).

As others have noted, the parameters for change in policy and practice are generally limited (Bochel et al, 2007). Commissioners of research and service development, operating within the current politically driven framework, may find it difficult to act on findings that fundamentally challenge practice or policy priorities. In the preceding years of research, our influence on policy has had limitations, but has also made a difference. We have had more success in influencing practitioners in their practice but the overarching framework continues overwhelmingly to cast the lives of teenage mothers in a negative light. This experience serves as a timely reminder that we, too, although critiquing aspects of the Teenage Pregnancy Strategy, are also part of the political structures that shape the lives of teenage mothers.

> In order to remain critically self aware about the decisions we take as researchers we need to be able to make explicit both the nature of the dilemmas we face and the losses as well as the gains that result from our decisions. (Alldred, 1998, p 147)

Acknowledgement

Many of the ideas that we have built upon in this chapter have developed from discussions and analysis undertaken across a body of research, evaluation and training relating to teenage pregnancy. Other researchers and colleagues have contributed at various points in time but most notably thanks go to Professor Gayle Letherby, who was instrumental in engaging us in this area of research and winning funding for the continuation of the work and has always encouraged our academic and personal development.

Endnote

Bibliographic details of the body of research that has been undertaken at Coventry University since 2001 are distributed throughout the references.

twelve

Involving young people in research: making an impact in public health

Louca-Mai Brady, with young researchers Ellie Davis, Amrita Ghosh, Bhavika Surti and Laura Wilson

Introduction

In this chapter we discuss the legislative and policy context for children and young people's participation in the United Kingdom (UK), and how this relates to the evidence base for their involvement in research. We then examine a specific project developed by the NCB (National Children's Bureau) Research Centre, called 'PEAR (Public health, Education, Awareness, Research): our voices, our health', which supported young people to contribute to public health research. We consider the lessons from this project for the involvement of children and young people (CYP) in research and policy, with contributions from four young people who are members of PEAR.

Children and young people's participation

The involvement of CYP in research needs to be placed within the wider context of their participation in other aspects of their lives as well as the international framework of children's rights. Participation[1] can be defined as the process by which individuals and groups of individuals influence decisions, which bring about change in them, others, their services and their communities (see Treseder, 1997; Participation Works, 2008). The United Nations Convention on the Rights of the Child (UNCRC) (UN, 1989) was ratified by the UK government in 1989. Article 12 of the UNCRC states that all CYP who are capable of forming their own views, have a right to express those views freely in all matters affecting them.

Since the UNCRC there has been a broad acceptance of children's right to be involved in decisions that affect them, or on behalf of other children (Sinclair and Franklin, 2000; Kirby et al, 2003). The UNCRC was supported in the UK by the introduction of legislation and policy such as the Children Act 2004, *Every child matters* (HM Government, 2003) and *The children's plan* (DCSF, 2007). Kirby et al (2003) have, however, concluded that there is still work to be done in ensuring that this participation is meaningful to young people, effective in bringing about change and sustained. More recently, Davey (2010), in research for the Office of the Children's Commissioner, found that although significant progress has been made in the last few years in relation to children's participation in decision making, many children continue to be denied opportunities to influence matters affecting their lives. Also, although adults report that services have improved as a result of participation, little progress has been made to evidence at a strategic level *how* children have contributed to this improvement (Davey, 2010).

There are several rights-based models of CYP's participation, as well as complementary models for user or 'patient and public' involvement in research. Hanley et al (2004) identified the different levels of user involvement in research as consultation, collaboration and user control. Arnstein's (1969) ladder of citizen participation was adapted by Hart (2008) to include children and consists of eight rungs:

- manipulation;
- therapy;
- informing;
- consultation;
- placation;
- partnership;
- delegated power;
- citizen control.

These eight rungs range from non-participation, through tokenism to the last three rungs, which are identified as citizen power or shared decision making. In *Building a culture of participation*, Kirby et al (2003) propose a model that could be seen to sit between these: their model takes as its starting point Article 12 of the UNCRC and therefore only includes participation (for instance not the lower three rungs of Hart's ladder). This model is non-hierarchical: the appropriate level is determined according to the circumstances and the participating CYP:

- *Children and young people's views are taken into account:* the information children provide is one source, among others, that adults use to make a decision.
- *Children and young people are involved in decision making:* children are directly involved at the point where decisions are made, but adults still hold ultimate responsibility for deciding the course of action.
- *Children and young people share power and responsibility for decision making:* similar to the previous category, but adults make a commitment to share power and to undertake joint decision making with children.

- *Children and young people make autonomous decisions:* recognising that the implementation of these decisions may be ultimately dependent on adult structures, responsibility and power.

Involving children in research

Advances in public and professional attitudes towards children's right to participate have, to some extent, been reflected in increasing interest in CYP's involvement in research (NCB, 2002; Kirby, 2004; Powell and Smith, 2009), both as participants and through their active involvement in the planning and process of research.

Involving those who are the focus of research can have a positive impact on what is researched, how research is conducted and the impact of research findings (eg Staley, 2009; INVOLVE[2]). In recent years there has been a theoretical and methodological shift among social researchers away from traditional approaches, which saw CYP mainly as objects of enquiry, and towards a view that CYP are social actors, with their own unique views and insight into their own reality (Prout, 2002; Greig et al, 2007). There is also increasing acknowledgement of their competence to contribute such insights and the power of the 'child voice' in research (Hill, 1997; Alderson, 2001; Sinclair, 2004; Powell and Smith, 2009). Although there is less of an evidence base in relation to CYP's involvement in research practice compared to adults (Brownlie, 2009), the case for their involvement has been explored in a number of publications (eg Alderson, 2001; Kirby, 2003; Kellett, 2005). The main arguments for involvement of adults in the research process are all valid to the involvement of CYP:

- the functional benefits to the research (validity, eg better understanding of young people's worlds, impact);
- the benefits to those who get involved (eg skills, experience, recognition);
- the ethics of participation (rights, inclusion and empowerment).

CYP can be involved in research at different stages (from developing a proposal to dissemination) and in different roles (from being part of a reference group for adult-led projects, to undertaking peer-led research). The degree to which CYP are involved in research will vary depending on the availability and interests of the individuals themselves, the nature of the research and the available resources (Alderson, 2001; Kirby, 2003; Powell and Smith, 2009). Although this can involve CYP as research participants (that is, sources of data), the concept of involvement discussed here is focused on their active involvement in research planning and processes.

Some of the specific challenges to children's involvement in research include:

- availability (many children are not available during term time and often have other commitments outside school or college) (McLaughlin, 2006);
- age and accrual (children grow older and, as well as interests and availability changing rapidly over time, also cease to be 'young researchers' when they reach adulthood);
- informed consent and the role of 'gatekeepers' (parents, teachers or staff in services) (Alderson, 2000; Powell and Smith, 2009);
- ethical issues regarding safeguarding and child protection, which need to be balanced against rights to participate.

Children who are perceived to be vulnerable, or at risk of social exclusion, can be denied opportunities to participate in research (Cahill, 2007; Powell and Smith, 2009). Along with issues of diversity and accessibility common to much adult user involvement in research (eg Steel, 2005; Staley, 2009), CYP who choose to get involved in research tend to be older and the voices of younger children can be excluded. Involvement of CYP can have resource implications for research projects in terms of both costs and researcher time, and involvement needs to be planned with this in mind as well as considering issues of availability, safeguarding requirements and lack of experience (McLaughlin, 2006).

Adult researchers also need to consider the extent to which they hold ultimate responsibility for maintaining quality standards, managing technical aspects of the research and ethical and legal issues. In the authors' experience these are areas of the research process in which CYP rarely want to get involved, but nonetheless the limits of CYP's involvement and influence should also be agreed with them at the outset and consulted on and updated as appropriate.

The PEAR project – involving young people in public health

The Young People's Public Health Reference Group (YPPHRG) was run by NCB Research Centre from November 2005 to February 2008, with support from the Public Health Research Consortium (PHRC)[3] and INVOLVE, as a pilot project to explore how young people could contribute to public health research in the UK (Brady et al, 2008). Funding from the Wellcome Trust enabled NCB to expand and extend the work of the pilot, and members of the group renamed the project 'PEAR (Public health, Education, Awareness, Research): our voices, our health'. The PEAR project supported young people to contribute to the UK public health agenda from 2008 to 2010 by:

- helping young people to learn about, inform and influence public health research and policy (eg contributing to the setting of priorities for public health research; involvement in research projects at proposal writing, design, literature review, analysis and dissemination stages; advising public health research bodies on how they could involve young people in their work; responding to government consultations);

- developing links between young people and public health researchers, research bodies and policy makers;
- producing and distributing information about public health issues and research to other young people (primarily through the website and conference – discussed later);
- seeking to demonstrate the impact of young people's involvement in public health research, and how this can be applied to policy and practice (Brady and Ghosh, 2009).

The PEAR project included regular meetings of 20 young people in groups based in Leeds and London. Group members worked with public health researchers and received training in research skills and public health, helped develop a website[4] and organise a conference, as well as commissioning their own research project on the impact of cyber bullying on young people's mental health.

Successes of the project

In the evaluation of the pilot project (Brady et al, 2008), the young group members felt that they had been able to influence public health research, and both those young people who were interested in 'having a say' and those with a specific interest in public health and/or research said that they had benefited from their involvement in the project. Adults involved felt that the group had 'brought to life' public health research for young people, that the group had provided a reality check to academic views and that methods of engaging young people had been tested and tangible outputs produced. The concrete outputs of the project (in particular research summaries) were really valued, by both young people and adults, and it was felt that the group's work had reached and generated interest among a wide audience.

PEAR group members – young people's views

The key successes of the project for group members included opportunities to learn about public health, gain research skills and have something to put on their CVs; having their voices heard by researchers and policy makers; helping to make research and policy more relevant to young people; commissioning their own research project; developing

---

the website; planning the conference; and letting other young people know about public health issues that affect them:

'We've been able to work with researchers and give our opinions. There's a mutual benefit, we've helped them and also gained knowledge ourselves.'

'There's lots of research about young people and public health – we deserve to have our voices heard.'

'The views of adults and young people are different – hearing what we have to say makes it [public health research and policy] more valid and useful.'

'It's important that ... our opinions are heard, not assumed.'

Challenges

Challenges faced by the pilot (Brady et al, 2008) included recruiting a diverse range of CYP to something quite academic and involving a long-term commitment. This was something the subsequent PEAR project sought to address (discussed in the next section). It was also hard to maintain attendance through the two years of the project, but recruiting new members was difficult as understanding of public health and research developed among the group. There were also challenges in balancing group members' and researchers' expectations. Researchers often wanted input from young people at particular stages of their project (eg when developing research tools or emerging findings), but group members were more interested in ongoing involvement and shaping researchers' ideas and thinking from the start of a project. There was also initial scepticism from some researchers about how young people could usefully contribute to research. Time and resource constraints limited how often the groups could meet (four one-day meetings a year during school holidays), and, because of the need to link in with research timetables and researcher availability, the agenda was often adult led. The fact that group members had school or college and other commitments, and that the age group interested in being involved tended to be in exam years, had implications for availability, as did the fact that availability and interests were likely to change over the course of the project.

PEAR group members – young people's views

Group members felt that it was really important to get feedback on the impact of their involvement:

'I think researchers we have helped should "drop us a note" about what they did with the information we provided.'

'It's important that we're involved in evaluating the project as well as being part of the group. We think the group should have met more often – as otherwise it's hard to stay engaged and to remember things we've learned.... As some people have left, or don't attend very often, it means that the meeting is smaller, and we think it would be better if there were more people at the meetings. It would also be good to have a wider range of young people in the groups.'

Children and young people's involvement in research – making an impact

PEAR group members – young people's views

Amrita Ghosh

'Involving young people in research has benefits for both young people and adults: we are taught new skills that we can put into action as we grow up and know that we are making a difference to public health research; and adult researchers get to see their research from our perspective, understand what our priorities are for public health and how our involvement can improve their research. In the group I have discovered that the adults and the young people often have different ideas on the same subjects, so involving us in planning research about young people's public health helps makes sure researchers are asking the right questions in the right way. The PEAR group has helped us to bridge the gap between young people and researchers. Since we've received feedback from researchers who have spoken to us I've realised the impact of our opinions and it has also made me more aware of public health systems and government policies.'

Ellie Davis

'It's very good to see some of [the research and policy process] done for young people as we only usually get to see the end result, and also to take part in some of the decision-making processes that have an effect on our lives. Through taking part in the group I have an increased awareness of just how much support is available for young people on public health issues.'

Bhavika Surti

'As a member of PEAR I feel like we have really achieved something and shown that it isn't just adults who are researchers but that young people can also be involved. As young people we have picked up on public health ideas that researchers haven't thought about, as we see things from a different perspective. I've learnt a lot and feel privileged that I could help researchers with their projects and I feel like I have made a difference. It's fascinating to see the difference in opinions from adults and children and it goes to show that involving children in projects like PEAR is beneficial.'

Laura Wilson

'Prior to being a member of PEAR, as a young person I was often aware of the vast amounts of research on people of my age by 'experts' who didn't seem to have come into contact with a diverse range of "real" young people, which I think can help create and promote stereotypes. But by being a member of the PEAR group and participating in research about and by young people, working alongside researchers and professionals, I feel that our voices are being heard more coherently. It has also allowed us to expand our knowledge and understanding of research as well as discovering the importance of public health. I feel we have also enabled researchers to understand young people's perspectives more fully, allowing their research and projects to become more accessible and relevant to young people.'

Evidence of impact emerged as a key issue in the pilot project, as group members wanted to see the impact of their work and evidence of how they were 'making a difference'. They wanted to see direct, practical results soon after their input into a project, but this was not always possible or did not always happen as quickly as they would have liked. There was also an issue of how to measure broader impact – for instance beyond the researchers the group worked with.

NCB attempted to address these various challenges in the PEAR project, for example through establishing a second group in Leeds and a wider recruitment base. Young people were involved in overall management of the project through representation on the project advisory group and, as well as working with adult researchers on their projects, the group also had areas of responsibility that they controlled with support from NCB staff (the website, conference and commissioning their own research project). As well as providing information from researchers on what the group can offer, there were clear expectations on what is expected in return, in particular ongoing involvement or timely feedback on impact and outcomes. The project team tried to do more to involve group members in between meetings. As can be seen from the co-authors' views mentioned earlier, seeing clear evidence of the impact of their involvement is really important for those involved as well as researchers and funders. So group members were also involved in the evaluation of the project, including defining objectives and outcomes and collecting data.

Nevertheless, there are clearly limitations to an advisory group model for involving CYP in research, particularly one that meets infrequently: it is difficult to keep some CYP engaged with the project in between meetings, it is difficult for access to the group to be available for researchers at the time they need it for their research, and there are issues of recruitment and retention as previously discussed. Obviously there are significant cost implications to more regular meetings, but these could to some degree be offset by writing the cost of input from the group into research projects at the planning stage – as the costs would still be considerably less than setting up a specific CYP's reference group for an individual project. We would therefore suggest that a better model may be a flexible approach with slightly more frequent meetings (eg every six to eight weeks, at weekends as well as during school holidays), combined with a secure online forum for discussion in between meetings and a network of organisations and CYP's groups with specific interests or needs (eg those who may not want to be part of a regular group or have an interest in a specific project or type of project) who can be called on when needed. So, for example, if researchers working on mental health wanted input from CYP, it would be possible to set up a meeting with a group of young mental health service users as well as with an established group of young researchers. This would give two different, but equally valid sets of CYP's perspectives.

What makes involvement meaningful?

CYP's involvement in research has benefits for researchers, research bodies, policy makers and CYP who are both involved in and affected by research. The authors therefore propose that for CYP's involvement in research and policy to be meaningful for all involved, it needs to:

- be planned from the outset;
- carefully consider who should be involved, how, where and when, and address issues of gatekeepers and parental or carer consent;
- provide genuine opportunities for meaningful decision making;
- have benefits for the research as well as the CYP involved;
- involve CYP in as many stages of the research project and process as possible;
- involve CYP in deciding if, when and how they want to be involved – and give them all the information they need to do so in appropriate and accessible formats, and clearly defined roles;
- be flexible and creative about models and methods of involvement, seeking to ensure accessibility to a wide range of CYP;
- provide appropriate and ongoing training and support;
- consider appropriate methods of reward and recognition;
- recruit, train, support and reward CYP appropriately;
- ensure safe and ethical working procedures;
- be properly resourced;
- have a clear exit strategy;
- build in systematic evaluation of, and feedback on, impacts and outcomes related to CYP's participation in research.

Notes

[1] Generally, 'participation' is the term used in work with CYP, but 'involvement' is more commonly used in the context of participative research.

[2] www.invo.org.uk

[3] www.york.ac.uk/phrc/

[4] www.ncb.org.uk/PEAR

Acknowledgements

With thanks to the other members of the PEAR young people's group who contributed to this work, Professor Catherine Law (Institute of Child Health), Anita Franklin (The Children's Society), Catherine Shaw and Deepa Pagarani (NCB Research Centre), Sarah Buckland (INVOLVE), the Public Health Research Consortium, Wellcome Trust and the many others who worked with and supported the PEAR project.

thirteen

Projects through partnership: promoting participatory values throughout the research process

Robert Kirkwood

Introduction

This chapter describes my development and facilitation of a participatory action research project engaging young people with varying levels of hearing loss. The project description serves as a helpful platform from which to critically reflect on issues of power and position when collaborating with young people (Fraser et al, 2004); social and cultural identities in relation to deafness and disability (Bauman, 2008); and the specific tensions I have encountered when seeking to develop a practice that fosters genuine partnerships and participatory values throughout the research process.

Within this context, the notion of 'partnership' represents both relationships between individuals or groups and the process through which their commonalities are mapped and outcomes subsequently unfold (Hostick and McClelland, 2002). 'Participation', on the other hand, seems to point to the characteristics or quality of engagement within these relationships and processes (Reason and Torbet, 2001). Increasingly within the social sciences, the need to evidence rigorous and authentic processes of inquiry has led to a politicisation of the word 'participation', which is now in many domains deeply imbued with humanitarian values drawn from equality, rights and empowerment discourses (Council of Europe, 2003; Kirby et al, 2003).

I write from a first-person perspective, recognising my own social situatedness within the project context. Locating the self within wider social and cultural parameters helps us gain a deeper understanding of how we interact with these phenomena and develop a greater participatory worldview (Heron and Reason, 1997).

Project inception

My motivation for developing a participatory action research project with young people with hearing loss was sparked by a body of literature suggesting that deaf young people receiving education within mainstream school settings are at increased risk of experiencing secondary mental and emotional difficulties linked with associated social stigma, isolation or exclusion (Hindley, 1994; Roberts and Hindley, 1999; Nunes et al, 2001; Powers, 2002; Ladd, 2003; Valentine and Skelton, 2007). However, there appears to be little within the literature to suggest that deaf young people themselves have explored their own identity on their own terms in the absence of a dominant predetermined question steering their endeavours. Such a dearth of participatory approaches fuelled my desire to examine whether an exploration of non-directive partnerships with the young people may generate effective methods applicable to clinical relationships with service users within professional practice. With this aim, the use of participatory action research was intended as a double-layered approach: to enable participants to investigate their own experiences, and to be tested as a therapeutic intervention in and of itself, building positive experiences that would counter the risk factors described in the literature.

I do not have hearing loss myself and am unavoidably no longer an adolescent. So, from a participatory perspective, I am already placed outside this specific field of lived experience on two counts. However, I have gained some proficiency in British Sign Language (BSL), which has led to a deeper awareness of practical and social issues faced by those with hearing loss. Additionally, in my professional capacity as an occupational therapist working within community child and adolescent mental health services, I engage with children and young people, allowing me to gain some insight into their concerns and to see circumstances from their perspective.

Occupational therapy as participatory practice

As a profession, occupational therapy claims to value a holistic view of human beings as principal actors within their worlds and transactors with their surroundings (WFOT, 2004). For occupational therapists, disabilities and health issues call for the adaptation of environmental processes to enable individuals to experience personally meaningful engagement, despite adversity (Wilcock, 1999). The concepts of 'partnership working' and 'participatory practice' share the same lens as the occupational therapy profession, privileging the views of the individual or community over and above knowledge claims that often seek to classify and compartmentalise from an a priori position that is outside of the individual/community's lived experience. From this perspective, any inquiry into the human experience is most useful when it is classified by, and for the benefit of, those who live through it. As Chambers (1997) posits, the action research method asks the question 'Whose reality counts?' Correspondingly, occupational therapy theory sets a precedent for engagement by suggesting that activity be used in partnership with the recipient to explore their responses to the question 'What does my reality mean to me?' The project discussed in this chapter attempts to explore the practical implications and lessons learnt from applying these principles within a specific context where there is potential to effect positive change.

Setting the scene

This community-based project has been undertaken as part of a professional doctorate in occupational therapy and has remained separate to my work within the National Health Service (NHS). However, it is hoped that the project outcomes can be applied to positively influence future practice within health services.

Over the space of an academic year, two small groups of young people met regularly to engage in an exploration of their views, their experiences and ultimately their identities. One group began in the September and a second project was subsequently instigated the following February; both running into the summer term.

Having gained ethical approval from the Faculty Research and Ethics Committee, information sheets for potential participants were forwarded by the local city council Sensory Needs Service to users of their service who they felt would benefit from the project. The Sensory Needs Service offers an educationally based service to all children within mainstream schools in its locality with a recognised hearing impairment. The service team, made up of teachers of Deaf people, had agreed to support the project, offering advice in the early stages of development and facilitating the recruitment process. The service team recognised a lack of skills and resources to meet what they saw as the very real mental and emotional needs that their young service users experience. As a team they welcomed a project initiative that sought to explore this further.

The project was preliminarily named 'See Yourself – A collaborative youth project' in an attempt to convey the project's intended exploratory and participatory principles. To give an initial shape to the project, the information sheets described one group lasting approximately eight months, gathering 10 to 15 young people from school years 8, 9 and 10, for two hours once a fortnight, probably after school. The aim of the project was framed as exploring the participants' identities and their shared experience of deafness and attending a mainstream school, through whatever creative means the group wanted to pursue. It was emphasised that the project would be led by the young people involved, based on their own ideas.

The first project community: young people from mainstream schools

An introductory open evening was held in July, a few weeks after the information sheets had been sent. Attendance was low with only three young people present, escorted by parents. However, all three signed up and agreed to start the project in September, deciding to meet fortnightly for three hours on a Saturday afternoon during term time.

By September, another two young people had been recruited to the project and the group then consisted of three boys and two girls ranging from 13 to 15 years of age (a third girl aged 13 would join the following February). All, bar one, attended mainstream schools in the local area. One of the girls, however, had a learning disability and attended a special school locally. The young people used English as their first language and minimal adjustment in communication was required to accommodate levels of hearing loss, supported by the use of hearing aids. However, the girl attending the special school benefited from Sign Supported English (where most spoken words are supported by their signed equivalent) to help her follow conversations. The project sessions were based in a large room, part of a larger local conference venue. A teacher of Deaf people from the Sensory Needs Service, involved in the project development stages, agreed to co-facilitate the sessions on a freelance basis. The first eight sessions were co-facilitated after which point the teacher was forced to withdraw due to personal circumstances. With the group's approval, I also recruited a 19-year-old female with experience of youth work to support the sessions. This role proved to be particularly useful in giving one-to-one support to the girl with special needs when necessary.

During the early sessions, various activities such as visual arts, role play, discussions, games and music were suggested by the group members and used to explore and express their thoughts and feelings. The members stated that their reason for attending the project was to meet other young people who shared the same problems and experiences as they did. Gradually, direction for the project developed culminating in the production of a 15-minute film constituting a sequence of photographs the young people had taken, overdubbed with excerpts of recorded discussions between the young people about their views on a range of topics including deafness and featuring music that they had devised, played and recorded in a studio with my support. By mutual agreement, the project was extended to last the full academic year and in May, towards the end of the project, the short film was screened at an event celebrating Deaf culture as part of a local arts festival. By this time, two of the boys had withdrawn from the project due to what they described as pressures from other commitments such as school work and other extramural activities. This left one boy and three girls as the core members.

Throughout the first project, the young people themselves voiced their desire for more members. However, despite their own attempts to enlist friends and my continued attempts to encourage the sensory needs team to recruit more young people, the membership only rose by one, reaching six young people at its peak. The project finished with a farewell party in early July, by which time the group had met for 19 sessions over a 10-month period.

The second project community: a school for Deaf children

At a review meeting with the Sensory Needs Service in the December we discussed a second formal recruitment drive and it was suggested that I approach a local non-maintained boarding school for Deaf people accommodating approximately 30 pupils, mostly placed from outside the county. Because so many of the pupils came under the responsibility of other local education authorities, the sensory needs team offered minimal provision to the school, but felt strongly that it would benefit from support regarding mental and emotional issues. I contacted the school in the January and received a swift and positive response to my proposal. The school appeared to be emerging from a longstanding oral tradition (pupils were not allowed to use sign language within their school day) to a position more open to the benefits of using sign language. However, opinions within the staff remained divided, making it a contentious issue. An open evening was arranged at the school for staff and pupils at the beginning of February. A brief presentation was followed by group work with the young people to explore their ideas about their own identity, their family networks and what 'community' meant for them. From the group work exercises, it became clear that there was a range of communication styles being used. Some pupils seemed more dependent on speaking English whereas others incorporated BSL. No pupil was solely using BSL and the majority employed varying degrees of Sign Supported English with varying lip-reading abilities. Having asked the pupils what they preferred, I communicated using Sign Supported English.

Following the open evening, five boys and three girls aged between 12 and 18 signed up to the project and parental consent was gained by the school. All eight young people either wore hearing aids or had cochlear implants fitted. The group agreed to meet for one and a half hours every Monday evening (term-time only) within the school's common room and drama studio. Just as the project began, pressing concerns started to emerge regarding the future of the school and information from the school governors was passed down to staff, parents and pupils in a piecemeal fashion over a number of weeks. Understandably, the young people's focus gravitated towards issues related to the school and their future within it. It soon became apparent that the school would close at the end of the academic year due to critical financial difficulties. This was unexpected and shattering news for all those involved with the school. However, in light of this decision, the project seemed well placed to offer an opportunity for these young people to explore with one another their reaction to this news and they chose to continue.

Between them, the young people decided to create a dramatic re-enactment of a set of events centring around a couple in the group who were dating. The girl had moved to the school a few weeks after the start of the academic year and shortly afterwards, the boy asked her out, sending waves of gossip through the close-knit school community. After several weeks of rehearsal, a professional media company (booked to film the drama) came to the school. At this point, the girl playing the lead role informed me that she wished to withdraw from the project for personal reasons. Despite this crushing news, the remaining group were swift to refocus, deciding to film themselves interviewing each other, giving candid accounts of their life experiences (such as experiencing bullying and isolation within the mainstream setting) and their views about friendships made at the school and expressing a deep sense of loss at its closure. On subsequent weeks the group advised on the editing and production of the footage and eventually a 13-minute documentary film was produced by the media company. The film was screened at the same Deaf culture event as the first group. The young people also presented it at a school assembly, receiving much praise and a surprising level of emotion from both staff and pupils. Shortly after this in early June, as the school began gearing down for closure, the remaining seven young people decided to disband the group, having met for 12 sessions over a four-month period.

Existing tensions

Having sketched out a brief summary of the project, I now look more closely at some of the engagement processes and their participatory qualities. All human inquiry processes will have their share of tensions specific to the field of engagement (Reason, 1994) and this work is no exception. Several themes have emerged, helping to explore the inherent tensions in greater detail.

The development phase

As emancipatory as this inquiry approach attempts to be, there remains a danger that action research can merely reflect the views of the facilitator (Winter, 2002), carrying a set of unchecked assumptions about what constitutes a problem and what might best help to change the situation for the better (David, 2002). From the project's inception, I found myself wrestling with how to introduce the project to potential participants in a style that did not merely throw a thin veil over a predetermined plan, but fostered a genuine intent to co-create and co-direct the project with the group. Independently outlining the project's structure and direction myself while championing non-directive participatory values seemed contradictory. Yet offering a basic context for the inquiry seemed a minimum requirement for a project. To my mind, answering the participants' question 'Why are we here?' with the response 'You tell me', felt somewhat disingenuous. So instead, accepting my role as instigator, my internal benchmark became 'To what degree am I merely offering a scaffold within which participants can build their own experience?'

My initial response to this question was to begin development of the project in partnership with a service that better understood the needs of the young people. However, having helped me develop appropriate recruitment parameters such as age and group size, the sensory needs team were then at risk, as gatekeepers, of applying another set of parameters regarding who they felt may or may not be appropriate for the project. I attempted to counter this bias by seeking a blanket mail-out to all those fitting the initial criteria, but nagging questions remained. How genuinely self-selecting was the recruitment process? Was I inherently seeking to impose classifications upon the young people? Harnessing these doubts proved effective in guiding my practice throughout the project.

The community contexts

There is a distinct difference in how each cohort connected as a group within their own community contexts, largely based on the different social contexts within which the groups were established: the first group, gathered by an external source to form a new community outside their existing experience; and the second, responding to the same external source by self-selecting within a school community, within which the project remained, and from which members already drew a strong shared identity.

Although small in number, the group attending mainstream schools took time to grow in confidence in their engagement with one another and became arguably stronger than if the group had been larger as I had originally intended. The unfamiliar setting for the sessions undoubtedly contributed to a longer period of adjustment. The group members had no contact outside of the sessions, other than three members attending the same large secondary school who suggested they only saw each other in passing. The second group, on the other hand, already knew each other and there was evidence of strong existing friendships within the group.

Communication

There was also a marked difference in communication styles within each context. In the first cohort, the young people's hearing loss did not significantly impact their language acquisition or verbal communication. As a result, ideas and views appeared to be exchanged freely and equitably across the group during the sessions and a shared interest in music emerged as a key bond. By comparison, the use of language within the second group carried deeper levels of complexity, significantly influencing their social interactions and shaping their status within the school. The remainder of this section focuses on the second project community's communication.

Throughout sessions, a creole of BSL and English was used between the young people themselves. There is a rich historical narrative regarding Deaf culture and identity, drawing from disability rights and cultural minority discourses (Bauman, 2008), within which BSL as a distinct language and sociopolitical conduit has held an important role (Ladd, 2003). This complicated subtext appeared very apparent within the second group's sessions as those who were not as fluent in BSL were often left at the fringes of some of the more quick-fire gossip, leaving them visibly isolated. It is worth noting that this specific subculture, where the use of BSL holds considerable power, stands counter culturally to the wider values of their school where greater weight was placed on the oral tradition. Inevitably, the complex and varied communication needs of the group led to frustrations between some of the young people. At a developmental stage, when identities are forming and social mastery is highly prized (Weare and Gray, 2003), those with a more fluent use of BSL could be seen to use this skill as a device to create pockets of exclusivity between themselves and deride, however humorously, those outside their posse.

These communication issues were compounded for the eldest member of the second project group for whom English was his second oral language and BSL a very recent addition. Frustrations played out between him and another group member in particular seemed to be borne out of his being treated with a lack of respect; seemingly denied due to his difficulties grasping both spoken English and BSL. This social process reflects similar dynamics found within many cross-cultural youth contexts where language holds such determining powers (Talbot et al, 2003). Nonetheless, the additional notion of accessibility, pertinent within both linguistics and the disability agenda, makes this account all the more complex and compelling.

The role of facilitator

Over the course of the project, an emerging distinction helped me make sense of my facilitatory approaches. The members of the first group had been gathered into a wholly new context. As the initiator, I was seen as a central point and main constant throughout the project. This was a position of authority I strove hard to disassociate from; deferring instead to the young people's views and choices. In contrast, the second group was part of an established community into which I had been parachuted. This placed me in what felt like a more vulnerable position as I negotiated my role within an already close-knit group. Given the participatory focus of the project, this was a situation I welcomed, if somewhat apprehensively. There was an ethnographic quality to this second experience that provided rich insight into a culture I would not otherwise have seen.

The groups' contrasting social contexts gave rise to different attitudes and responses to my role as facilitator; an approach that was arguably incongruent with that of other adults the young people encountered. Within a school context, for example, engagement with the young people is more likely to be negotiated from a presupposed position of authority (Rowling, 2007). My concerns with issues of position and power and the counteracting participatory approach I attempted to employ made me acutely aware of times I felt the young people wished for an authoritative response from me. Boundaries will always shape a structure and the testing of them in this way is well documented within group development, especially with young people. So, when I sought to place the responsibility of boundary setting back into their hands and not react in the way they may have been expecting, the members reacted in several ways.

For a while, the first group continued to look to myself as the 'project leader' for answers and direction. This seemed appropriate for a group gathered into such a new context. As the weeks progressed, so the group members became more comfortable in making decisions for themselves. One fascinating development was their shared enthusiasm for playing hide and seek. I turned my initial frustrations at the lack of inquiry focus of this activity into an appreciation of the game as a metaphor for the young people's experiences, and their intentional or unintentional exploration of the relationships between discovery and safety; social boundaries and bonding; separated-ness and connection.

The second group found an initial frisson of excitement in the freedom the informal project tone set within an environment normally associated with their school routine. My minimal approach to intervention led to surprising leadership qualities emerging within the group. However, there were times when the group seemed to become frustrated at their own inability to regulate or control the behaviour of their peers. This led in turn to episodes of disengagement, often towards the end of sessions when tiredness set in. My response ranged from self-doubt in my ability as a facilitator to control a group of young people, to careful consideration of what support the individuals needed to help them engage more purposefully with one another, without prescribing an agenda. I began to feed in trigger questions but felt that I was often ignored by the group. On the one hand, this left me feeling despondent and ineffectual, and on the other, it reassured me that I was clearly not falling into an overly authoritative role! Through trial and error, a pattern emerged whereby I would talk to one specific young person who was then usually able to hold the group's attention for long enough to initiate a brief discussion. Through this method, agreements were reached that served the interests of the young people and placed us shoulder to shoulder.

Conclusion

This chapter has been an attempt to capture the essence of the inquiry process by describing my own insights and reflections. I would hope that it brings a deeper understanding of the broader issues related to participatory practice as well as raising further questions about the topic. Yet paradoxically, the extent to which these insights might make sense to the young people personally involved in co-creating the project that I describe is worth questioning. For example, if the young people found difficulty in articulating their own feelings towards the project, would this negate their experience or imply they have drawn less meaning from their involvement because of their lack of familiarity with certain concepts? If they disagree with what I have written, would this render my own experience meaningless? The privileging of experiential knowledge (that which is truly known through personal experience) within participatory action research (Reason and Bradbury, 2001) would indicate not. But this question does capture the perpetual struggle that exists when trying to conjoin the roles of co-researcher and co-facilitator. The expression and comprehension of experiential meaning often seems highly dependent on the ability to communicate it, and where levels of language or cognitive ability vary between inquiry partners, equitable access to emerging knowledge can be complicated (Powers, 2002). However, lived experience can still affect personal change whether it is articulated to others or not.

Where there are barriers to communication, disputes and frustration will surely arise and, in participatory action research, short cuts may be sought. Being aware of these issues in practice dramatically reduces the risk of falling into such traps. From a personal perspective, I have attempted to use my facilitative role to suggest to the young people ways of achieving what they wish to, without overly directing them. My meta-view of the project's development afforded opportunities to access funding and resources that the young people may not have otherwise requested. Additionally, my concern for equitable balances of power led me to seek an exploration with both the young people and the adults around them regarding the appropriate negotiation of power relationships. This, surely, is the starting point for any partnership; resting on the ability to communicate intentions to one another and to reach mutually acceptable agreements. For example, although the classification of hearing impairment served as a starting point for the inquiry, this did not serve as a focus for the project work itself until the young people raised it themselves, which they did in fact choose to do. In this way, the young people classified their own personal and corporate experiences for the purposes of learning about themselves and others (Kemmis, 2006).

The process has attempted to offer the young people genuine benefits from their involvement in the project in terms of enhancing skills, providing opportunities to widen their experience, broadening their social networks and their gaining a greater sense of accomplishment within a community. As facilitator and co-researcher, I have also benefited in all these ways through my own involvement.

fourteen

Involving older people in research: empowering engagement?

Lizzie Ward and Beatrice Gahagan

Introduction

Over recent years the drive to give older people 'a voice' has gained momentum. Involving older people in the design, delivery, commissioning and monitoring of services has become part of United Kingdom (UK) government policy (DH, 2001a, 2009a; DWP, 2005, 2009). In part this can be understood as a response to demographic change as more people are living longer and healthier lives and assumptions about old age have been increasingly challenged. However, the framework of involvement has generally been located within a consumerist approach, with a focus on older people as 'customers'.[1] Although there has been some recognition of the skills and experience that older people contribute to decision-making processes, the need to increase older people's involvement has also been expressed in terms of equity and empowerment: 'To create a more equal and just society which values all citizens, we must empower older people to have a say in the governing of their communities' (DWP, 2009a, foreword).

In relation to academic research on ageing, there has also been somewhat of a shift towards recognising the value of participatory approaches and actively involving older people in producing knowledge about the lived experiences of ageing and later life (Walker, 2007). Researchers working from a critical gerontology perspective have argued that participatory approaches directly challenge the power relations embedded in traditional gerontology, which remains dominated by biomedical perspectives that frame ageing as a 'problem' and where older people themselves are viewed as research 'subjects' (Ray, 2007). In contrast, research that involves older people as 'active' subjects is crucial for producing knowledge that can address the concerns of older people and issues related to ageing and later life.

In a review of studies that have involved older people, Barnes and Taylor (2007) identify reasons for involvement as:

- to produce research that is considered relevant and important by older people;

- to understand what ageing means to older people;
- to ensure that research has a bigger impact;
- to develop skills among older people;
- to challenge ageist assumptions;
- to generate data to be used as a campaigning resource by older people.

While the involvement of older people (both in research and across a range of spheres) has moved towards the mainstream, the complexities of how this might translate into practice are not so universally understood. There is an ever-present danger that 'involvement' may be superficial and the challenge, as Bernard and Scharf (2007, p 7) observe, is to move 'beyond the platitudinous claims about simply needing to "hear the voice" of older people'. Moreover, along with the benefits outlined earlier, there are challenges and tensions thrown up by involving older people in the research process. Some of these are practical, such as having sufficient time and resources to support involvement properly; others strike a chord with dilemmas that are common in participatory research, such as who gets involved, whose voice is heard and how far can participatory approaches address equality of 'voice'?

In this chapter we reflect on our experiences of working together on research with older people. Although it is written primarily from our own perspectives (one of us as a practitioner and the other an academic researcher), it has been informed by the reflections and feedback from those we involved in the research process. The research projects were undertaken in Brighton and Hove (UK) as part of a collaborative partnership between Age Concern, a local voluntary sector organisation working exclusively with older people, and academic researchers from the Social Science Policy and Research Centre (SSPARC) at the University of Brighton. We explore the tensions between the social outcomes of enabling older people to be actively involved and our own research agendas, negotiating how we use older people's experiential knowledge in non-exploitative ways and trying to ensure that the research has an impact, yet still genuinely involves everyone who takes part. We aim to show that meaningful involvement is a complex and sometimes difficult process through which 'empowerment' does not necessarily emerge. The particular needs of the people you seek to involve and the power relations embedded within research and knowledge hierarchies need to be carefully considered. In this chapter we discuss the ways in which we have attempted to address these issues using an *ethic of care* framework. We argue that involving older people in research is not just a matter of inclusion in a set of activities, but also crucially it is the nature of the relationships developed during the process that is key to understanding involvement as potentially empowering.

Developing research relationships

The research relationship between us (as community partner and academic researcher) has developed through two distinct research projects involving older people. Several significant features were present from the outset in the ways we developed our partnership and approach. These included a shared commitment to the value of 'experience' in producing knowledge; the importance of recognising and valuing our different areas of expertise; and crucially, the desire to place older people's experiences at the centre of the research and work in a participatory way. We also started from a position that recognises the very category 'older people' as potentially problematic in that it suggests a homogenised group of people and conceals the vast range of differences between older people, in terms of socioeconomic status, gender, ethnicity and sexuality and in relation to individual personal biographies. 'Old age' covers a spectrum of time and people who belong to different cohorts in terms of chronological age and generation. This prompts an initial question 'what do we mean by "older people"?' Clearly, it is important to be mindful of the differences between older people and for us that also entailed a commitment to involving 'older' older people (in their late seventies and eighties) and thinking through how we might achieve this in practice.

As our research relationship has developed we have become aware of the significance of shared values that have implicitly shaped our approach. These were already present in both the person-centred practice of Age Concern and the commitment to collaborative working of the academic research centre. We have sought to make our shared values an explicit part of our work by using an *ethic of care* framework. This is a framework originating from feminist philosophy, which draws attention to the moral dimensions of care and caring relationships (Tronto, 1993; Sevenhuijsen, 1998). The framework sets out the interconnected principles of *attentiveness*, *responsibility*, *competence*, *responsiveness* and *trust* as a requisite for 'good care'. These principles can also be effectively applied to research practice. They offer context-specific ways of understanding and responding to the ethical challenges of undertaking participatory research, such as power differences between us, and help us to reflect on how we handle these differences in practice. This framework has also enabled us to recognise different experiences, break down the boundaries between expert and lay knowledge and encourage mutual recognition, sharing and validating of different areas of expertise (Ward and Gahagan, 2010). As our research team has developed we have found that the ethic of care principles have acted as guide ropes for managing the process and relationships.

The evolving process of how we involved older people

In addition to the reasons for involving older people in research already outlined, part of Age Concern's remit is to enable older people to continue to be active citizens by providing opportunities through volunteering. We have been able to adapt the organisation's existing volunteering policies and recruitment processes to develop co-researcher roles that also met the requirements of the University of Brighton's ethical procedures. The aim has been to involve older volunteers in the research at a number of levels: in the design and development of the research; carrying out fieldwork; analysing data; ongoing advisory roles; and in dissemination.

Our first research project explored older people's experiences of alcohol (Ward et al, 2008). In this project we recruited older people through Age Concern's volunteer base in two ways. First, as co-researchers who, through a series of group training sessions, developed the detailed research design and subsequently carried out interviews and focus groups with other older people about their alcohol use. Second, as members of a reference group who met regularly over the course of the project and acted as a 'sounding board' to advise on the design, content, findings and dissemination. Work descriptions and draft terms of reference were drawn up for both roles and information about the research was distributed via Age Concern's volunteer database and through local older people's groups and networks. The result was a team of four 'younger' older people (in their early sixties) who were recruited as co-researchers and a reference group that comprised 'older' volunteers (in their late seventies and eighties) who were interested in the research but did not feel able to take such an active role.

From the start we were aware of the tension between our responsibilities for completing a time-limited research project and our desire to offer learning opportunities to those with little or no previous research experience. This was coupled with an initial anxiety that we might implicitly exclude people above a certain age because of the timescales and the levels of support and flexibility we could realistically offer. When we subsequently began working on our next research project on wellbeing, which had a longer timescale, we made the decision to form a single research team so that we could develop different roles and levels of activity to enable people to take part at a level they felt comfortable with yet ensure that everyone felt part of the research team. Again, members were recruited from Age Concern's volunteer base, some having taken part in the previous research and others who were already involved in another area of the organisation. Adopting a more open and flexible approach resulted in many of the 'older' members of the team being involved in active tasks such as carrying out interviews, facilitating focus groups, coding and analysing the data and dissemination.

Who got involved ... older people bringing more than just themselves

In relation to the specific make-up of our team, both research projects benefited from involving older people who already had direct experience of older people's issues. Most members of the team had many years' experience of working as volunteers for Age Concern and were motivated by a desire to help and support other older people. They had fulfilled a variety of roles such as counselling, information and advice, home visiting, assisting clients with computer technology and monitoring clients receiving help in the home. They brought this practice-based experience to the research so that they were not just representatives of their own personal experiences of ageing, but a much wider spectrum of insight into many issues of ageing more generally. As Age Concern volunteers, they were already skilled at working in a person-centred way to 'get inside' the problems of another older person, understand their point of view and yet work within boundaries. In addition, two team members were also members of the local Older People's Council, bringing their experience at a strategic level, of lobbying the local council on issues affecting older people locally. Thus, a distinctive feature of the research project was the accumulated knowledge and in-depth understanding of the team members.

The unfolding challenges

The process of developing the research as a team has brought to the fore a number of significant issues, which we explore here. These have arisen from our different relationships to the research as we negotiated a pathway through what we hoped would be our different but equal contributions without assuming a false equality between us. It is here that an *ethic of care* framework has been useful in providing principles to guide us through the challenges presented in this type of participatory research, in particular, managing the pace, expectations and responsibilities within the research team.

Different roles and different paces

One of the challenges of working with a larger team that spans a broad age range (from early sixties to late eighties) has been learning how to manage the process. Team members took on different roles and activities and this meant individuals working at different paces. This had several implications. In order to remain fully inclusive and cater for individual needs, it took longer to progress the research. It also highlighted the importance of ensuring good communication within the team so that everyone was in touch with all aspects of the research. Regular meetings and a newsletter that was produced helped to ensure that all members of the team were fully informed and kept up to date with the different activities that team members were carrying out. One advantage of working in this way was more flexibility to respond to team members' changing needs. This included, for example, responding to health-related disruptions, which may occur more often in later life, in such a way that allowed members to have periods of time out without 'giving up' being part of the research team.

Different expectations of the research and involvement

Another area in which differences were apparent related to expectations of the research. For some of the older team members there was more of a sense of ambivalence and uncertainty about taking part. During a feedback and reflection session early in the project it became evident that team members needed a clear sense of the purpose and to know both what the research would achieve and how their own input would bring about change. This revealed a tension between their expectations and assumptions that the research would bring 'a solution' to a problem and the reality of what was likely to happen in terms of changes in policy and practice. This highlighted the need for us to be clear and honest about the outcomes of research and how it may have less visible immediate impact on policy or policy makers. Although we may offer reassurances that our work will make a contribution by adding to and building on a body of knowledge, this may ring hollow for team members who are concerned that action should result from the research and who experience frustration at the lack of immediate change.

Different responsibilities

We attempted throughout to ensure that all team members felt genuinely included in decision making and shaping the research process while acknowledging that ultimate responsibility for the project lay with us. There was a tension, therefore, at times between being inclusive and 'getting the job done'. The challenge was to get the balance right between providing an infrastructure and direction, at the same time as ensuring that members were genuinely involved and able to shape the research. It took us some time to feel comfortable that we were getting this balance right. Learning when to give direction and when to sit back evolved with the development of the team. In practice this ranged from paying attention to the details of arrangements for meetings, such as timing, access and refreshments, to how to manage what are often experimental research processes, usually done by a single researcher, being unravelled as a group process.

One area where we clearly do have responsibility relates to research ethics, which require us to take account of the potential impact of the research on participants. In our project we also needed to ensure that the team members, as well as the participants, were treated with respect and not harmed in the research process. We were conscious that members of the team might be affected by the research on a personal level by virtue of the fact that they were researching issues of ageing that were pertinent in their own lives. Our concern was to ensure that being involved as co-researchers was a worthwhile experience for each member of the team and ensure that no one was negatively affected by taking part in data collection, analysis or in general discussions of the findings. This aspect needed constant reflection to build awareness of the possibility of identifying with the experiences of the research participants. We made time during team meetings to acknowledge and share our different personal responses to the circumstances of those being interviewed as well as offering opportunities for individual support.

We worked through these unfolding challenges by using the ethic of care principles in our planning, thinking and organisation to exercise our responsibilities in ways that allow for different but equal contributions to the research process and to build relationships of trust.

Conclusion

We have highlighted some of the complexities of involving older people in research and the need for careful consideration of the many dimensions of involvement. Evidently it throws up many challenges for us as 'professionals' (both academic and practitioner) and for those who take part as co-researchers. Our concern was to ensure that while researching the topic of wellbeing, our older co-researchers were given an experience that was conducive to their own wellbeing. Partly this was afforded by the opportunity for team members to continue making a contribution to something they have cared about throughout their life. But for us it has also been an ongoing learning process involving reflection and being open to receiving feedback from those we have involved. Through this process we have developed a deeper understanding of the issues that may present themselves over the course of a research project, how these issues relate to later life experiences and how we might adapt our ways of working to take account of them. In negotiating a pathway between the different needs and aims of the project the key issues to address involve when to lead and provide structure, when to step back and how to ensure that ethic of care principles are upheld within the research relationships. Our experience so far is that this creates an environment that is conducive to genuine input from older people across a broad spectrum of age. It is a way of researching and producing knowledge of older people's lives that is greatly enhanced by their involvement and contribution to it.

Note

[1] See, for example, the Better Government for Older People programme introduced in 1998, which set up pilot projects such as the social research evaluation of the Benefits Agency Better Government for Older People (BA BGOP) prototypes. These tested a series of service design features, including integrated working, information surgeries, home visits, road shows, telephone advice lines and new information technology services. The aim of the evaluation was to evaluate customer, staff and stakeholder attitudes towards BA BGOP prototypes, and to explore their experience of these new ways of delivering benefit advice and information to older people (those aged 50 years and over) (Chang et al, 2001).

fifteen

'Still out there?' Is the service user voice becoming lost as user involvement moves into the mental health research mainstream?

Kati Turner and Steve Gillard

Background

Service user involvement in mental health research in the United Kingdom (UK) has moved on from the pioneering research that characterised the turn of the millennium: surveys of service provision environments supported by the Sainsbury Centre's User Focused Monitoring initiative (Rose, 2001); emancipatory user- and survivor-led research typified by the Strategies for Living project supported by the Mental Health Foundation (MHF, 2000); the Service User Research Enterprise's bold work on electroconvulsive therapy, challenging ideas about who decides what should be measured, and how, as research outcomes (Rose et al, 2003). More recently, policy changes are promoting individualised mental health and social care, and requirements that Patient Reported Outcomes are central to the evaluation of new forms of service delivery (DH, 2009b, 2010a). The National Institute for Health Research (NIHR) stipulates that an appropriate level of public and patient involvement should be incorporated into the design and implementation of all centrally funded mental health research (NIHR, 2007). Recently completed large-scale national research projects commissioned by NIHR either have incorporated substantial 'user-led' modules (Burns et al, 2009; Price et al, 2009) or have integrated service users into a comprehensive, collaborative research approach (Gillard et al, 2010a). Service user involvement in mental health research is no longer confined to small-scale initiatives led by pioneering individuals. Service user involvement in research has mainstreamed and has moved into the university.

A recent review of the impact of public and patient involvement across health and social care research highlighted a range of benefits and negative impacts of involvement, both for those involved and for the research itself (Staley, 2009). However, that review did not explore the extent to which service user researchers have felt able to voice their service user identity

189

in particular research environments. The authors of this chapter were involved in a small qualitative study exploring stakeholder engagement in organisational change in a mental health trust (Gillard et al, 2010b). In that study the collaborative research team reflected on the extent to which the service user researchers involved had 'retained' their service user voice as they became embedded into the research team. In this chapter we will develop that reflective process, tracking our parallel, but very different journeys into the mental health research mainstream.

Who we are

Kati Turner has worked as a service user researcher in the Section of Mental Health, Division of Population Health Sciences & Education (PHSE) at St George's, University of London (SGUL) since 2005. Kati undertakes freelance training and consultation in the mental health field as an 'expert by experience' and has had experience of using mental health services and of involvement, as a service user, in mental health service and strategy development work over the last 25 years.

Steve Gillard is a Senior Lecturer in Social and Community Mental Health in the Section of Mental Health, Division of PHSE at SGUL, having previously worked as a researcher in the voluntary sector with a local association of the mental health charity Mind. In both jobs his research has focused on enabling service users to work as researchers, as well as studying the impact of that involvement on the research process.

Aim

Our primary aim in this chapter is to explore the question: 'Is the service user voice becoming lost as user involvement moves into the mental health research mainstream?' We reflected on our different, but overlapping research journeys, first of all on paper, sending each other questions about our respective experiences, considering our responses and making notes. We then interviewed each other 'live' at the Critical Perspectives conference in Brighton in April 2009. Subsequently, we reflected further on our answers and wrote more detailed responses. Here we present an edited version of those more detailed responses.

Kati – the service user researcher's account

How did you first become involved in research?

Via a chance meeting with a clinician with whom I had been in treatment previously and had worked with in the service user involvement field. He had received funding for a small, local research project and wanted involvement from service users. A telephone conversation and informal interview with a university researcher followed and I joined the research team on a fixed-term contract as a service user researcher.

What was it that made you want to become involved in research?

My personal experience of mental distress and of services over many years – not always positive – made me want to make my voice heard, try to make a difference to services, and challenge the huge amount of stigma and discrimination still alive in mental health. It helped that I had positive experiences of other work in the service user involvement field. After many years of not working, becoming involved in an environment where my mental health experience was seen as an asset rather than a drawback, and where I would be trained to learn new skills, appealed to me.

Did you have any expectations, and if so, what were they?

I had no previous direct experience of research so had little idea of what to expect. However, I had been approached in the past by clinicians as a research participant and asked to fill out lots of questionnaires: this left me with a sense of research being 'done' to me rather than 'with' me. I developed a dislike of quantitative research methods as a primary means of obtaining information from service users: I felt these could be limited in scope and not allow the full experience of treatment to be recounted. I hoped that the research I would be involved in would be of a type where service users' stories could be told rather than just ticking endless boxes.

I did have quite high expectations of the research team as I knew and respected the clinician involved. I was pleased that another service user researcher was also recruited to the project as I felt this would provide not only some 'safety in numbers', but also a variety of views from the service user perspective.

Were there any obstacles to becoming involved and how were these overcome?

I had to satisfy the Occupational Health (OH) doctor that I was 'fit for work' – a rather tricky negotiation seeing as my personal experience of mental health issues was part of my job description. The process was facilitated by letters written by the university researcher confirming that ongoing support was available. I was also fortunate that the OH doctor was knowledgeable about mental health and supportive of my position.

Another obstacle was dealing with the labyrinthine benefits system. Fortunately, the university researcher had the experience and foresight to be aware of potential pitfalls and arranged support from the local mental health trust benefits advice centre. This made an enormous difference and I was able to begin the slow but steady transition from dependence on state benefits to independence.

What role did you play in the research?

I began as a service user researcher on a multidisciplinary research team (clinical, university and service user researchers). I helped to plan the research design, undertook interviews and focus groups, analysed the data, and contributed to producing and disseminating the final report. We worked in a collaborative manner so I never undertook these tasks in isolation.

After this project finished I was invited to take part in other projects. As I gained more experience I began mentoring and guiding other service user researchers and taking responsibility for ensuring that service user perspectives were properly reflected throughout a project's life.

More recently I have also taken on the role of promoting the culture of service user involvement throughout the department, talking to other researchers and advising them on service user involvement best practice. I set up a new group, PEER (Peer Expertise in Education and Research), made up of service users interested in contributing to research and acting as a resource for the whole department. I also teach on two Masters courses at St George's on service user involvement in services and research.

What was it like working in a research team? Were there any challenges? How did you deal with them?

Initial challenges arose from my inexperience in research, not knowing the majority of the team and returning to a work environment after many years. I remember feeling quite intimidated by the professional roles of clinicians and researchers. However, from the beginning we invested time in group meetings, discussing and refining the scope and design of the project and getting to know each other and our different perspectives. This set the tone for the rest of the project and by the time we arrived at the analysis stage, feeling overawed was a thing of the past. The climate we managed to create – one of mutual respect and commitment to include all our perspectives – meant that the research felt meaningful and owned by the whole team. Since then I have been a member of five research teams and have learned to adapt to different personalities and perspectives. It has helped that the original university researcher has been consistently involved throughout:

his support and our experience of working together over a number of years has enabled us to talk through and resolve any sticking points.

New challenges arose when working with other university researchers who had not previously worked with service user researchers. They were willing to enter into a dialogue but sometimes – when personal issues arose for service user researchers as a result of the research – the tendency was to 'pathologise' the distress and emotions felt, steering it away from the research team and into what they felt were 'safer waters' (eg the university counselling service). It could be argued that this added layer of 'emotion' or personal disclosure is a vital and unavoidable part of the service user researcher role. If service users are to be involved in research on the basis of their personal experience and what that brings to the research, it is perhaps not surprising that contact with people and environments that may have previously been a source of trauma can sometimes produce a level of identification and emotional distress that the traditional research assistant may not experience. The challenge for the research team is to find safe and supportive ways of managing this instead of labelling it as 'over-emotional' or a 'problem', which can lead to the service user researcher feeling stigmatised. For example, in a project with people who had been detained under the Mental Health Act a couple of challenging interviews took place on wards where I had spent time as a patient in the past. The debriefing and regular supervision built into the project provided a safe space that allowed me to talk about my feelings and make a distinction from interviewees' distressing experiences, which we were then able to capture in the analysis and final project report.

What have you gained by the experience?

I have increased confidence in the workplace and have learned – am still learning – new and valuable skills. Being involved in research and returning to paid employment has played an important part in my continued mental wellbeing (a rehabilitation effect?). It has allowed me to use past negative or painful experiences in a positive way, both for myself and hopefully for others. It is also exciting to be part of this relatively new area, especially looking at the impact of service user involvement on the research process and findings, which is still in its infancy.

Steve – the university researcher's account

How did you first become involved in mental health research, and in service user involvement in research?

I took a research job with a local branch of the mental health charity Mind. I had been doing research about young people and their experiences of conflict internationally, but having started a family I wanted a job that was geographically closer to home. A lot of that research had been about how people respond to trauma, and at about the same time a couple of people who I was very close to had had difficult, but very different experiences of mental health issues. It seemed like both a natural and an important move. Also, the research I had done with young people had been about 'giving voice' to individuals living in very oppressive societies who had no other means to talk about their experiences, and I took that approach into the work I did in mental health. I found out about the 'Strategies for Living' project at the Mental Health Foundation (MHF, 2000) and then managed to secure funding from the local mental health trust and social services department to train and pay a team of service user researchers to undertake a piece of research called 'All talk: Exploring how people talk about their mental health experiences' (Gillard and Stacey, 2005).

You mentioned that you worked in the voluntary sector initially. Why did you decide to take a job in a university?

I think it was frustration in a way. There was a sense that we were doing great collaborative research but that reports were still ending up on the shelf at the end of the day. Yes, the *All talk* report (SULC 2004) did provide evidence that helped the primary care trust locally to commission more psychological therapies, but what the team felt were the really powerful findings (about how relationships between service users and mental health professionals shaped individuals' aspirations and expectations of their mental health) went pretty much unnoticed. I still felt that the service user voice wasn't being heard clearly enough and wondered if findings might have more impact if they came from a university department.

And did it work?

It was a strange experience initially. I had been employed partly to support service user involvement in research in the department, and quite soon I became involved in a number of mental health trust funded projects that employed service user researchers, where there were high levels of collaboration and where the service user voice remained strong and distinctive. But there was still a sense that service user involvement in research felt outside of the main business of the department, as if our team and our relatively small projects were somehow 'ghettoised' at the end of the corridor. No one else was really involving service users in their research and people remained sceptical; voicing the usual criticisms that service user researchers would have an axe to grind and could not be expected to bring anything other than their personal experiences to a project.

So what changed?

First of all we were successful, perhaps against expectations, in applying for funding from one of the NIHR funding streams for a reasonably substantial project that would explore the way mental health trusts nationally supported people in their self-care (Gillard et al, 2010a). The whole study was informed by a service user involvement approach and had service users and carers on the research team, guiding the project, and collecting and analysing data. At around the same time, expectations of service user involvement in all NIHR-funded research were increasing, with a requirement that lead investigators should indicate in their funding applications how patients and members of the public would be involved in designing and undertaking the research. Those tick boxes on the applications forms obliged people to take service user involvement a bit more seriously.

Surely that was a good thing?

Yes, the research team in our 'Self Care' project was very committed to service user and carer involvement in research, and we worked very well as a collaborative team, producing a much better piece of research as a result. But for me the real test would come when an academic, who previously had shown little interest in service user involvement in research, would get funding to do a project involving service users. I suppose I had a fear that they would pick the nearest willing service user, stick them into a traditional and often very demanding research assistant (RA) role, with no investment in the sort of support that might be necessary to ensure that the researcher had a good experience of doing the research and was able to make the most of their expertise as a service user.

And has that happened?

To some extent. I was involved in another project that employed a service user researcher to carry out and analyse qualitative interviews. There were lots of positives about the project, the researcher was very talented and the team was committed to service user involvement as an asset to the research. But at the same time I think the university culture – the way things are habitually done in research teams – was not quite up to speed with our expectations.

First, it often seems that the academic environment is not very supportive of RAs in general. There is a prevailing sense that these are academic jobs and that RAs should not need, for example, emotional support to undertake their work. And so if the researcher does become distressed after a particularly demanding interview, and is also a service user, they are easily made a scapegoat: 'they became distressed because of their mental health issues and it is not the academic team's responsibility to support them.'

Second, there was a sense in which the service user researcher was at times pathologised, indirectly and inadvertently, by the casual way in which difficult mental health issues were discussed within research teams. When the 'them' that were the research participants were discussed and characterised in research team meetings there was, at times, a collective lack of awareness that 'them' also included the team's service user researcher.

Third, there was sometimes a sense that, in order to be doing good research ,it was important to check how *reliable* the service user researcher's input was, for example through exploring the 'inter-rater reliability' of their analysis with other researchers on the team. The service user voice was perceived as having validity where it was shown to be in agreement with those more conventional research voices. In the study referred to above, 100% agreement of other researchers with the service user researcher was indicated in 65.5% of allocations of thematic 'codes' to interview data, and 75%+ agreement in 84% of allocations. Some members of the team suggested that this lack of distinctive analysis signified that service user involvement had been a success; that the service user was a good researcher. In contrast, in our earlier study of people detained under the Mental Health Act, service user researchers offered very different interpretations of interview data to the conventional university researchers on the team. They focused on interviewees' experiences and feelings about detention, rather than the processes and procedural issues highlighted by the university researchers (Gillard et al, 2010c). A reductive approach to involvement would have questioned the validity of the analysis and impoverished the study's findings.

So what are the potential effects of this on the service user voice in mental health research?

I think it can be stifling, can result in self-censorship. The researcher stops speaking up at team meetings, or at least does not speak up in the same way. Rather than giving of themselves as someone who has experienced mental health issues, they focus instead on performing well in a conventional RA role, and then the added value to the research of that explicit 'expertise by experience' is lost. If those experiences are not actively voiced throughout the research process then that dimension to the research is absent. It is as though the *service user* goes underground and only the *researcher* is heard. I know more than one very good service user researcher who does not want to be identified as such at research conferences for fear that someone in the audience, a senior academic, might interview them for a research job in the future and remember that they stood up and said they were a service user.

That, I think, is the worst-case scenario; that where the university culture does not look critically at itself and recognise the extent to which it is potentially an oppressive environment, the service user voice, far from remaining 'out there', will be suppressed and lost to mainstream mental health research. On the other hand, I think most of our experiences demonstrate that it is possible, not only to preserve, but also to amplify the service user voice, at the heart of mainstream mental research, where the research team is able to reflect on how it operates and properly include the service user researcher as a full team member.

Discussion

Clark et al (2004) demonstrate that provision of inadequate support for service user researchers, by the research team, can have a detrimental impact on their mental health. Our experience has shown that there has to be a commitment, from the outset, by the university department and lead researchers, in order for service user involvement in research to be an acknowledged success. Because service user and carer involvement in research is now an obligation rather than a choice, it is more important than ever that researchers understand the principles behind it and are acquainted with best practice guidelines (Hanley et al, 2003). Otherwise the experience can very easily turn into a negative one for all concerned: frustration, distrust and accusations of tokenism and stigmatisation. Appropriate support systems, requiring adequate time and resources (both human and financial), need to be factored in when planning research. If the challenging issues of Occupational Health checks and negotiating the complex benefits system are not addressed at an institutional level then many potential service user researchers will feel unable to step into a mainstream research environment at the outset, and their voices will be silenced.

Mental health service user researchers have noted how they have felt powerless to change the direction of a research project once it has begun (Faulkner, 2004). Genuine collaboration and a safe space for expression and reflection, by both conventional university and service user researchers, are necessary to allow for disagreements and difficult emotions to be expressed. An atmosphere of equality and mutual respect must be aimed for, and continually worked on as the project progresses, with the recognition that for the service user researcher, being involved in research is often both a personal and professional journey.

Our experiences, as our research has moved into the mainstream, have shown that tension can arise between the twin roles and identities of service user and researcher. The challenge has been not to draw a clear line between these two identities, but to help foster an environment where they are able to co-exist. We have found that some service user researchers identify

197

more readily with the role of researcher than of service user and do not want their personal experiences to define their professional lives. Others enter the research field with no experience of research and so may identify more readily as service users. This identification may shift more towards the 'researcher' role as the service user researcher becomes familiar with research and the university environment. On the other hand, increased confidence and experience in the 'researcher' role can enable greater self-assurance in expressing a service user identity and using this productively in research. Within the research team, and within the wider university environment, the researcher needs to feel able to articulate their service user identity, and to be supported and respected in so doing, if the research is to benefit from that source of insight that comes from outside of the conventional university research team.

We wondered whether the problem lies with the 'service user researcher' label; the term 'service user researcher' automatically discloses a level of personal information that conventional university researchers are not expected to make public to their colleagues. Part of the solution is to allow individual researchers to exercise control over that degree of disclosure. However, our experiences have also suggested that responsibility here should not lie entirely with the service user researcher; to be thick skinned and to get on with it. Responsibility for nurturing service user involvement in mainstream mental health research lies instead with the university culture, which has traditionally not been over supportive of its junior researchers (RCUK, 2008), and additionally finds it difficult to accept more radical approaches – from 'non-scientists' – that challenge the conventional academic wisdom of what makes 'good science' (Nowotny et al, 2001). If mental health service users are invited onto university research teams, but then made to feel uncomfortable about wearing a 'service user researcher' label and so retreat behind the traditionally 'silent' RA role, then there is a real risk that the service user voice becomes 'sanitised' and devalued.

So have the distinctive voices of service user researchers, heard clearly but situated somewhat on the margins during those pioneering years of the 1990s, retained the radical edge as they speak from within the university? Is service user involvement in research 'still out there'? Remaining 'out there' requires commitment on the part of both the university researcher and the service user researcher to be constantly alive to the challenges that the service user voice brings to the university environment: challenges in terms of a different, sometimes unwelcome, voice being heard, which may be at odds with conventional academic research processes and priorities (Gibbons et al, 1998). As discussed earlier in this chapter, the reductive approach of seeking reliability through agreement – triangulation by perspective (Patton, 1990) – can serve to blunt that radical edge. However, exploring what is meaningful about difference can enhance the quality and critical scientific rigour of research: the articulate service user researcher obliges the conventional research team to reflect on the way it usually does things.

Our experiences have indicated that the principal obstacles to this radical involvement seem to originate in the university culture, rather than with individual university researchers who might mistrust and resist involvement. Cultural obstacles exist both at an institutional level, where procedures around recruitment and employment can act as a barrier, and within the academic environment, where prevailing scientific practice can act to sanitise or stifle the service user voice. Prior, considered investment by the research team in both these areas must be complemented with support for the individual service user researcher to enable them to rise to the challenges they are likely to meet. Still out there? Potentially yes, as long as the mental health research mainstream can also move to meet the service user researcher.

sixteen

Service user-led research in the NHS: wasting our time?

Patsy Staddon

Introduction

Leading my own research into women's alcohol use and its treatment, funded by a local National Health Service (NHS) mental health trust, was both exciting and demanding. It helped me to understand better the relationship between service user and service provider, to develop different ways of seeing and to challenge the conventional and medical standpoints on 'alcoholism'. Unfortunately, this publicly funded research may not influence practice, since few alcohol treatment specialists will hear about it. Medical journals remain uninterested in small-scale, qualitative work, which, no matter how rigorous the ethical procedures, may be described as 'grey', or not scientifically proven. Fortunately, my university took a different view, awarding me a PhD in the sociology of women's alcohol use and its treatment in August 2009.

In this chapter I explain in the first section – 'Initial involvement and setting the agenda – how I came to do this research, with its service user perspective. The next section – 'Findings' – summarises the research results. Then, in 'Risks and rewards', I look at some of the difficulties that occurred along the way, particularly the problems I encountered when attempting to place the research in substance use journals. Finally, in the last section – 'Wasting our time?' – I emphasise the crucial importance of changing this situation, and suggest some ways forward. These include the need for local NHS trusts not only to fund service user-controlled research, but also to publish it, whatever its conclusions.

Initial involvement and setting the agenda

As a sociologist who had survived alcoholism, alcohol treatment and mental health problems, I felt that something was very wrong in the way the issues were approached, particularly for women. Women have an iconic role (Ettorre, 2007), which is damaged by their being defined by a shaming condition such as 'alcoholism'. I knew from first-hand experience that very many people left, or avoided, both treatment and Alcoholics Anonymous

(AA) for that very reason. When I learnt that our local NHS mental health trust was interested in sponsoring service user-led research, I really wanted to see whether my experiences in alcohol treatment were typical, and if so, why such treatment was as it was. I sought a different, critical perspective, to assess women's alcohol use and treatment provision.

I therefore applied to the University of Plymouth to do a research-based PhD in the sociology of women's alcohol use, and to the local NHS mental health trust for research funding, ethical approval for the research and general support. I planned first to interview women from the wider community who had, or had had, alcohol issues, to hear whether they had had help, and if so, what was effective and what was not. A second project would involve interviewing general practitioners (GPs) and treatment providers, to hear how they felt about women with alcohol issues, what sort of training they had had and what their views were about available treatment.

The first hurdle was the excruciatingly difficult task of proving to the Research Ethics Committee, and separately to the university, that the research was honest, consistent, had considered all sorts of possible harms and repercussions to respondents, and would provide answers to the research questions. The Ethics forms were very complex, and the director of research for the trust spent many hours on the telephone explaining the process to me, but it was as if we were speaking different languages. However, after lengthy struggles, ethical approval was granted. I would recommend anyone who wants to do such research to seek support early on from people with experience of these forms and formalities, since they may differ between universities and health authorities.

I still had much to learn about the service user movement as a parallel to other cultures of resistance, such as the black, the feminist, the disability and the lesbian/gay/bisexual/transgender (LGBT) movements. Shaping Our Lives, the national service user group, helped me reach a better understanding of the social control of minorities. There was already acknowledgement that (dis)ability was caused for the individual by society, rather than the other way around (Oliver, 1989). Applying this perspective to women's alcohol use confirmed my concerns about addiction treatment approaches. Whatever the reasons for men to drink, those for women included a greater burden of poverty, loneliness and abuse as the 'second sex' (De Beauvoir, 1997), while their treatment emphasised their shame and failure to live up to ideals of iconic womanhood (Ettorre, 1997). I also came, through feminist sociological research theory (Letherby, 2003), to understand the enormous value of an approach to 'doing the research' that acknowledged the full partnership and reciprocity of respondents, and examined reflexivity in the researcher.

My background in sociology, that most argumentative of sciences, together with being an active feminist, inclined me to a critical stance towards received wisdom. I did not see myself as a flawed person, 'powerless over alcohol', since I had chosen of my free will to stop using it, before I ever went for 'treatment'. This 'powerlessness' interpretation of alcohol problems, common in treatment and with the public, reinforces the very social expectations of women that have precipitated these issues (Hall, 1994). My awareness of 'alcoholism' as a social construct developed as the research progressed.

The director of research for the NHS trust had suggested I acquire a research advisory group (RAG) of other women who had also recovered from alcoholism. This was a great success. The 12 women I recruited (through advertisements in shops, health centres and wherever there was a free notice board) had all been recovered for a minimum of two years; some, like me, for over 10. Most had found alcohol treatment unhelpful and 'mutual aid' groups generally unsuitable. However, one or two RAG members had found such organisations useful at some stage. We had lost our alcohol dependence for different reasons, at different points in our lives and in different ways. The women in RAG were not respondents, but helped to design the interviews and focus groups, discuss best ways of working and talk over the findings. They were active in distributing flyers and mailing letters to clinics. I analysed the findings myself, since respondent identity was confidential, but the results were discussed and commented on in the group. Members would also come with me to talk about our research at treatment provider training sessions and at GP training sessions. They also made themselves available to talk to me over the telephone when I was distressed. The group ran for four years, from 2003 to 2007, and we organised two major research projects, 'Making a Start' and 'Treatment Approaches', both funded by the NHS trust.

'Making a Start' was designed to find out how women felt about their drinking and about what help was available. I believed that it essential to draw respondents from the community, rather than recruiting from treatment centres. Much data about alcohol problems have been derived from residential treatment centres, where women are less likely to go (Greenfield et al, 2007) and indeed recruiting women respondents from any clinical settings will inevitably produce skewed results for the same reason (Ettorre, 1997). I advertised in newspapers, on local radio and on notice boards for women who had, or had had, alcohol issues. I 'came out' publicly about myself, even being photographed for the local paper, believing that women were more likely to want to talk in confidence to someone like me, since peer group experience tends to inspire trust (Soyez et al, 2004). At the same time, the fact that the research was being carried out under the auspices of the NHS implied professional governance and credibility.

All 23 women respondents were interviewed, usually in their own homes, and all were invited additionally to small focus groups. These provided a safe and welcoming environment to discuss what they saw as the most important issues; probably a first-time experience (Crossley, 2003). Several women were keen on meeting others in a similar position. Respondents ranged in age from 25 to 57; all were white, several were lesbian/bisexual and most had children. My own alcohol background seemed to give respondents confidence, and helped me to draw out a number of factors in women's alcohol use that have a low profile in most alcohol research (Ettorre, 2007).

A great deal of their unhappiness centred on the responses of GP and treatment centre assessors. Consequently, in the following project, 'Treatment Approaches', I interviewed GPs and treatment assessors on their behalf, asking what they thought about women's alcohol issues. Obtaining these interviews with professionals was time consuming and difficult, but again, once they realised I had the consent of the local NHS trust, this made a difference. Perhaps too some GPs wanted to meet that 'non-existent phenomenon', a recovered (as opposed to 'in recovery') 'alcoholic'.

Findings

'Making a Start' emphasised the effect of gender on all the women involved. Their alcohol use challenged social stereotypes, even while it was often a response to them. For example, social expectations had meant that several women, such as Helen[1] and Deirdre, had become mothers at a young age. Family members had tried to push women into caring roles, for example trying to restrict Margaret's career so that she could help more in the home. Other social pressures had been applied outside the family; both Anne and Deirdre had been laughed at for being drunk on the street. These humiliations would have been less likely for men, for whom such behaviour is seen as part of growing up and adopting a male identity (Harnett et al, 2000). Women had frequently been led to subordinate their own needs, often at great cost, in order to feel loved and wanted (Doyal, 1995). Alcohol had often become their only friend and safe place, even when they were aware of current and potential costs to their lives.

Information of this sort was given to me freely and trustingly. They knew I had 'been there' and only sought greater understanding. They told me how they had often been able to use alcohol to suppress anger, express anger, make a point, or effectively change a situation they disliked. They had also been able to be themselves, enjoy time out and relax. In interviews, and then focus groups, women felt free to talk about these things, often for the first time. The focus groups led to the development by respondents and members of RAG of Women's Independent Alcohol Support (WIAS), a user-controlled women's group to encourage building social networks.

Women often found it hard to approach GPs for advice. By the time they had made up their minds to go, they might have numerous additional problems, particularly abuse and depression. They found that GPs knew little of what resources existed, and often had attitudes that implied moral judgement of their lives. If they went to AA, or into treatment, they met this moral approach again based on the same perceptions of how women should behave, what was good for their health and what was good for their families. These perceptions reinforced such views as those of Margaret's family: "They gave me an ultimatum: I had to cut the hours I worked and do more at home or leave ... so I left."

Large, mixed-sex treatment groups reinforced a view that they had misbehaved and needed to acknowledge their 'fault'. The presence of men in such a situation added greatly to the women's distress. In addition, they could seldom acknowledge that alcohol might have enabled them to enjoy play and at least a brief freedom from constraint, as young men have typically been able to do.

When the time came for me to interview GPs, I found that they had received minimal training about 'alcoholism' and that what there was had described it as an incurable condition, evidencing low moral standards. A common term for 'alcoholics' was 'dirty work patients'. All the GPs recommended AA, although none knew of anyone who had recovered through attending. Typically, they would know of one or two of the 10 treatment centres locally available, but little about how they worked. Similarly judgemental approaches occurred in the treatment centres, where treatment assessors often saw the drinking as a cause, as opposed to a consequence, of distress: "it's quite tempting to oversimplify and say it's because of this in their background, it's because of that....' (treatment assessor).

Few treatment centres adopted a more holistic approach, questioning the necessity to stop using alcohol, and recognising its possible value in achieving or enacting authenticity. For some people, substances are an essential part of the balance between reality and unreality (Aaslid, 2006). This made a non-judgemental environment such as WIAS of particular value to the women who accessed it.

Risks and rewards

There is no doubt about the value and qualifications of 'experts by experience' (Faulkner and Layzell, 1999), but emotional risks for us can be high (Lowes and Gill, 2006). Receiving telephone calls from women in response to the advertisements was very stressful (see Staniszewska et al, Chapter Ten). I took basic information while being continually aware that for the caller what I said might be critically important. The interviews that took place later were less stressful, but were still emotionally draining. This was the case with both the women alcohol users, with whom I identified, and the GPs and treatment professionals, with whom I did not. Even my first-hand knowledge of the field of alcohol treatment could be disempowering as well as enriching (Cotterill and Letherby, 1993). I had suffered from the culture of the treatment centre, where the greater worth of staff, and therefore the indisputability of their assertions, goes unquestioned. This may leave the patient feeling that they are 'only' 'service users' (Beresford and Campbell, 1994). I feared that my research would not 'count'; I did not 'really' know much. My service user history made me slow to accept that my own observations had validity (Raine, 2001). Naples (1996) refers to such a position as holding numerous positions of 'knower', but it was a lonely and frightening place to be.

However, without such a background, and perhaps, without such a sense of insecurity, the research findings would not have spoken out so clearly of pain, rage and treatment failure. A short version of the report was sent to all the GP practices and treatment centres in the city, and workshops were offered, although only three out of 10 treatment centres, and no GP practices took advantage of these. I presented the findings, often helped by members of RAG and members of WIAS, at conferences around the country. We arranged service user-controlled workshops, meetings and events, and for a while operated a telephone line to give information about what help we knew to be available. Yet for me what was particularly relevant was the involvement of the women respondents, two of whom had never spoken of their alcohol issues before to anyone. This reassured me that the methodology was the right one; those for whom the research mattered most were favourably impressed.

Unfortunately, it is difficult to convince doctors and treatment advisers unless findings have been published in medical journals, which are unlikely to publish service user-led research (Rose, 2003). There is said to be little evidence of the effect of service user involvement on improvement in health and social care outcomes (McLaughlin, 2009b), but as long as our more collaborative and challenging research comprises a tiny proportion of research outputs, that is likely to remain the case. 'Service user involvement … can easily be degraded, diluted and devalued….' (Branfield et al, 2006, p ix). Unreported in peer-reviewed journals, it will not influence policy. Perhaps most sadly, the NHS trust that had sponsored the research regretfully declined to publish its findings on its website, because they had not been peer reviewed in their entirety. It would have been a simple thing to indicate that the findings came from the research of someone who was 'only' a service user, and more senior researchers might have taken up the ideas presented.

Once research is reported, it may be cited, beginning a powerful movement for change. Was it a factor that the results of service user-controlled research are very likely to be controversial and to run counter to established knowledge, created by professionals? An article I submitted to an addiction journal was criticised because I had described myself as an ex-alcoholic and, the reviewer wrote, 'as AA tells us, there is no such thing'. In the alcohol field, such knowledge is often premised on an understanding of the experience of service users still in treatment, or newly emerged from treatment, which has a strong AA bias (Walters, 2002). There has not been time for the effectiveness or suitability of the treatment to be assessed. In addition, since most people who recover from alcohol issues do not enter treatment at all (Hall et al, 2001), these people's experiences are even less reliable as a guide to 'what works'.

This was not the case with my research, which drew its participants from the community as a whole, thus including a far wider range of people. Like the work of many service users (Beresford, 2007), it was challenging, questioning medical ideas and performance. The role of medicine in social control is visible and acknowledged in every sphere of life (Lupton, 2003 [1994]), and service users who protest are perceived as 'dissident' (Beresford, 2009b). For this and other reasons, I am now pursuing publication in the sociological journals, who may be interested in my dissident perspective.

Wasting our time?

Are there ways forward from this impasse? The sociologist in me is sceptical. It is difficult to move established power from its position and service users are far from united in their opposition. Too many, as I was myself, are so grateful to be heard, and still more, to be funded, that they let their stories be used without checking what use will be made of them, and whether results that show treatment to be misdirected and ineffective will ever be published. Perhaps most tragic of all is the way that most alcohol treatment inclines service users to believe that when they were drinking they were 'bad', and that to be 'good' requires acceptance of the very social conditions that may have led them to drink in the first place (Ettorre, 2007). Sociological appraisals should demonstrate the role of medicine in the social control of deviance (Campbell, 2000).

Service users do not, as they could, unite under a national organisation such as Shaping Our Lives, which has a political agenda of helping them to challenge and to affect the ways that they are treated, insisting on respect and proper representation. Such respect might be given to all, whether they wish to give up using alcohol or not; whether they are 'dissident' or not. Service user research could inform policy and change systems, but first it must cease to be discounted as 'grey'. Such a change would, of course, challenge the privileged position of academics as the 'knowers' (Naples, 1996); dangerous ground.

It is difficult to feel hopeful about the future of service user-controlled research that is able to assure service users that they are not being involved in research as local colour or a useful line in a grant application. It is likely to cost more and be seen as biased (Turner and Beresford, 2005, cited in McLaughlin, 2009b). It would also benefit from a study of feminist sociological research theory, which has already studied issues of power in the research process, and how to address them (Fish, 2006). But of all the rejections and disappointments that our research is heir to, the worst to me is the failure of the NHS, which all citizens finance, to publish the research findings of those citizens, because they have not obtained the rubber stamp of professional scrutiny. Until and unless that rubber stamp, 'peer-reviewed findings', is obtained, we may well have been wasting our time.

Note

[1] All names are pseudonyms.

seventeen

Should we? Could we? Measuring involvement

Rachel Purtell, Wendy Rickard and Katrina Wyatt

Introduction

The issue of how to measure the success or impact of involving service users, patients, carers and the public within health and social care is a live and active debate within the public and voluntary sectors. Currently there is no agreed measure of success and, presumably as a consequence, no coherent evaluation of impact (see Barber et al, Chapter Eighteen). It is indeed reasonable to suggest that as public monies are spent on the activities of involvement then there needs to be some validation of both the individual initiatives and the wider policy context that has been the impetus for involvement in recent years. In this chapter the focus is on involvement in research. Much of the knowledge is drawn from the authors' experiences and the particular experience of Folk.us (www.folkus.org.uk), a Department of Health-funded programme to enhance and support service user, patient and carer involvement in health services and social care research, based in Devon. It does not propose any hypothesis or indeed solution to the debate, but highlights concerns that measuring involvement at this time may be too soon for this way of working.

Defining involvement

At the outset it is important to define what we mean by 'involvement'. For the purposes of this chapter we accept that, as a general definition, involvement means: (to be included on an equal basis) 'with participation in decisions which affect how much and what kinds of support (people) receive' (Lindow and Morris, 1995, p 1). At Folk.us we also use the definition: 'service users, patients and carers to inform and guide research at all stages' (Folk.us, 2009). Using these two different definitions highlights one of the issues about creating a measurement of success and impact of involvement, namely that there is no universal definition of what is meant by 'involvement'. This raises the problem that, if there is no one encompassing term that has an agreed, shared meaning, then the attempt to establish a universal measure is fraught with difficulty. There are and have been moves away from the term 'involvement' in the Department of Health: 'engagement' has become a common term, but for the purposes of this chapter we will focus on 'involvement'. Through the work of Folk.us and many others (eg 'Shaping Our Lives': www.shapingourlives.org.uk), it would seem clear that the different meanings of involvement are essential for good involvement to thrive and are necessary for the very nature of involvement as a living and developing process.

Involvement needs different activities within different structural contexts. For instance, someone may be involved in a committee making decisions about awarding research funding, another person may work as a co-researcher on a research project and yet another may review and comment on a research idea for their clinician. These are all involvement activities. As there is no one set of activities that can be called 'involvement' and, indeed, the Folk. us experience would imply that it would be a mistake to try and make all activities 'uniform', this again causes a problem for the development or establishment of a universal measure of involvement. Involvement activities must remain flexible on two levels: first, to be able to respond to the needs of those being involved; and second, to be open to how involvement is informing the need for change to the project, structure or work itself. This raises the question: 'what is to be measured?'

The purpose of involvement

It is vital that the purpose of involvement be considered from the outset, yet in practice there is rarely room for what might seem a more philosophical discussion about 'what is it all for?' In other chapters in this book the different histories and developments within social movements have been discussed in relation to involvement, and it is clear that there are at least two distinctly different approaches to involvement in research. These have historically been called the 'consumerist approach' and the 'emancipatory approach' (Beresford and Campbell, 1994; Oliver, 1997). Involvement in research that is explicitly trying to facilitate the furthering of the rights of those we seek to involve, to share or transfer power and to change the context of research, is described as adopting an emancipatory approach. If these are the intentions then crucially the point of research has to be overtly about such aims along with clear implementation that achieves them. Alternatively, involvement may be aimed at ensuring that research, which has been decided on in advance, is better informed and there can be claims of accountability to the taxpaying public, for example a consumerist approach. The consumerist approach is predominantly about who pays, and the act of paying gives a voice. In many ways this can only perpetuate the status quo of who gets a say, whereas the emancipatory approach is about who is most affected and who should have their rights furthered in an unequal society to address and reduce inequality.

The reality of many projects is that they end up in a grey area of neither one nor the other. So again this raises the question about what is to be measured. Is it whether the research achieved its aim? Or is it whether the people involved benefited in some way (eg through having greater knowledge of something or feeling more able to do something)? These are very different questions.

Currently there is evidence and discussion about the need for better reporting of involvement in research and some thoughts on developing guidance to help with decisions about what information is captured to explain involvement in projects (Staniszewska et al, 2008; Staley, 2009). However there has been little discussion in recent times of the overriding purpose of any research involvement that is being developed in well-established organisations such as the National Health Service (NHS). These discussions seem to have slipped off the agendas in the general consensus that involvement is now, at least in some disciplines, part of an acceptable way of doing research. Few projects actually explicitly think about which approach is underpinning the involvement. Most discussions in involvement activities tend to be very function led, as in what is needed from patients, service users and carers, thinking about questions such as 'what is it that patients are expected to do' or 'what is needed by the project'?

Involvement in practice

Earlier discussions have resulted in ways of describing involvement in research, of which the best known is the INVOLVE (2004) definition of consultation, collaboration and user control. This is useful but it does not explain all the variations that many people experience. For instance, at Folk.us there have been at least three projects where a patient has directly suggested the basis for a research question to their clinician (on two occasions the suggestions were to consultants in mental health and diabetes and on the other one occasion the suggestion was to a general practitioner GP). In the first two projects the patients did not want to have any involvement in the creation of the subsequent project, but work was developed as a result. These are really interesting scenarios because they do not fit into any of the existing descriptions of involvement. 'Consultation' has been about inviting people to comment on and contribute to existing ideas and structures. A good example of this currently being developed through a joint project with the Joseph Rowntree Foundation and the Carnegie UK Trust (Carnegie UK Trust, 2010) is called Power Tools. They describe this approach as 'invited spaces'. Typically, these will be events such as research conferences, patients' days, or a specific activity where patients are asked about a specific research idea or proposal.

Our first two examples do not fit into the 'collaboration' definition either, as there was no ongoing involvement in the steering, designing or development of the projects. However, the third example does fit into the collaboration definition as it became a piece of research that was undertaken both by the GP practice and by the patient who initially brought the idea to the clinician. The patient then went on to have training in research methods and the whole project was conducted collaboratively. The project continues as a PhD placement and details can be found on the Folk.us website and in paper publications in peer-reviewed journals (Blake et al, 2007; Ruel, 2007). The two examples with consultants are not service user led, or patient led, so the 'user led' definition does not work either. The ideas came from patients but they did not go on to control any element of what happened as a result of their idea (because they did not wish to). These two examples of patients saying 'this is an issue you need to look into' do not fit with any of the existing descriptions, yet the research projects that stem from those encounters would not have existed otherwise, so these would seem to be very important involvement activities. These are the issues with involvement: it rarely fits into neat definitions; and there is still no really comprehensive way to define all the activities, which again raises questions about what measurement would look at.

Issues of guidance and practice

The inexplicit nature of the approaches to involvement is not surprising when looking at the difference between policy guidance documents themselves and then the absence of mechanisms to implement them. This was captured in Faulkner's (2004) *A story of colliding worlds*, which focused on a project where service users were researchers and highlights many of the practical difficulties that were encountered. These practical difficulties continue to date, with problems such as paying people to be involved as there are still no mechanisms to do this, despite guidance stating that people should both be reimbursed for their expenses and have their time paid for. However, in reality, this can mean all kinds of difficulties for people receiving benefits and paying tax. This is a huge gap between policy and practice as the Department of Health, the Department for Work and Pensions and HM Revenue and Customs have no working agreement on the issue of involvement or a definition of what activities of involvement might be, and therefore could be exempt from being seen as work or income.

It seems unrealistic to measure the impact or success of involvement when such fundamental support for involvement practice, such as a payment system, is still lacking. To be able to measure the success or impact of involvement in any equitable way surely requires there to be a way of making its practice universal in terms of national systems; however, currently these national systems are working directly against the policy aspirations. The implication is that success or impact of involvement can be, and is, completely subject to how well people (staff and service users) can work around the barriers of the national systems, which does not seem the right set of indicators for involvement.

In broader terms there are issues about practices that result from the lack of a comprehensive approach to involving people. For instance, the conference entitled 'Critical Perspectives on User Involvement' at the University of Brighton, which is the impetus for this book, encountered its own issues. There is no agreement about whether conferences that invite service users, patients and carers should or should not charge for places. This conference did and so do many others including INVOLVE, although many do give bursaries if people apply for them. Folk.us held its fourth conference this year – 'Turning the Tide'. Folk.us does not and never has charged for places and in addition all travel and care expenses for service users, patients and carers are met. This is not a criticism of any practice, just another example of how inconsistent practices are across the UK. The absence of the support systems available or of agreed practices does imply that involvement activities follow a consumerist model and are not about furthering the rights of people involved.

There may be nothing inherently wrong with the consumerist approach to involving people, providing there is honesty about the limits of what can be influenced and most importantly what and whose purpose is actually being served. However, for many who have had a long association with the ideas and ideals of involving people, it has been the emancipatory approach that has been of interest. Involvement was, and still is, about changing how things are done. The need for involvement has been borne from previous failures to get things right for people using services, so if it becomes simply about carrying on the same way but with a few people on board and with involvement not changing anything, it does seem a little futile.

Another area where there are some examples of the confusion in research involvement is on ethics committees and funding committees where many lay people who serve on these committees have previous experience of being professors or healthcare staff. Again, there is nothing wrong with this per se, but the expectation of what those roles within the committee hope to achieve is rather important. Is it about a 'different' kind of expert or an allied opinion? This leads back to the issues of both the definition and the purpose of involvement. There are undoubtedly a number of different people who should be involved in different activities, from the taxpaying public, to people who have to rely on services to support them. There is no coherent way to explain all these different roles or experiences and with the gaps in policy and practice, again it raises the question as to which activities and whose activities should be measured.

What *part of* involvement is to be measured?

In practice, involvement can mean very different things to different people. For some it can be seen as a way of working, to be embedded into our everyday practice, stemming from the expectation that if, as a service user or patient, you are someone who is potentially going to have a stake in the work proposed, then you have a right to say, 'I want to be part of those decisions.' Or it may be viewed as an 'add-on' piece of activity that can be singled out and brought away from the whole and scrutinised separately. These two approaches are clearly at odds with each other. It is doubtful whether involvement can become an effective way of working if it is continuously 'dug out' and treated as a separate thing. There is a danger of involvement being singled out for its own special treatment, as discussed earlier, to be measured for impact or success, yet still without comprehensive support systems and definitions. It appears that there is a drive to measure this thing called 'involvement' when it still has an awful lot to contend with. Research now requires multidisciplinary teams to address the issues and yet we do not ask for measures of impact of the 'statistician' or the 'health economist' – there is an underlying assumption that their expertise is necessary for the project – why then are we concerned with determining the impact of involving service users and carers?

The final point we want to make is that the demand for measuring involvement is based on ideas of needing to know that 'we are getting it right' or at least 'not damaging people'. This seems to be the most worrying part of all – if the process and the relationships of involvement are not giving that knowledge then surely the question must be, what is the involvement process? It is too late to wait for an external measurement to be applied if the need is for this kind of knowledge. The first and most golden rule of involving people is that it does not cause damage and that the process is sufficiently responsive that it can change, adapt and be open to seeing and hearing any potential issues long before they become a major problem. It is unlikely that any type of measurement is going to resolve these sorts of issues and there is an inherent danger to the practice of involvement if yet more sets of rules are created that imply that it does not matter how the process goes on because it will all be explained at the end. It is not the activities of involvement that need to be homogenised, but the issues around equality and fairness that currently stand in the way of good practice.

Conclusion

In this chapter there has been an attempt to play 'devil's advocate' in the debate about measuring involvement. It is not an anti-measurement stance as there are very good reasons why measuring impact or success of involvement may well be useful and helpful. However, it does feel premature to rush into designing or creating measures when there are still fundamental and universal barriers in the systems that involvement is governed by. These barriers seem to have been forgotten or are getting lost in an academic debate about evidence. We are sceptical that it is possible to collect evidence about involvement that would prove that it is worth doing to a critical research practitioner or funder; we think the best we may do is to establish that involvement creates diverse ways of practising research and that research is more connected to the lived experience of those it has been about.

The history of involvement is not a scientific one; we cannot and should not reduce it to something that looks like a randomised controlled trial. Involvement has been and is still about the development of rights and it remains a concern that the very reason involvement is important may be destroyed in an attempt to turn it into measurable, neat pieces of activity. At Folk.us the central concern is that people have real influence and are supported to do so, no matter what the definition is, no matter what the subject, no matter what the method. As has been said earlier, in most other cases the success or impact of research projects is measured by their results, and it is unclear as to why involvement is singled out as needing its own measure. It appears that involvement practice still has many barriers to overcome. Perhaps when the playing field is more even and these barriers are considerably reduced, a discussion about measure, success and impact would seem more fitting. Until then, for many, the day-to-day battles of creating spaces where people are involved in research in a way that can be done equitably and has real influence to change research questions, designs, methods and implementations, is challenge enough. For many of the big systems such as the NHS, involving patients in research is still in its infancy; we may be asking it to stand up against the tape measure attached to the wall before it can yet stand up at all. We should not be lured into the idea of proving something about involvement if by the very process of achieving that we destroy what made involvement worth doing in the first place.

eighteen

Evaluating the impact of public involvement on research

*Rosemary Barber, Jonathan Boote, Glenys Parry,
Cindy Cooper and Philippa Yeeles*

Introduction

There has been a substantial increase in public involvement in research both in the UK and internationally during the past decade (Caron-Flinterman et al, 2006; National Health and Medical Research Council, 2002; National Institutes of Health Director's Council of Public Representatives, 2010; UKCRC, 2011). The public is now involved in many different types of research activities in a variety of ways, including identifying and prioritising research topics, carrying out research, analysing data and interpreting and disseminating the findings (Hanley et al, 2003). Yet, surprisingly, there have been few attempts to assess the impact of public involvement in a systematic way (Staley, 2009), and there are limited theoretical models and frameworks to inform the development of impact measures (Boote et al, 2002; Oliver et al, 2004; Telford et al, 2004; Brett et al, 2009). This chapter suggests why it is important to investigate the impact of public involvement in health and social research, presents a brief overview of what we know already and highlights some of the challenges. We use the term 'public' to include patients, people who use health and social services, informal carers and organisations that represent people who use health and social services, and the INVOLVE (Hanley et al, 2003) definition of public involvement: 'Many people define public involvement in research as doing research "with" or "by" the public, rather than "to", "about" or "for" the public.'

The value of public involvement in research is contested, with both substantive and normative arguments being made (see Purtell et al, Chapter Seventeen). Substantive arguments consider public involvement as a means to an end, for example in terms of its potential to improve the quality and relevance of the research. Normative arguments view public involvement as an end in itself; a democratic right, associated with public accountability and transparency, taking into account moral and political values such as fairness and justice (Caron-Flinterman et al, 2006). It might be assumed that those who deem public involvement to be of intrinsic value view attempts to evaluate its impact as irrelevant. However, a recent Delphi study found that many Delphi panellists (comprised of members of the public, researchers, research managers, commissioners, policy makers and analysts) viewed public involvement to be of intrinsic value, while at the same time asserting the importance of investigating the difference that it makes (Barber et al, 2011).

There are persuasive reasons for evaluating the process and impact of public involvement: to find out how best to involve the public meaningfully in different types of research activities; to examine the possibility of deleterious effects; to try to achieve value for money; and to increase knowledge and understanding. There is much to learn about the effectiveness of different models, contexts and structural aspects, such as support and remuneration, that will facilitate or inhibit successful public involvement. It is possible to approach the impact from a variety of perspectives. This chapter considers the impact of public involvement on research processes, outcomes and key stakeholders, drawing on three recent reviews of the literature (Brett et al, 2009; Staley, 2009; Boote et al, 2010).

A brief summary of the impact of public involvement

Considerable evidence is emerging of the promising positive effects of public involvement on research processes, such as identifying, prioritising and commissioning research topics, research design, collecting and analysing research data, and interpreting and disseminating the findings. Current evidence is dominated by brief narrative descriptions, and systematic studies are rare. Involving the public is said to increase the range of research topics, alerting researchers to issues important to patients and the public (Rhodes et al, 2002; McCormick et al, 2004; Bryant and Beckett, 2006; Caron-Flinterman et al, 2006; Hewlett et al, 2006; McLaughlin, 2006; Staniszewska et al, 2007; Serrano-Anguilar et al, 2009). Boote et al (2010) have drawn attention to the benefits of public involvement at the research design stage, where members of the public helped to improve trial consent procedures (Ali et al, 2006), leading to a more ethically acceptable research design (Koops and Lindley, 2002; Collyar, 2005). Staley (2009) presented evidence that the public can have a positive impact on recruitment and accrual rates, providing researchers access to participants through their networks, or by doing the recruitment themselves.

Some research projects have included the public as co-researchers and interviewers. This appears to have led to more candid and in-depth responses from interviewees, resulting in higher-quality data (Clark et al, 1999; Faulkner, 2006). There are few reports of public involvement in analysing data. Staley (2009) has summarised the main benefits: adjusting researchers' misinterpretations (Savage et al, 2006); highlighting new themes (Fisher, 2002); identifying findings most pertinent to the public (Ross et al, 2005);

and challenging the interpretations of researchers and making adjustments to how findings are reported (Rose, 2004; Faulkner, 2006).

Information is available on some aspects of the impact of public involvement on outcomes: disseminating research, implementing research findings and the quality of research and/or research-related activities. One study showed how involving the public led to the identification and incorporation of an additional outcome measure (quality of life), in a national hormone replacement therapy trial as a result of consulting the public (Marsden and Bradburn, 2004). In another study, the focus of outcomes was changed, to reflect more accurately the views and wishes of the public (Trivedi and Wykes, 2002). When the public were involved in disseminating research findings, the findings were said to be more powerful and credible (Smith et al, 2008) and offered possibilities for the public to disseminate more widely through their own networks (Barnard et al, 2005), allowing the findings to be more accessible (McLaughlin, 2006).

There have been few attempts to evaluate the impact of public involvement on the quality of research, and this remains a challenge. One study indicated that an integrated approach between a charity, its professional and patient members, and researchers in a multi-centre randomised controlled trial (Langston et al, 2005) appeared to lead to a higher quality of trial information and also well-targeted sharing of research findings, through newsletters, presentations and web-based media. The impact of collaborating closely was thought to have resulted in well-informed and motivated participants, and in turn, a higher number of completed questionnaires, thus improving the quality of the trial data.

While there is accumulating evidence to support public involvement in research processes and outcomes, some deleterious effects have also been noted in the literature. In one instance the process of peer interviewing had a negative impact on data collection, primarily due to the inexperience of the interviewers, which, it was said, could be addressed by support and training (Bryant and Beckett, 2006). Wyatt et al (2008) queried whether it is appropriate for the public to bring their own agenda to the research process. Boote et al's (2010) review of public involvement at the design stage of primary health research identified a series of tensions and barriers that can exist when members of the public are involved at this stage of the research process: tensions between different stakeholder groups; variable levels of understanding of members of the public of health research methods (especially the rationale for randomisation in clinical trials); time and cost; the perceived representativeness of the public participating in research design activities; and the potential for the public to be put off by the complex language and jargon used by researchers.

A number of studies have given detailed accounts of the impact of public involvement on key stakeholders. Public involvement is strongly associated with empowerment and strengthening of the public voice (Macaulay et al, 1999; Beresford, 2002). Findings from studies that have examined the experiences of the public involved in the research process indicate that involvement can have positive effects, for example, in increasing knowledge, skills and confidence (Kai and Hedges, 1999; Rhodes et al, 2002). This suggests that public involvement in research can support self-empowerment. However, it is important to note that negative consequences for the public have also been reported, including feeling overburdened (Clark et al, 2004) and having to relive distressing memories (Cotterell et al, 2008).

Less is known about the effects of public involvement on researchers (Brett et al, 2009; Staley, 2009). However, researchers have been reported to develop a deeper understanding of patient and community issues (Hewlett et al, 2006; Lindenmeyer et al, 2007), prompting them to challenge their own beliefs and assumptions (Hewlett et al, 2006). In some cases, public involvement was said to move researchers 'from compliance to enthusiasm' (Paterson, 2003). Frustrations have been voiced concerning additional time and resources required, and the slower nature of the research process (Rhodes et al, 2002; Wright et al, 2006; Wyatt et al, 2008). Researchers have also expressed concerns about perceived threats to professional skills and knowledge (Thompson et al, 2009), and the surrender of some power (Lindenmeyer et al, 2007). One author suggested that different research skills are needed by researchers who work collaboratively with the public (McLaughlin, 2006).

Challenges to evaluating the impact of public involvement

Recent attempts to map and review the literature on the impact of public involvement on health and social research reflect a growing interest in this subject (Oliver et al, 2004; Staley, 2009; Boote et al, 2010; Brett et al, 2009). These reviews have also highlighted difficulties inherent in the process. As discussed in the Introduction to this book, there is no consistency in the literature regarding the use of the terms to describe public involvement. The lack of consistency with language highlights the complexity of the different ways in which public involvement is conceptualised and carried out. Different models and frameworks for public involvement have been put forward (Arnstein, 1969; Oliver et al, 2004; Pivik et al, 2004; Telford et al, 2004; Dewer, 2005). For instance, Telford et al (2004) presented principles and indicators of successful public involvement in research, developed through consensus methods. However, no comprehensive theoretical model of public involvement has been developed that takes into account the full range of the complexities, and which could be used to develop and test different evaluation methods. Clarifying the specific contribution and influence of the public in relation to various research activities that take place in different contexts and organisations is difficult, particularly when decisions are made after lengthy deliberation and debate.

None of the major health databases (Medline, CINAHL, EMBASE and PsycINFO) has a subject heading specifically to describe public involvement in the research process, and it is not yet common practice for public involvement to be routinely described in the abstracts of journal articles. Therefore, when undertaking reviews of the evidence, it is possible that articles that report on public involvement will be missed if the public involvement in the study is described solely in the body of the paper. Accounts of public involvement are often brief narrative descriptions, lacking important details that would allow replicability.

To ensure that public involvement is more routinely recorded in published accounts of health research, agreement is needed among the editors of health and social care related journals on the best ways for this to be done. There are three aspects of public involvement that need to be recorded in published research (preferably routinely and consistently), to improve the inclusivity and accuracy of future systematic reviews:

- whether members of the public were actively involved at all in the research;
- if they were involved, who were involved and how were they involved;
- if they were involved, the impact(s) that they had.

Whether or not the study had public involvement could be recorded in a statement in the study abstract. Details of which members of the public were involved, and an account of how they were involved, could be recorded in the methods section. Details of the impact(s) of public involvement could be detailed in the results or discussion section of the paper. Once the method and the impact of public involvement become routinely and consistently recorded in published accounts of health research, then critical appraisal checklists can be developed to appraise the evidence base. This would assist in the teaching of good practice on public involvement for the benefit of all stakeholders.

Public involvement is essentially an interpersonal process (Smith et al, 2008), dependent on mutual trust and learning (Lindenmeyer et al, 2007). Researchers and the public will bring different aspirations, values and perspectives to the research, and will almost certainly have differing views on the relevance and importance of key impact issues, such as outcomes, outputs and quality issues. The 'public' is, of course, comprised of different stakeholders with various perspectives. Negotiations will be necessary to incorporate diverse views when deciding what to evaluate and why, and when interpreting the findings. For instance, Fisher (2002) highlighted the work of Morris (1995) in describing how the focus of research on young carers of parents who were ill or disabled, changed to an inquiry on the absence of adequate care, following the involvement of disabled people. Ross et al (2005) noted that public involvement in the analysis of interview data added 'another layer of insight to interpretation'.

It can be difficult to capture the interpersonal processes that may either facilitate or inhibit productive public involvement. Not surprisingly, recent research suggests that researchers' attitudes to public involvement can be influential (Thompson et al, 2009). Much depends on the receptiveness and skilfulness of researchers to consider, evaluate and embrace new and different ways in which public involvement can impact positively on research. Learning about the conditions that need to be in place for public involvement to prosper is at an early stage (Brett et al, 2009).

A fundamental difficulty in assessing the impact of public involvement has been, until recently, a lack of funding from commissioners to resource impact research. It can be very costly to carry out complex comparative studies. Many of the benefits of public involvement can be longer term, and may evolve in an organic way, while research projects are traditionally shorter and more discrete, with little room to take account of emerging ideas during the research process. Do we have adequate research methods to address the complexities of evaluating the impact of public involvement? It has been suggested that traditional research methods have limitations, and there is a need to develop innovative techniques (McCormick et al, 2004). Qualitative research methods predominate in studies of public involvement, although randomised controlled trials are not unknown (Guarino et al, 2006). There is current interest in using methods to evaluate complex interventions. These take account of interventions with many interacting components, are tailored to more local circumstances, emphasise early piloting of the methods, and model processes and outcomes to examine important uncertainties (Craig et al, 2008). Revised and updated guidance on this promising approach is available (MRC, 2008).

Are there limits to evaluating public involvement in research? Are some impact issues more feasible to evaluate than others? A recent Delphi study (Barber et al, 2011) found consensus that it was feasible to evaluate the impact of public involvement on health and social research on five out of 16 impact issues:

- identifying topics to research;
- prioritising topics;
- disseminating the results;
- the public involved in the research;
- the researchers.

These five impact issues could provide a promising focus for future research.

There are reports that involving the public at the early stages of research, such as identifying and prioritising topics, can help to focus research on topics of direct interest to the public (Staley, 2009). Investigating these processes in greater detail could show how and in what way research agendas have been influenced by the public, and the consequences of this.

The potential benefits of public involvement in disseminating research are important because they include not only the possibility of wider awareness of research findings (particularly among those who will benefit most from the research), but also a greater likelihood of the findings being implemented (Staley, 2009). The quality of research outputs and the wider impact of research are now part of the Higher Education Funding Council for England's (2011) assessment of the quality of research in the UK. Further research on the impact of public involvement in disseminating research is therefore likely to be of great interest to a number of different stakeholders.

As was mentioned earlier in this chapter, the impact of public involvement on the public involved in the research and on the researchers appears to be associated with negative as well as positive consequences (see Staniszewska et al, Chapter Ten). Additional research could help to identify the processes and circumstances that are associated with more positive benefits of public involvement both for the public involved in the research and for the researchers.

There is a growing interest in researching the impact of public involvement on research, and there are many different ways of understanding the potential benefits. The challenge is to undertake research that is robust and informative, and that addresses questions of interest to researchers, the public and the wider research community, including research commissioners and policy makers.

Part Three

User involvement in research

Questions for reflection

Part Three had the most contributions in this volume – perhaps because of the origin of the chapters in a conference organised and hosted by a university. But it does indicate that research has become an important focus for user involvement and this raises important issues about the way knowledge is produced and what sort of knowledge is valued. We suggest that the following questions will help us to reflect on both the current situation and how both service users and researchers might want to develop this area of activity:

- How different is research conducted with or by service users from that conducted by researchers who have no experience of service use? How may user-led research enable us to think differently and produce different outputs?
- There has been a great expansion in user involvement in research and many funders now require researchers to demonstrate how they have involved users in developing proposals and will continue to involve them in carrying out the research. Does all research require user involvement? Has user input made a real difference to what research is being done and how it is being done?
- Is involvement in research more or less threatening, to service planners and providers, than direct action or involvement in service delivery? Is developing user input to research a diversion from taking action to change services or policies that have important impacts on people's lives, or is it a route to fundamental change?
- Who gets most benefit from user input to research: users or researchers? (Assuming users do not identify themselves as researchers.)
- How is user research evaluated? Is there a need for alternative ways of disseminating such research from the traditional peer-reviewed journals that bestow recognition on academic research? Can and should user research try to adopt methods that bestow academic respectability?

Conclusion

Critical and different perspectives on user involvement

Marian Barnes and Phil Cotterell

In this final chapter we offer our own perspectives on the issue of 'critical perspectives' on user involvement. This book has deliberately sought to include views from those who have participated in, researched and reflected on user involvement from different positions within academia, practice and user movements. Some contributors occupy more than one of those positions, at the same or at different times. These diverse contributions have demonstrated different ways in which user involvement might be understood and assessed, and they reflect different views about key issues (eg 'to measure or not to measure' outcomes of involvement). They also illustrate ways in which competing understandings and interpretations of events or actions can lead to different conclusions and sometimes conflict over 'the facts'. Such differences are not restricted to accounts and analyses of user involvement. All social phenomena are subject to competing interpretations of meanings and significance and reality itself can be considered to be 'socially constructed' (Berger and Luckmann, 1967). In the context of user involvement, recognition of these epistemological issues is directly related to the political significance of such activities. As many of the contributions to this volume have shown, particularly those that have considered the significance of user involvement in the process of generating knowledge through research, struggles over who has the authority and power to determine meaning are fundamental to the objectives of many user organisations. Thus, it is impossible either to take action or to study user involvement without considering one's own positionality in relation to this. There is no 'view from nowhere' and a reflective stance is necessary to understanding, promoting or critiquing the activities of public officials who have 'invited' users to get involved, of researchers who have sought to develop methodologies through which knowledge can be co-produced and of service users themselves who have adopted diverse ways of shaping not only public services, but also broader social relationships.

Thus, in this final chapter we (the co-editors) reflect on our positions in relation to the 'subject' of user involvement, in relation to both our personal and professional identities and our histories of working in this area. We were both based in academia as we were working on this project, but neither of us has only worked in academia and in disciplinary terms we bring different academic perspectives. But it is not just our positions as 'academics' or as workers that have influenced our view of user involvement. We reflect here on aspects of our personal identities that we think are significant in order to challenge assumptions that identity is singular and that one aspect of identity will determine how we (and others) approach user involvement. We are mindful here of work by Tregaskis (2004), who reflects on her various identities as a woman, a professional, a disabled person, a researcher and others, and how these intersect in constructing her relationships with workers and users of a leisure centre she is researching. We hope that it is helpful to offer our different perspectives as a way of contributing to understanding what we can learn from different perspectives.

Marian

My professional identity is as a social scientist and researcher, although I have not always worked in universities. Nor did I start out working in social policy or social welfare. My initial postgraduate work was in information studies, I worked in libraries and my PhD is in librarianship – although the topic is significant. I studied what happened when users of public libraries asked questions of librarians – how did the librarians respond and seek to resolve information needs? Hence my interest focused on the interactions between providers and users of library services. My earliest experiences of undertaking evaluations of social care services was when I was employed in the late 1970s/early 1980s as a research officer in social service departments. With no previous experience or specific training in evaluation it appeared self-evident to me that evaluation was not possible without understanding what those on the receiving end thought of services. Thus, the evaluations I undertook were built around interviews with service users. As I became more established in this work and started to read relevant books and articles, I discovered that such an approach was considered rather radical. A key text at the time was entitled *The client speaks* by Mayer and Timm (1970), a study of service user opinions of social work, referred to by a service manager in the department in which I worked as *The client squeaks* – in cynical reflection on the strength of what would now be called the 'user voice'. Thus, in rather different contexts I found myself interested in the frontline interactions between providers and users of public services, how these were negotiated and what were the experiences of service users.

When I moved into an academic research post I had the opportunity to pursue my growing interest in ways in which users' and carers' voices were starting to be heard in different public services (Barnes et al, 1990; Barnes and Wistow, 1994), and then in particular to research ways in which disabled people and mental health service users were organising within their own groups outside the control of service providers (eg Barnes, 1999; Barnes et al, 1999). A growing reputation as someone who 'knew about' user involvement led to opportunities to take part in national policy initiatives, such as the Patient Partnership Reference Group, which advised the Department of Health on developing a strategic approach to patient and public involvement, and the group developing guidelines for user involvement in research within the National Health Service (NHS) (Hanley et al, 2000). Locally I started to have contact with groups and initiatives through which user involvement was developing and a link with Age Concern, Scotland led to me becoming adviser to and evaluator of an innovative project using community development approaches to enabling frail older people to influence services (Barnes and Bennet, 1998). As well as studying involvement and collective organisation, as a researcher I was developing participatory research practice and I was also playing a local and national role in policy and practice development. Such activities have continued and also broadened out to encompass public participation in processes of governance and service delivery across a range of policy areas (Barnes et al, 2007).

An academic position is a privileged one in a number of ways. One such is the possibility of pursuing lines of enquiry in which one is intellectually interested and to which one has a value commitment. It is a position that also offers the possibility of drawing on research to play a part in influencing policy and practice (although the relationship between research and influencing policy is by no means a straightforward one). My 'choice' of user involvement and user movements as topics for study was based in a belief that such action was important, not only to ensure that services that are more appropriate, responsive and helpful, but also because such action was necessary for social justice. I sought to use my position to develop opportunities and practices for involvement as well as to study them. At the same time, as a social scientist I have been committed to use the tools of social science disciplines to help understand the dynamics and challenges of such action. Lewin (1951) suggested that there is 'nothing as practical as a good theory' and I have drawn on a range of theoretical work to develop analyses of user involvement, public participation and user movements. My chapter with Colin Gell in this volume (Chapter Two) does not make explicit reference to this, but could not have been written without an understanding of power and of mental health user groups as social movement organisations that I have developed elsewhere (Barnes and Bowl, 2001). These analytical frameworks offer opportunities for critical analysis of practices encompassed within the broad terrain of user involvement. They suggest explanations for tension, conflicts and failure as well as offering guidance for successful action. For example, with colleagues I have explored the micro-dynamics of participation, drawing on critical theories of deliberative democracy to account for the ways in which some voices may be silenced or de-legitimised within participation initiatives (Barnes et al, 2004). Thus, I do not believe that recognising and valuing experiential knowledge should also mean ignoring or devaluing theoretical knowledge.

I do not bring to work on user involvement personal experience of living with a disability, mental health problems or long-term physical health problems, nor of living in poverty or being dependent on health and social services for support in everyday life. I do not and cannot identify myself as a disabled person and thus cannot claim the experiential knowledge of those who do. In some contexts my legitimacy to speak on such issues has been challenged as a result. I, like most people, have close friends and relatives who have experienced mental health problems, illness, increasing frailty and the need for support in old age. I have some limited experience of negotiating with services in relation to help for my mother, and more extensive experience of the impact of dementia on a loved one and on her relationships with family members. Like us all, I am ageing and in some categorisations now qualify as an 'older person'. My personal experiences in these contexts have affected how I look at questions about rights, care and justice that I think are relevant to understanding the nature and significance of action by services users and carers. I have always been committed to a voice for lay carers as well as for service users (Barnes, 2011), and I think that the absence of such a voice in this book is a limitation. While I continue to believe that many of the issues that service users campaign about should be seen as civil and human rights issues, I no longer consider that a commitment to rights should mean the devaluation of care. Rather, along with many feminist scholars I consider that we need to broaden our concept of 'social justice' by encompassing care as a personal and political value within this (Tronto, 1993; Sevenhuijsen, 1998). The questions I ask, the issues that I want to explore and understand, and the frameworks that I use have developed and been influenced by personal experience as well as by working with user and carer groups and by knowledge of social science theory and research.

Phil

The position from which I connect with user involvement is one that is arrived at by way of a journey. My disciplinary identity has been closely allied to the health professions, and nursing practice in particular, but many other things contribute to influence my perception of my identity construction at this point in time. I have professional, academic and, to a degree, user identities. In terms of user identity I am referring here to living with two long-term medical conditions that necessitate continued reliance on medication and being in contact with health professionals on a regular basis. I also have irregular but ongoing contact with professionals in social care as a 'user'. My direct interest and activity with user involvement has come about within the last decade, but I trace a commitment to user experience back to my early nursing career.

Commencing training as a psychiatric nurse, I recall being attracted to the idea of being an advocate for people, of tuning in to people's experience and thoughts, and of helping them through a difficult time. It seemed challenging and looked like you could really make a difference in people's lives. Of course I was very naïve, idealistic and unworldly. I was ripe for an extreme shock. I cannot say that this experience was wholly negative but I was very uncomfortable with the seemingly implicit institutionalisation and I felt deep sadness working in this environment at times. A desire to engage with people rather than to assume or impose things upon them did not seem to fit into the culture of the organisations I worked in. This may not have been typical but I did not go on to pursue a career in psychiatry.

At a later point, moving into palliative care and working with people approaching the end of their lives was an opportunity to practice nursing in a setting that prioritised holistic care and acknowledged the importance of viewing individuals as part of a family unit and wider community. Involvement at the individual level was enacted where at all possible. For example, patients were involved in decision making about issues concerning them, and relationships between staff and patients and their families were usually built on a collaborative basis. It was in this hospice setting, when I was working as a nurse specialist, that my interest in user involvement took hold and developed. I became aware over time of the need for some service users to 'have a say', or to be involved to a greater extent in voicing their needs and shaping those things that affected their lives. For me there was also a desire to assist with challenging paternal barriers that sometimes prevented service users with palliative and/or end-of-life care needs from becoming actively involved.

My focus on user involvement originated in practice then and also from hearing of the ideas and possibilities during attendance at a particular conference. Hearing an influential figure in involvement discuss its possibilities led me to consider the relevance of user involvement to palliative care and to research. I saw this involvement as fitting with certain principles inherent to palliative care. Cicely Saunders was a widely acknowledged leader in the development of hospice and palliative care in the United Kingdom (UK) and her original aims were not only 'to be a voice for the voiceless....' but also to 'enable people who were facing the end of their lives ... to speak to people outside....' (Oliviere, 2000, p 103). Building on from this, the philosophy may be seen not only as a way of listening and learning from service users, but also as a call for engagement with and being led by service users. Indeed, Cicely Saunders' encounter with David Tasma, a dying man she met in her role of hospital almoner, was an example of action developing from practice (Du Boulay, 1984, p 57). It was this relationship, in which user and professional were able to see the need for improvements in care for people with life-limiting conditions and how they could go about changing attitudes and practice, which was one of the precursors to the inception of the modern hospice movement.

It was while working in a hospice that I began my PhD and, through commencing a participatory study, met with and brought together a small group of people with life-limiting conditions to work with me on my doctoral research (Cotterell, 2006). This small group became the Service User Research Advisory Group (SURAG) that met with me 32 times over a three-year period of study. People with life-limiting conditions have been described as vulnerable and as a hard-to-reach group of people (Steel, 2005, p 19). In this instance, however, access was not difficult and as a group, myself and surviving members have written about the difficulties and positives encountered in actively involving service users with life-limiting conditions in research (Cotterell et al, 2007, p 101; Cotterell, 2008). This experience was revelatory for me in terms of working closely and over time with the group and in terms of accessing certain material. Of key influence was work from the discipline of disability studies, and in particular Hunt's (1981) paper 'Settling accounts with the parasite people'. This was a call both for 'doing research differently' and for social justice. The conduct of my research was also greatly influenced by the social model of disability (Oliver, 1990) and the more feminist interpretation of this (Thomas, 2007). Taking theoretical direction in this way led me to challenge preconceived ideas derived from a disciplinary background dominated by the biomedical model. The research and the frame through which we all worked, myself and the SURAG, became more and more open to the factors that shape social relations.

I have continued to have a focus on service user involvement in the field of cancer and palliative care and I have been involved in a range of studies exploring how involvement has been played out both in cancer service delivery (Sitzia et al, 2006) and in cancer research (Brown et al, 2006). More recently I have worked with colleagues to focus on the impacts that involvement can have on those service users who become involved in various activities (Cotterell et al, 2011). We describe a wide range of significant personal impacts for those service users who become involved and we argue for greater attention to be paid to emphasising these personal impacts in practice.

Less tangible than academic outputs is the change that involvement has the potential to bring about. I am referring here to the changes that are possible at the level of people's lives. The lived experience of involvement is an almost too esoteric way to refer to this, but what I mean is the movement, the change possible through involvement activities. Over the years I have worked with many service users as active members of research teams. I know from both their and my experience that involvement has the capacity, given the right circumstances, to empower and to enable people to see things in a different way. As we have seen in this book, it is not a panacea and we have to be careful about presenting involvement as an unassailable good, but it is clear that it can present both service users and researchers with opportunities to learn and to develop new skills and attitudes on the way to producing robust research. Finally, though, we must remember that involvement is often not entered into for personal gain. This may be one important outcome but impact on policy and practice is of paramount importance – 'to act is vital' (Cotterell et al, 2009).

What are 'critical perspectives'?

From our different positions, both of us start from a commitment to the involvement of people who use services in individual and collective decision making about services, and in research that concerns their lives and the policies and services that affect them. We also celebrate collective action by carers, disabled people, older people and others who use health and social care services, but whose social change objectives extend well beyond reform or even transformation of public services. But we do not think that commitment implies an uncritical questioning of such action. We suggest that there are at least three ways in which a critical perspective can contribute to understanding and progressive development.

First, critical social science analysis implies questioning based in conceptual and theoretical analysis and by drawing on research data that might be generated using participatory or non-participatory research methods. For example, we might offer a critique of claims by policy makers that service users are 'empowered' through participation by undertaking a conceptual analysis of the way that power operates. But we might also critique the practice of user groups by considering the power dynamics within groups themselves. Social movement theory can suggest questions about the way in which user movements generate collective identities or an 'oppositional consciousness' (Mansbridge and Morris, 2001) and help us understand the way in which their growth and development may be helped or frustrated by the political context in which they operate (Tarrow, 1998).

Reflective practice can also facilitate a critical, learning perspective. 'Practitioners' in this context might be user activists, workers in health and social care seeking to enable involvement or researchers developing participatory research practice. Standing back and reflecting on what worked and what did not, the nature of the relationships that have been generated, and both expected and unexpected changes that have resulted from involvement, is an important way of learning about and developing effective ways of ensuring a voice. It requires the ability to be self-critical as well as trusting of relations between those engaged in self-reflection.

The importance of understanding what the world looks like from the perspective of those who have little power to determine the way in which the world is structured, is fundamental to an understanding of user involvement as necessary to social justice (Barnes et al, 2010). Thus, a critical perspective on user involvement necessitates service users offering a critique of policy makers, practitioners and researchers based on their personal experiences of 'being involved'. One way in which this happens is through emancipatory research that is relevant politically and to the people who are the focus of the research; that reverses existing hierarchies and ensures that disabled people are at the centre of the research in terms of control (Stone and Priestley, 1996).

Critique is by its nature challenging and can be uncomfortable. Claims that it is based solely on sound research evidence or robust theoretical analysis ignore the political nature of user involvement and the different stakes that activists have in comparison with external analysts. But we also suggest that people are not 'right' solely because of the position they occupy and that there is value in learning from the insights enabled by different types of critical analysis, as well as recognising the different positionality of users themselves.

Conclusion

This volume reflects the enduring significance of user involvement in the context of health and social care services, policy and research. Such involvement is taken for granted in a way that would have been unimaginable to many of those involved in initiatives from the 1970s and 1980s. Achievements such as the profound challenge offered to the medical model by the social model of disability have transformed the landscape of health and social care. But critique builds and develops. The social model has itself been subject to critique, from inside as well as outside the disability movement (eg Shakespeare, 2006). While the widespread adoption of individual budgets as the preferred means of 'empowering' service users via the exercise of choice and control is hailed as evidence of the success of the disability movement, there are also concerns about the impact of their introduction in the context of a reduction in state spending (Boxall et al, 2009), and about the impact of personalisation more generally on collective responsibility and the 'social' aspect of service delivery and use (Barnes, 2008a). We do not know what impact a much more 'personalised' approach to service delivery will have on user involvement that has been strongest when it has been built on collective action among service users. The need to sustain an independent, vigorous challenge from users, alongside critical analysis from researchers and with support from crucial reflective practitioners will remain as we start to learn what the transformation of personalisation has in store for all of us.

This volume also demonstrates that user involvement does and will continue to generate different views and ideas, and that the new types of relationships between users, researcher and practitioners through which its potential can be delivered require hard work and ethical as well as political sensibilities. Different voices are expressed in different ways and it is important not to mute such differences to conform to some presumed deliberative or stylistic norm. The results of this can be uncomfortable, but are also the source of the unsettling of established assumptions that can bring about change. Thus, we do not attempt to draw a final overall conclusion from this volume. Rather, we hope that the contributions stimulate a continued critical engagement with the possibilities for change in both service and social relationships resulting from different modes of user organisation and action.

References

Aaslid, F. S. (2006) 'Facing the dragon: exploring a conscious phenomenology of intoxication', Dr. Polit. thesis, Department of Social Anthropology, NTNU Trondheim: Norwegian University of Science and Technology.

Alborz, A. (2002) 'Are primary care groups and trusts consulting local communities?', *Health and Social Care in the Community*, vol 10, no 1, pp 20-7.

Alderson, P. (2001) 'Research by children', *International Journal of Social Research Methodology*, vol 4, no 2, pp 139-53.

Ali, K., Roffe, C. and Crome, P. (2006) 'What patients want: consumer involvement in the design of a randomised controlled trial of routine oxygen supplementation after acute stroke', *Stroke*, vol 37, pp 865-71.

Alldred, P. (1998) 'Ethnography and discourse analysis: dilemmas in representing the voices of children', in Ribbens, J. and Edwards, R. (eds) *Feminist dilemmas in qualitative research: Public knowledge and private lives*, London: Sage Publications.

Alldred, P. and David, M. (2009) 'What's important at the end of the day? Young mothers' values and policy assumption', in Duncan, S., Edwards, R. and Alexander, C. (eds) *Teenage parenthood: What's the problem?*, London: Tufnell Press.

Alderson, P. (2000) *Young children's rights: exploring beliefs, principles and practice.* London: Jessica Kingsley

Anderson, W. and Florin, D. (2001a) *Patient and public involvement in primary care groups and trusts: North Lewisham case study*, draft report, London: King's Fund Primary Care Programme.

Anderson, W. and Florin, D. (2001b) *Patient and public involvement in primary care groups and trusts: Dagenham case study*, draft report, London: King's Fund Primary Care Programme.

Anderson, W. and Florin, D. (2001c) *Patient and public involvement in primary care groups and trusts: Harrow East and Kingsbury case study*, draft report, London: King's Fund Primary Care Programme.

Anderson, W. and Florin, D. (2001d) *Patient and public involvement in primary care groups and trusts: City and Hackney case study*, draft report, London: King's Fund Primary Care Programme.

Arai, L. (2009) *Teenage pregnancy: The making and unmaking of a problem*, Bristol: The Policy Press.

Archer, M. (1995) *Realist social theory: The morphogenetic approach*, Cambridge: Cambridge University Press.

Ardron, D. and Kendall, M. (2010) 'Patient and public involvement in health research: what is it, and why is it so important?', *International Journal of Palliative Nursing*, vol 16, no 4, pp 160-2.

Armes, D. G. (2006) 'Enablement and exploitation: the contradictory potential of community care policy for mental health services user survivor led groups', PhD thesis, University of Bedfordshire/Luton.

Arnstein, S. (1969) A ladder of citizen participation, *Journal of the American Institute of Planners*, vol 35, no 4, pp 216-24.

Attree, P., Morris, S., Clifton, M., Hinder, S. and Vaughan, S. (2009) *Exploring the impact of user involvement on health and social care services for cancer in the UK: Final report*, London: Macmillan Cancer Support.

Aveyard, B. and Davies, S. (2006) 'Moving forward together: evaluation of an action group involving staff and relatives within a nursing home for older people with dementia', *International Journal of Older People Nursing*, vol 1, pp 95-104.

Baggott, R., Allsop, J. and Jones, K. (2005) *Speaking for patients and carers: Health consumer groups and the policy process*, Basingstoke: Palgrave.

Bailey, N. Brown, G. Di Marco, H. Letherby, G. and Wilson, C. (2004) Teenage pregnancy and young motherhood: medical encounters. *British Journal of Midwifery*, 12:11

Bailey, N., Brown, G., Letherby, G. and Wilson, C. (2002) 'Young motherhood: "insider" and "outsider" views', *HealthWatch*, newsletter (West Midlands Centre for Health Action Research and Training).

Barber, R., Boote, J. D. and Cooper, C. (2007) 'Involving consumers successfully in NHS research: a national survey', *Health Expectations*, vol 10, no 4, pp 380-91.

Barber, R., Boote, J., Parry, G., Cooper, C. Yeeles, P. and Cook, S. (2011) 'Can the impact of public involvement on research be evaluated? A mixed methods approach', *Health Expectations*, doi: 1111/j.1369-7625.2010.00660.x.

Barnard, A., Carter, M., Britten, N., Purtell, R., Wyatt, K. and Ellis, A. (2005) *The PC11 report: An evaluation of consumer involvement in the London Primary Care Studies Programme*, Exeter: Peninsula Medial School.

Barnes, C. (1994) *Disabled people in Britain and discrimination: A case for anti-discrimination legislation*. London: Hurst & Co.

Barnes, C. (2003) 'What a difference a decade makes: reflections on doing "emancipator" disability research', *Disability & Society*, vol 18, no 1, pp 3-17.

Barnes, C. and Mercer, G. (2004) *Implementation of the social model of disability: Theory and research*, Leeds: The Disability Press.

Barnes, C. and Mercer, G. (1997) *Doing disability research*, Leeds: The Disability Press.

Barnes, M. (1997a) *Care, communities and citizens*, Harlow: Addison Wesley Longman.

Barnes, M. (1997b) *The people's health service?*, Birmingham: Health Services Management Centre, University of Birmingham.

Barnes, M. (1999) 'Users as citizens: collective action and the local governance of welfare', *Social Policy & Administration*, vol 33, no 1, pp 73-90.

Barnes, M. (2002) 'Bringing difference into deliberation: disabled people, survivors and local governance', *Policy & Politics*, vol 30, no 3, pp 355-68.

Barnes, M. (2005) 'Same old process? Older people, participation and deliberation', *Ageing and Society*, vol 25, no 2, pp 245-59.

Barnes, M. (2007) *A final brick in the wall? A history of the Nottingham Advocacy Group*, Brighton: University of Brighton, www.brighton.ac.uk/sass/contact/details.php?uid=mb129

Barnes, M. (2008a) 'Is the personal no longer political? A response to Charles Leadbeater, Jamie Bartlett and Niamh Gallagher's *Making it personal* (Demos, 2008)', *Soundings*, no 39, pp 152-9.

Barnes, M. (2008b) 'Passionate participation: emotional experiences and expressions in deliberative forums', *Critical Social Policy*, vol 28, no 4, pp 461-81.

Barnes, M. (2009) 'Authoritative consumers or experts by experience? User groups in health and social care', in Simmons, R., Powell, M. and Greener, I. (eds) *The consumer in public services*, Bristol: The Policy Press.

Barnes, M. (2011) 'Caring responsibilities: the making citizen carers?', in Newman, J. E. and Tonkens, E. (eds) *Active citizenship in Europe*, Amsterdam: University of Amsterdam Press.

Barnes, M. and Bennett, G. (1998) 'Frail bodies, courageous voices: older people influencing community care', *Health and Social Care in the Community*, vol 6, no 2, pp 102-11.

Barnes, M. and Bowl, R. (2001) *Taking over the asylum: Empowerment and mental health*, Basingstoke: Palgrave.

Barnes, M. and Shardlow, P. (1996) 'Identity crisis: mental health user groups and the "problem" of identity', in C. Barnes and G. Mercer (eds) *Exploring the divide: Illness and disability*, Leeds: The Disability Press.

Barnes, M. and Taylor, S. (2007) *Involving older people in research: Examples, purposes and good practice*, Sheffield: ERA-AGE European Research Area in Ageing Research, http://era-age.group.shef.ac.uk/content/228/

Barnes, M. and Walker, A. (1996) 'Consumerism versus empowerment: a principled approach to the involvement of older service users', *Policy & Politics*, vol 24, no 4, pp 375-93.

Barnes, M. and Wistow, G. (eds) (1992) *Researching user involvement*, Leeds: Nuffield Institute for Health Services Studies.

Barnes, M. and Wistow, G. (1994) 'Achieving a strategy for user involvement in community care', *Health and Social Care in the Community*, vol 2, pp 347-56.

Barnes, M., Bauld, L., Benzeval, M., Judge, K., Mackenzie, M. and Sullivan, H. (2005) *Health Action Zones: Partnerships for health equity*, London: Routledge.

Barnes, M., Gell, C. and Thomas, P. (2010) 'Participation and social justice', in I. Greener C. Holden and M. Kilkey (eds) *Social policy review: Analysis and debate in social policy 2010*, Bristol: The Policy Press.

Barnes, M., Harrison, E. and Murray, L. (2011) 'Ageing activists: who gets involved in older people's forums?' *Ageing and Society*, vol 31, pp 1-20, doi:10.1017/S0144686X11000328.

Barnes, M., Harrison, S., Mort, M. and Shardlow, P. (1999) *Unequal partners: User groups and community care*, Bristol: The Policy Press.

Barnes, M., Knops, A., Newman, J. and Sullivan, H. (2004) 'The micro politics of deliberation: case studies in public participation', *Contemporary Politics*, vol 10, no 2, pp 93-110.

Barnes, M., Newman, J. and Sullivan, H. (2007) *Power, participation and political renewal: Case studies in public participation*, Bristol: The Policy Press.

Barnes, M., Prior, D. and Thomas, N. (1990) 'Social services', in N. Deakin and A. Wright (eds) *Consuming public services*, London: Routledge.

Bate, P. and Robert, G. (2007) *Bringing user experience to healthcare improvement: The concepts, methods and practices of experience based design*, Oxford: Radcliffe Publishing.

Bauman, H.-D. L. (ed) (2008) *Open your eyes: Deaf studies talking*, Minneapolis, MN: University of Minnesota Press.

BBC (British Broadcasting Corporation) (2010) *Panorama: The cuts – can you fight back?*, Broadcast on BBC One, 17 May.

Begum, N. (2006) *Doing it for themselves: Participation and black and minority ethnic service users*, Participation Report 14, London: Social Care Institute for Excellence.

Beresford, P. (1999) 'Making participation possible: movements of disabled people and psychiatric system survivors', in Jordan, T. and Lent, A. (eds) *Storming the millennium: The new politics of change*, London: Lawrence and Wishart, pp 34-50.

Beresford, P. (2002) 'User involvement in research and evaluation: liberation or regulation?', *Social Policy & Society*, vol 1, no 2, pp 95-105.

Beresford, P. (2003) *It's our lives: A short theory of knowledge, distance and experience*, London: OSP for Citizen Press.

Beresford, P. (2007) 'The role of service user research in generating knowledge based health and social care: from conflict to contribution', *Evidence & Policy: A Journal of Research, Debate and Practice*, vol 3, no 2, pp 329-41.

Beresford, P. (2008) 'Welfare users and social policy', in Alcock, P., May, M. and Rowlingson, K. (eds) *The student's companion to social policy* (3rd edition), Oxford: Blackwell Publishing, pp 259-66.

Beresford, P. (2009a) 'Co-production from a user perspective', in *Co-production in action: A Social Care Institute for Excellence expert seminar*, 1 October, event report, London: SCIE, pp 5-7.

Beresford, P. (2009b) 'Developing a social model of madness and distress to underpin survivor research', in Sweeney, A., Beresford, P., Faulkner, A., Nettle, M. and Rose, D. (eds) *This is survivor research*, Ross-on-Wye: PCCS Books.

Beresford, P. (2010) 'A tale for would be voters', Blog, *Society Guardian*, 30 April, www.guardian.co.uk/society/joepublic/2010/apr/30/general-election-voting-rights

Beresford, P. and Branfield, F. (2006) 'Developing inclusive partnerships', *Health and Social Care in the Community*, vol 14, no 5, pp 436-44.

Beresford, P. and Campbell, J. (1994) 'Disabled people, service users, user involvement and representation', *Disability and Society*, vol 9, no 3, pp 315-25.

Beresford, P. (1992) Researching Citizen Involvement: A Collaborative or Colonising Enterprise? in Barnes, M., & Wistow, G. (eds) (1992) *Researching User Involvement*. Leeds, UK: Nuffield Institute for Health Services Studies

Beresford, P. and Croft, S. (1990) *From paternalism to participation: Involving people in social services*, London: Joseph Rowntree Foundation and Open Services Project, with a foreword by Sir Roy Griffiths and Lady Wagner.

Beresford, P. and Croft, S. (1993) *Citizen involvement. A practical guide for change*, Basingstoke: Macmillan.

Beresford, P. and Croft, S. (2004) 'Service users and practitioners reunited: the key component for social work reform', *British Journal of Social Work*, vol 34, no 1, pp 53-68.

Beresford, P. and Evans, C. (1999) 'Research note: research and empowerment', *British Journal of Social Work*, vol 29, pp 671-7.

Beresford, P. and Rose, D. (2009) 'What is research?, in Sweeney, A., Beresford, P., Faulkner, A., Nettle, M. and Rose, D. (eds) *This is survivor research*, Ross-on-Wye: PCCS Books, pp 11-22.

Beresford, P., Croft, S., Evans, C. and Harding, T. (1997) 'Quality in personal social services: the developing role of user involvement in the UK', in Evans, A., Haverinen, R., Leichsenring, K. and Wistow, G. (eds) *Developing quality in personal social services*, Aldershot: Ashgate, pp 63-81.

Berger, P. L. and Luckmann, T. (1967) *The social construction of reality: A treatise in the sociology of knowledge*, Harmondsworth: Penguin.

Bernard, M. and Scharf, T. (eds) (2007) *Critical perspectives in ageing societies*, Bristol: The Policy Press.

Berry, S. H. (ed) (2008) *Kingston Hospital and Kingston Primary Care Patient and Public Involvement Forums: The legacy of their work*, New Malden: Number 11 Publishing.

Best, S. (2002), *Introduction to politics and society*, London: Sage Publications.

Blake, S., Ruel, B., Seamark, C. and Seamark, D. (2007) 'Experiences of patients requiring strong opioid drugs for chronic non-cancer pain', *British Journal of General Practice*, February, www.folkus.org.uk/files/Opioid_Project.pdf

Bochel, C., Bochel, H., Somerville, P. and Worley, C. (2007) 'Marginalised or enabled voices? "User participation" in policy and practice', *Social Policy and Society*, vol 7, no 2, pp 201-10.

Bode, I. (2003) 'Flexible response in changing environments: the German third sector model in transition', *Nonprofit and Voluntary Sector Quarterly*, vol 32, no 2, pp 190-210.

Boote, J., Baird, W. and Beecroft, C. (2010) 'Public involvement at the design stage of primary health research: a narrative review of case examples', *Health Policy*, vol 95, pp 10-23.

Boote, J., Telford, R. and Cooper, C. (2002) 'Consumer involvement in health research: a review and research agenda', *Health Policy*, vol 36, pp 213-36.

Borkman, T. (1976) 'Experiential knowledge: a new concept for the analysis of self-help groups', *Social Service Review*, vol 50, pp 445-56.

Bovaird, T. (2007) 'Beyond engagement and participation: user and community co-production of public services', *Public Administration Review*, vol 67, no 5, pp 846-60.

Boxall, K., Dowson, S. and Beresford, P. (2009) 'Selling individual budgets, choice and control: local and global influences on UK social care policy for people with learning difficulties', *Policy & Politics*, vol 37, no 4, 499-515.

Bradwell, P. and Marr, S. (2008) *Making the most of collaboration: An international survey of public service co-design*, Demos report 23, London: Demos.

Brady, L. and Ghosh, G. (2009) 'Involving young people in public health research', *INVOLVE newsletter: Summer 2009*, www.invo.org.uk/Newsletters.asp

Brady, L. M., Law, C. and Gibb, J. (2008) *Young People's Public Health Reference Group: Pilot project: Final report*, London: NCB, www.york.ac.uk/phrc/YPPHRG_FR_1.08.pdf

Brand, D. (2009) 'SCIE perspective on co-production', in *Co production in action: A Social Care Institute for Excellence expert seminar*, 1 October, event report, London: SCIE, pp 4-5.

Brandsen, T. and van Hout, E. (2006) 'Co management in public service networks: the organizational effects', *Public Management Review*, vol 8, no 4, pp 537-49.

Brandsen, T. and Pestoff, V. (2006) 'Co production, the third sector and the delivery of public services: an introduction', *Public Management Review*, vol 8, no 4, pp 493-501.

Branfield, F. and Beresford, P. (2011) *Beyond the usual suspects: Developing diversity in involvement*, London: Shaping Our Lives

Branfield, F. and Beresford, P. with Andrews, E. J., Chambers, P., Staddon, P., Wise, G. and Williams-Findlay, B. (2006) *Making user involvement work: Supporting service user networking and knowledge*, York: Joseph Rowntree Foundation.

Braye, S. (2000) 'Participation and involvement in social care', in Kemshall, H. and Littlechild, R. (eds) *User involvement and participation in social care: Research informing practice*, London: Jessica Kingsley Publishers.

Brett, J., Staniszewska, S., Monkford, C., Seers, K., Heron-Marx, S. and Bayliss, H. (2009) *The PIRICOM Study: A systematic review of the conceptualisation, measurement, impact and outcomes of patients and public involvement in health and social care research*, London: UK Clinical Research Collaboration.

British Society of Rehabilitation Medicine (2003) Vocational Rehabilitation: The Way Forward. London, UK: BSRM Cited in The Sainsbury Centre for Mental Health (2004) Benefits and work for people with mental health problems: A briefing for mental health workers. Briefing 27. London, UK: The Sainsbury Centre for Mental Health

Brown, G., Brady, G., Wilson, C. and Letherby, G. (2009) 'Teenage pregnancy and young parenthood: questioning the inevitability of risk, lone motherhood and social exclusion', in Johns, N. and Barton, A. (eds) *Evaluating the political achievement of New Labour since 1997*, Lampeter: Edwin Mellen.

Brown, I. (1994) 'Community and participation for general practice: perceptions of general practitioners and community nurses', *Social Science and Medicine*, vol 39, no 3, pp 335-44.

Brown, V., Cotterell, P., Sitzia, J., Richardson, A., Kelley, K. and Willers, R. (2006) *Evaluation of consumer research panels in cancer research networks*, London: Macmillan Cancer Support.

Brownlie, J. (2009) 'Researching, not playing, in the public sphere', *Sociology*, vol 43, no 4, pp 699-716.

Bryant, L. and Beckett, J. (2006) *The practicality and acceptability of an advocacy service in the emergency department for people attending following self-harm*, Leeds: University of Leeds.

Burns, T., Catty, J., White, S., Clement, S., Ellis, G., Jones, I.R., Lissouba, P., McLaren, S., Rose, D. and Wykes, T. (2009) 'Continuity of care in mental health: understanding and measuring a complex phenomenon', *Psychological Medicine*, vol 39, pp 313-23.

Cahill, C. (2007) 'Doing research with young people: participatory research and the rituals of collective work', *Children's Geographies*, vol 5, no 3, pp 297-312.

Campbell, J. and Oliver, M. (1996) *Disability politics: Understanding our past, changing our future*, London: Routledge.

Campbell, N. D. (2000) *Using women: Gender, drug policy, and social injustice*, New York, NY: Routledge.

Campbell, P. (1996) 'The history of the user movement in the United Kingdom', in Heller, T., Reynolds, J., Gomm, R., Muston, R. and Pattison, S. (eds) *Mental health matters: A reader*, Basingstoke: Macmillan in association with The Open University, pp 218-25.

Carey, G., Braunack-Mayer, A. and Barraket, J. (2009) 'Spaces of care in the third sector: understanding the effects of professionalization', *Health (London)*, vol 13, no 6, pp 629-46.

Carlsson, C. and Nilbert, M. (2007) 'Living with hereditary non-polyposis colorectal cancer: experiences from and impact of genetic testing', *Journal of Genetic Counselling*, vol 16, pp 811-20.

Carnegie UK Trust (2010) http://democracy.carnegieuktrust.org.uk/democracy/power_tools

Carney, L., Jones, L., Braddon, F., Pullybank, A. M. and Dixon, A. R. (2006) 'A colorectal cancer patient focus group develops an information package', *Annals of the Royal College of Surgeons of England*, vol 88, pp 447-9.

Caron-Flinterman, J. F., Broerse, J. E. W. and Bunders, J. F. G. (2005) 'The experiential knowledge of patients: a new resource for biomedical research?', *Social Science & Medicine*, vol 60, pp 2575-84.

Caron-Flinterman, J. F., Broerse, J. E. W., Teerling, J., Van Alst, M. L. Y., Klaasen, S., Swart, L. E. and Bunders, J. F. G. (2006) 'Stakeholder participation in health research agenda setting: the case of asthma and COPD research in the Netherlands', *Science and Public Policy*, vol 33, no 4, pp 291-304.

Carr, S. (2007) 'Participation, power, conflict and change: theorising dynamics of service user participation in the social care system of England and Wales', *Critical Social Policy*, vol 27, no 2, pp 266-76.

Carr, S. (2004) *Has service user participation made a difference to social care services?*, London: Social Care Institute for Excellence.

Cater, S. and Coleman, L. (2006) *'Planned' teenage pregnancy: Perspectives of young parents from disadvantaged backgrounds*, Bristol and York: The Policy Press and Joseph Rowntree Foundation.

Cavet, J. and Sloper, P. (2004) 'The participation of children and young people in decisions about UK service development', *Child Care, Health and Development*, vol 30, no 6, pp 613-21.

Chamberlin, J. and Unzicker, R. (1990) *Psychiatric survivors, ex patients, and users: An observation of organizations in Holland and England*, by Judi Chamberlin and Rae Unzicker.

Chambers, R. (1997) *Whose reality counts? Putting the first last*, London: Intermediate Technology.

Chang, D., Spicer, N., Irving, A., Sparham, I. and Neeve, L. (2001) *Modernising service delivery: The Better Government for Older People prototypes*, DWP Research Report no 136, London: DWP.

Charles, C., Gafni, A. and Whelan, T. (1997) 'Shared decision-making in the medical encounter: what does it mean? (Or it takes at least two to tango)', *Social Science and Medicine*, vol 44, no 5, pp 681-92.

Charles, N. (2004) 'Feminism, social movements and the political order', in Todd, M. J. and Taylor, G. (eds) *Democracy and participation: Popular protest and new social movements*, London: Merlin Press, pp 248-72.

Charlton, J. I. (1998) *Nothing about us without us: Disability, oppression and empowerment*, Berkeley, CA: University of California Press.

Church, K. (1996) 'Beyond "bad manners": the power relations of "consumer participation" in Ontario's community mental health system', *Journal of Community Mental Health*, vol 37, pp 22-5.

Clark, C. C., Scott, E. A., Boydell, K. M. and Goering, P. (1999) 'Effects of client interviewers on client reported satisfaction with mental health services', *Psychiatric Services*, vol 50, no 7, pp 961-3.

Clark, M., Glasby, J. and Lester, H. (2004) 'Cases for change: user involvement in mental health services and research', *Research Policy and Planning*, vol 22, no 2, pp 31-8.

Collyar, D. (2005) 'How have patient advocates in the US benefited cancer research?', *Nature Reviews Cancer*, vol 5, pp 73-7.

Cooper, C., Moore, J., Telford, R., Boote, J. and Repper, J. (2005) *Evaluation of the NTCRN Consumer Research Panel*, Sheffield: School of Health and Related Research, University of Sheffield.

Cotterell, P. (2006) 'Living with life limiting conditions: a participatory study of people's experiences and needs', PhD thesis, School of Health Sciences and Social Care, Brunel University.

Cotterell, P. (2008) 'Exploring the value of service user involvement in data analysis: "our interpretation is about what lies below the surface"', *Educational Action Research*, vol 16, no 1, pp 5-17.

Cotterell, P., Clarke, P., Cowdrey, D., Kapp, J., Paine, M. and Wynn, R. (2007) 'Becoming involved in research: a service user research advisory group', in Jarrett, L. (ed) *Creative engagement in palliative care: New perspectives on user involvement*, Abingdon: Radcliffe Publishing.

Cotterell, P., Harlow, G., Morris, C., Beresford, P., Hanley, B., Sargeant, A., Sitzia, J. and Staley, K. (2008) *Identifying the impact of service user involvement on the lives of people affected by cancer: Final report*, London: Macmillan Cancer Support.

Cotterell, P., Harlow, G., Morris, C., Beresford, P., Hanley, B., Sargeant, A., Sitzia, J. and Staley, K. (2011) 'Service user involvement in cancer care: the impact on service users', *Health Expectations*, 14, (2). 159-169 doi: 10.1111/j.1369-7625.2010.00627.x

Cotterell, P., MacFarlane, A. and Findlay, H. (2009) 'Patient and carer narratives and stories', in Oliviere, D. and Gunaratnan, Y. (eds) *Narrative and stories in healthcare: Illness, dying and bereavement*, Oxford: Oxford University Press.

Cotterell, P., Sitzia, J. and Richardson, A. (2004) 'Evaluating partnerships with cancer patients', *Practice Nursing*, vol 15, no 9, pp 430-5.

Cotterill, P. and Letherby, G. (1993) 'Weaving stories: personal auto/biographies in feminist research', *Sociology*, vol 27, no 1, pp 67-80.

Council of Europe (2003) *Revised European Charter on the Participation of Young People in Local and Regional Life*, Strasbourg: Council of Europe.

CQC (Care Quality Commission) (2009) *Voices into action: The Care Quality Commission's statement of involvement*, London: CQC.

Craig, P., Dieppe, P., Macintyre, S., Mitchie, S., Nazareth, I. and Petticrew, M. (2008) 'Developing and evaluating complex interventions: the new Medical Research Council guidance', *British Medical Journal*, vol 337, pp 979-83.

Crawford, M. J., Aldridge, T., Bhui, K., Rutter, D., Manley, C., Weaver, T., Tyrer, P. and Fulop, N. (2003) 'User involvement in the planning and delivery of mental health services: a cross-sectional survey of service users and providers', *Acta Psychiatrica Scandinavica*, vol 107, pp 410-14.

Crossley, M. L. (2003) '"Would you consider yourself a healthy person?": using focus groups to explore health as a moral phenomenon', *Journal of Health Psychology*, vol 8, no 5, pp 501-14.

Crossley, N. (1999) 'Fish, field, habitus and madness: the first wave mental health users' movement', *British Journal of Sociology*, vol 50, no 4, pp 647-70.

Crossley, N. (2006) *Contesting psychiatry: Social movements in mental health*, London: Routledge.

CSIP and DH (Care Services Improvement Partnership and Department of Health) (2007) *Mental well-being impact assessment: A toolkit: 'A living and working document'*, London: CSIP and DH.

CYPU (Children and Young People's Unit) (2001) *Learning to listen: Core principles for the involvement of children and young people*, Annesley: Department for Education and Skills.

d'Agincourt-Canning, L. (2005) 'The effect of experiential knowledge on construction of risk perception in hereditary breast/ovarian cancer', *Journal of Genetic Counselling*, vol 14, no 1, pp 55-69.

Davey, C. (2010) *Children's participation in 2010: A summary report*, London: National Children's Bureau.

David, M. (2002) 'Problems of participation: the limits of action research', *National Journal of Social Research and Methodology*, vol 5, no 1, pp 11-17.

Davis, K. (1993) 'On the movement', in Swain, J., Finkelstein, V., French, S. and Oliver, M. (eds) *Disabling barriers: Enabling environments*, London: Sage Publications in association with The Open University.

Davis Smith, J., Rochester, C. and Hedley, R. (1995) 'Introduction', in Davis Smith, J., Rochester, C. and Hedley, R. (eds) *An introduction to the voluntary sector*, London: Routledge, pp 1-8.

DCSF (Department for Children, Schools and Families) (2010) *Teenage pregnancy strategy: Beyond 2010*, London: DCSF.

DCSF (2007) *The children's plan: Building brighter futures*, London: DCSF.

De Beauvoir, S. (1997, 1953 translation, 1945) *The second sex*, Reading: Vintage Classics.

Dearden-Phillips, C. and Fountain, R. (2005) 'Real power: an examination of the involvement of people with learning difficulties in strategic services development in Cambridgeshire', *British Journal of Learning Disabilities*, vol 33, pp 200-4.

Dewer, B. (2005) 'Beyond tokenistic involvement of older people in research – a framework for future development and understanding', *Journal of Clinical Nursing*, vol 14, suppl 1, pp 48-53.

DH (Department of Health) (1995) *A policy framework for commissioning cancer services (the Calman-Hine report)*, London: DH.

DH (2000) *The NHS cancer plan*, London: DH.

DH (2001a) *The national service framework for older people*, London: DH.

DH (2001b) *The expert patient programme: A new approach to chronic disease management for the 21st century*, London: DH.

DH (2001c) *The report of the public inquiry into children's heart surgery at the Bristol Royal Infirmary 1984-1995*, London: DH.

DH (2001e) *Involving Patients and the Public in Health Care: a discussion document.* London: DH

DH (2005) *Research governance framework for health and social care* (2nd edition), London: DH.

DH (2006) *Best research for best health: A new national health research strategy*, London: DH.

DH (2007a) *Cancer reform strategy*, London: DH.

DH (2007b) *Putting people first: A shared vision and commitment to the transformation of adult social care*, London: DH.

DH (2009a) *Shaping the future of care together*, London: DH.

DH (2009b) *New horizons: A shared vision for mental health*, London: DH, www.dh.gov.uk/prod_consum_dh/groups/dh_digitalassets/@dh/@en/documents/digitalasset/dh_109708.pdf

DH (2010a) *Equity and excellence: Liberating the NHS*, London: DH.

DH (2010b) *Government response to the Health Select Committee report on social care (third report of session 2009-10)*, London: DH

DH (2010c) 'Health Secretary outlines vision for locally led NHS service changes', press release, 21 May, www.dh.gov.uk/en/MediaCentre/Pressreleases/DH_116290

DiLapi, E. M. (1989) 'Lesbian mothers and the motherhood hierarchy', *Journal of Homosexuality*, vol 18, no 1-2, pp 101-21.

Doyal, L. (1995) *What makes women sick: Gender and the political economy of health*, Basingstoke: Macmillan.

Du Boulay, S. (1984) *Cicely Saunders: The founder of the modern hospice movement*, London: Hodder & Stoughton.

Duffy, J. (2008) *Looking out from the middle: User involvement in health and social care in Northern Ireland*, Stakeholder Participation Report 18, London: Social Care Institute for Excellence.

Duncan, S., Edwards, R. and Alexander, C. (eds) (2010) *Teenage parenthood: What's the problem?*, London: Tufnell Press.

Durkin, L. (1972) 'Patient power – review of a protest', *Social Work Today*, vol 3, no 15, p 14.

DWP (Department for Work and Pensions) (2005) *Opportunity age: Meeting the challenge of ageing in the 21st century*, London: DWP.

DWP (2009) *Empowering engagement: A stronger voice for older people*, London: DWP.

Entwistle, V. A., Renfrew, M. J., Yearley, S., Forrester, J. and Lamont, T. (1998) 'Lay perspectives: advantages for health research', *British Medical Journal*, vol 316, no 7129, pp 463-6.

Etchegary, H., Potter, B., Howley, H., Cappelli, M., Coyle, D., Graham, I., Walker, M. and Wilson, B. (2008) 'The influence of experiential knowledge on prenatal screening and testing decisions', *Genetic Testing*, vol 12, no 1, pp 115-24.

Ettorre, E. (1997) *Women and alcohol: A private pleasure or a public problem?*, London: Women's Press.

Ettorre, E. (2007) *Revisioning women and drug use: Gender, power and the body*, Basingstoke: Palgrave Macmillan.

Evans, C. (1995) 'Disability, discrimination and local authority social services 2: users' perspectives', in Zarb G. (ed) *Removing disabling barriers*, London: Policy Studies Institute, pp 116-23.

Evans, C. and Fisher, M. (1999) 'Collaborative evaluation with service users: moving towards user-controlled research', in Shaw, I. and Lishman, J. (eds) *Evaluation & Social Work Practice*, London: Sage Publications, pp 101-17.

Evans, C. and Hughes, M. (1993) *Tall oaks from little acorns*, Trowbridge: Wiltshire Social Services/Wiltshire Users' Network.

Evans, C. and Jones, R. (2005) 'Really making it happen in Wiltshire: the experience of service users evaluating social care', in Lowes, L. and Hulatt, I. (eds) *User involvement in health and social care research*, London: Routledge, pp 132-9.

Evans, C., Carmichael, A. and members of the Direct Payments Best Value Review Group of Wiltshire and Swindon Users Network (2002) *Users' best value: A guide to good practice in user involvement in best value reviews*, York: Joseph Rowntree Foundation.

Farr, M. and Cressey, P. (2010) 'Public service employee and user collaboration: creating change from the ground up', Paper presented at the British Sociological Association Annual Conference, Glasgow Caledonian University, 7-9 April.

Faulkner, A. (2004) *Capturing the experiences of those involved in the TRUE project: A story of colliding worlds*, Eastleigh: INVOLVE.

Faulkner, A. (2006) *Beyond our expectations: A report of the experiences of involving service users in forensic mental health research*, London: Department of Health.

Faulkner, A. (2009) *Service user and carer involvement in the National Mental Health Development Unit: Scoping report November 2009*, London: NSUN.

Faulkner, A. and Layzell, S. (1999) *Strategies for living: A report on user-led research*, London: Mental Health Foundation.

Ferguson, I. (2008) *Reclaiming social work: Challenging neo-liberalism and promoting social justice*, London: Sage Publications.

Finkelstein, V. (1980) *Attitudes and disabled people: Issues for discussion*, New York, NY: World Rehabilitation Fund.

Finkelstein, V. (1993) 'Disability: a social challenge or an administrative responsibility', in Swain, J., Finkelstein, V., French, S. and Oliver, M. (eds) *Disabling barriers: Enabling environments*, London: Sage Publications.

Fischer, F. (2000) *Citizens, experts and the environment: The politics of local knowledge*, Durham and London: Duke University Press.

Fish, J. (2006) *Heterosexism in health and social care*, Basingstoke: Palgrave Macmillan.

Fisher, M. (2002) 'The role of service users in problem formulation and technical aspects of social research', *Social Work Education*, vol 21, no 3, pp 305-12.

Folk.us (2009) *Annual report 2008-2009*, Exeter: Folk.us, www.folkus.org.uk

Formby, E., Hirst, J. and Owen, J. (2010) 'Pathways to adulthood: reflections from three generations of young mothers and fathers', in Duncan, S., Edwards, R. and Alexander, C. (eds) *Teenage parenthood: What's the problem?*, London: Tufnell Press.

Fraser, S., Lewis, V., Ding, S., Kellett, M. and Robinson, C. (eds) (2004) *Doing research with children and young people*, London: Sage Publications.

Freire, P. (1972) *Pedagogy of the oppressed*, New York, NY: Herder and Herder.

Fudge, N., Wolfe, C. D. A. and McKevitt, C. (2008) 'Assessing the promise of user involvement in health service development: ethnographic study', *British Medical Journal*, vol 336, pp 313-17.

Furedi, F. (2004) 'Foreword: reflections on some uncomfortable realities', in Todd, M. J. and Taylor, G. (eds) *Democracy and participation: Popular protest and new social movements*, London: Merlin Press, pp viii-xviii.

Fyfe, N. R. (2005) 'Making space for "neo-communitarianism"? The third sector, state and civil society in the UK', *Antipode*, vol 37, no 3, pp 536-57.

Fyfe, N. R. and Milligan, C. (2003) 'Out of the shadows: exploring contemporary geographies of voluntarism', *Progress in Human Geography*, vol 27, no 4, pp 397-413.

Gallacher, L. and Gallacher, M. (2005) *Participatory methods in research with children: A critique*, Edinburgh: School of Geosciences, University of Edinburgh, www.geos. ed.ac.uk/homes/s0453363/brunelpaperpdf

Gaskin, K. and Vincent, J. (1996) *Co-operating for health*, Loughborough: Centre for Research in Social Policy, Loughborough University:

Gibbons, M., Limoges, G. Nowotny, H., Schwartzman, S., Scott, P. and Trow, M. (1998) *The new production of knowledge*, London: Sage Publications.

Gillard, S. and Stacey, E. (2005) 'All talk: experiencing user led research', *A life in the day*, vol 9, no 2, pp 27-30.

Gillard, S., Edwards, C., White, S., White, R., Adams, K. and Davies, L. (2010a) *Identifying the barriers and facilitators of supporting self care in Mental Health NHS trusts: Report for the National Institute for Health Research Service Delivery and Organisation Programme*, London: HMSO, www.sdo.nihr.ac.uk/files/project/165-final-report. pdf

Gillard, S., Turner, K., Lovell, K., Norton, K., Clarke, T., Addicott, R., McGivern, G. and Ferlie, E. (2010b) '"Staying native": coproduction in mental health services research', *International Journal of Public Sector Management*, vol 23, no 6, pp 567-77.

Gillard, S. Borschmann, R., Turner, K., Goodrich-Purnell, N., Lovell, K. and Chambers, M. (2010c) 'What difference does it make? Finding evidence of the impact of mental health service user researchers on research into the experiences of detained psychiatric patients', *Health Expectations*, doi: 10.1111/j.1369-7625.2010.00596.x.

Glendinning, C., Challis, D., Fernandez, J.-L. Jacobs, S. Jones, K., Knapp, M., Manthorpe, J., Moran, N., Netten, A., Stevens, M. and Wilberforce, M. (2008) *Evaluation of the Individual Budgets Pilots: Final report*, York: Social Policy Research Unit, University of York.

Goodare, H. and Lockwood, S. (1999) 'Involving patients in clinical research: improves the quality of research', *British Medical Journal*, vol 319, pp 724-5.

Goss, S. and Miller, C. (1995) *From margin to mainstream: Developing user and carer centred community care*, York: Joseph Rowntree Foundation.

Gott, M., Stevens, T., Small, N. and Ahmedzai, S. H (2000) *User involvement in cancer care: Exclusion and empowerment*, Bristol: The Policy Press.

Graham, H. and McDermott, G. (2005) 'Qualitative research and the evidence base of policy: insights from studies of teenage mothers in the UK', *Journal of Social Policy*, vol 35, no 1, pp 21-37.

Greenfield, S. F., Brooks, A. J., Gordon, S. M., Green, C. A., Kropp, F., McHugh, K. R., Lincoln, M., Hien, D. and Miele, G. M. (2007) 'Substance abuse treatment entry, retention, and outcome in women: a review of the literature', *Drug and Alcohol Dependence*, vol 86, no 1, pp 1-21.

Greig, A., Taylor, J. and MacKay, T. (2007) *Doing research with children*, London: Sage Publications.

Griffiths, R. (1988) *Community care: Agenda for action*, London: HMSO.

GSCC (General Social Care Council) (2006) *Social work education in England: Listening, learning and shaping*, London: GSCC

Guarino, P., Elbourne, D., Carpenter, J. and Peduzzi, P. (2006) 'Consumer involvement in consent document development: a multicenter cluster randomized trial to assess study participants' understanding', *Clinical Trials*, vol 3, pp 19-30.

Habermas, J. (1972) *Knowledge and human interests*, translated by J. J. Shapiro, Boston, MA: Beacon Press.

Hall, J. M. (1994) 'The experiences of lesbians in Alcoholics Anonymous', *Western Journal of Nursing Research*, vol 16, no 5, pp 556-76.

Hall, M., Bodenhamer, B., Bolstad, R. and Hamblett, M. (2001) *The structure of personality*, Carmarthen: Crown House Publishing.

Hanley, B. (1999) *Research and development in the NHS: How can you make a difference?*, Leeds: NHS Executive.

Hanley, B., Bradburn, J., Barnes, M., Evans, C., Goodare, H., Kelson, M., Kent, A., Oliver, S., Thomas, S. and Wallcraft, J. (2003) *Involving the public in NHS, public health and social care research: Briefing notes for researchers*, (second edition) Eastleigh: INVOLVE.

Hanley, B., Bradburn, J., Gorin, S., Barnes, M., Evans, C., Goodare, H., Kelson, M., Kent, A., Oliver, S. and Wallcraft, J. (2000) *Involving consumers in research and development in the NHS: Briefing notes for researchers*, Winchester: Consumers in NHS Research Support Unit, Help for Health Trust (second edition published 2003).

Harding, S. (1993) 'Rethinking standpoint epistemology: what is "strong objectivity"?', in Alcoff, C. and Potter, E. (eds) *Feminist epistemologies*, London: Routledge.

Harnett, R., Thom, B., Herring, R. and Kelly, M. (2000) 'Alcohol in transition: towards a model of young men's drinking styles', *Journal of Youth Studies*, vol 3, no 1, pp 61-77.

Harrison, S. and Mort, M. (1998) 'Which champions, which people? Public and user involvement in health care as a technology of legitimation', *Social Policy and Administration*, vol 32, no 1, pp 60-70.

Harrison, S., Barnes, M. and Mort, M. (1997) 'Praise and damnation: mental health user groups and the construction of organisational legitimacy', *Public Policy and Administration*, vol 12, no 2, pp 4-16.

Hart, R. A. (2008) 'Stepping back from "the ladder": reflections on a model of participatory work with children', in Reid, A., Jensen, B. B., Nikel, J. and Simovska, V. (eds) *Participation and learning: Perspectives on education and the environment, health and sustainability*, Houton, the Netherlands: Springer.

Hayden, C. and Boaz, A. (2000) *Making a difference. Better government for older people evaluation report*, Warwick: Local Government Centre, University of Warwick.

Heater, D. (1999) *What is citizenship?*, Malden, MA: Polity PressHeginbotham, C. (ed) (1992) *Listening to local voices*, Birmingham: NAHAT.

Henwood, K., Griffin, C. and Phoenix, A. (eds) (1998) *Standpoints and differences: Essays in the practice of feminist psychology*, London: Routledge.

Hernandez, L., Robson, P. and Sampson, A. (2008) 'Towards integrated participation: involving seldom heard users of social care services', *British Journal of Social Work*, Advance Access published online 9 September.

Herron-Marx S, Putz, R, Staniszewska S (2009) The current state of patient and public involvement in NHS Trusts across England. National Centre for Involvement. Department of Health. Project report

Heron, J. and Reason, P. (1997) 'A participatory inquiry paradigm', *Qualitative Inquiry*, vol 3, no 3, pp 274-94.

Hewlett, S., de Wit, M. D., Richards, P., Quest, E., Hughes, R., Heiberg, T. and Kirwan, J. (2006) 'Patients and professionals as research partners: challenges, practicalities, and benefits', *Arthritis and Rheumatism*, vol 55, pp 676-80.

Heywood, A. (2007) *Political ideologies: An introduction: Fourth edition*, Basingstoke: Palgrave Macmillan.

Higher Education Funding Council for England (2011) *Decisions on assessing research impact,* Bristol: Higher Education Funding Council for England.

Hill, C., Martin, J. and Roberts, A. (1975) *A directory of the side effects of psychiatric drugs*, London: Hackney Mental Patients Union.

Hill, M. (1997) 'Participatory research with children', *Child and Family Social Work*, vol 2, no 3, pp 71-183.

Hill Collins, P. (1990) *Black feminist thought: Knowledge, consciousness, and the politics of empowerment*, London: Routledge.

Hindley, P. (1994) 'Psychiatric disorder in Deaf and hearing impaired children and young people: a prevalence study', *Journal of Child Psychology and Psychiatry*, vol 35, pp 917-34.

HM Government (2003) *Every child matters*, London: HMSO.

Hodge, S. (2005) 'Participation, discourse and power: a case study in service user involvement', *Critical Social Policy*, vol 25, no 2, pp 164-79.

Hostick, T. and McClelland, F. (2002) '"Partnership": a co-operative inquiry between community mental health nurses and their clients: 2: the nurse–client relationship', *Journal of Psychiatric and Mental Health Nursing*, vol 9, pp 111-17.

Hubbard, G., Kidd, L. and Donaghy, E. (2008) 'Involving people affected by cancer in research: a review of the literature', *European Journal of Cancer Care*, vol 17, pp 233-44.

Humphries, B., Mertens, D. M. and Truman, C. (2000) 'Arguments for an "emancipator" research paradigm', in Truman, C., Mertens, D. M. and Humphries, B. (eds) *Research and inequality*, London: UCL Press.

Hunt, J. (2001) *The union of the physically impaired against segregation*, internet publication, www.labournet.net/other/0107/upias1.html

Hunt, P. (1981) 'Settling accounts with the parasite people: a critique of "A life apart" by E.J. Miller and G.V. Gwynne', *Disability Challenge*, 1 May, pp 37-50.

Hunter, S. and Ritchie, P. (eds) (2007) *Co-production and personalisation in social care*, London: Jessica Kingsley Publishers.

Hurst, R. (2009) 'The right to be heard and co-production', Paper presented at the Critical Perspectives on User Involvement Conference, University of Brighton, 24 April.

Iedema, R., Merrick, E., Piper, D. and Walsh, J. (2008) *Emergency department co-design stage 1 evaluation: Report to Health Services Performance Improvement Branch NSW Health*, Sydney: Centre for Health Communication, University of Technology, Sydney.

Insight (1996) *Resourcing and performance management in community health councils*, London: Insight Management Consulting.

Irwin, E., Mitchell, L., Durkin, L. and Douieb, B. (1972) 'The need for a mental patients' union – some proposals', http://studymore.org.uk/mpu.htm#FishPamphlet

Jenkins, K. (2005) 'No way out? Incorporating and restructuring the voluntary sector within spaces of neoliberalism', *Antipode*, vol 37, no 3, pp 613-18.

Johnson, C. and Osborne, S. P. (2003) 'Local strategic partnerships, neighbourhood renewal, and the limits to co-governance', *Public Money & Management*, vol 23, no 3, pp 147-54.

Jones, C., Ferguson, I., Lavalette, M. and Penketh, L. (2004) *Social work and social justice: A manifesto for a new engaged practice*, Social Work Action Network, www.socialworkfuture.org/index.php/swan-organisation/manifesto

Jones, R. (2000) *Authorities to introduce more direct payments for disabled people*, London: ADSS Inform.

Jones, R. (2007) 'A journey through the years: ageing and social care', *Ageing Horizons*, vol 6, pp 42-54.

Jones, R. (2009) 'Social work and management', in Barnard, A., Horner, N. and Wild, J. (eds) *The value base of social work and social care*, Maidenhead: Open University Press, pp 145-61.

Jones, R. and Evans, C. (2006) 'Engagement and empowerment, research and relevance: comments on user controlled research', *Research Policy and Planning*, vol 22, no 2, pp 5-13.

Kai, J. and Hedges, C. (1999) 'Minority ethnic community participation in needs assessment and service development in primary care: perceptions of Pakistani and Bangladeshi people about psychological distress', *Health Expectations*, vol 2, pp 7-20.

Kelleher, D. (2001) 'New social movements in the health domain', in Scambler, G. (ed) *Habermas, critical theory and health*, London: Routledge.

Kellett, M. (2005) *How to develop children as researchers*, London: Paul Chapman.

Kelly, J. (2007) 'Reforming public services in the UK: bringing in the third sector', *Public Administration*, vol 85, pp 1003-22.

Kelson, M. (1995) *Consumer involvement initiatives in clinical audit and outcomes*, London: College of Health.

Kelson, M. (1997) *User involvement: A guide to developing effective user involvement strategies in the NHS*, London: College of Health.

Kemmis, S. (2006) 'Participatory action research and the public sphere', *Educational Action Research*, vol 14, no 4, pp 459-76.

Kemshall, H. and Littlechild, R. (eds) (2000) *User involvement and participation in social care: Research informing practice*, London: Jessica Kingsley Publishers.

Kendall, J. and Knapp, M. (1995) 'A loose and baggy monster: boundaries, definitions and types', in Davis Smith, J., Rochester, C. and Hedley, R. (eds) *An introduction to the voluntary sector*, London: Routledge, pp 66-95.

Kidger, J. (2005) 'Stories of redemption? Teenage mothers as the new sex educators', *Sexualities*, vol 8, no 4, pp 481-96.

Kirby, P. (2003) *A guide to actively involving young people in research, for researchers, research commissioners and managers*, Eastleigh: INVOLVE.

Kirby, P., Lanyon, C., Cronin, K. and Sinclair, R. (2003) *Building a culture of participation: Involving children and young people in policy, service planning, delivery and evaluation*, London: DfES.

Koops, L. and Lindley, R. I. (2002) 'Thrombolysis for acute ischaemic stroke: consumer involvement in design of new randomised controlled trial', *British Medical Journal*, vol 325, no 7361, pp 415-7.

Ladd, P. (2003) *Understanding Deaf culture: In search of deafhood*, Clevedon: Multilingual Matters.

Langston, A. L., McCallum, M., Campbell, M. K., Robertson, C. and Ralston, S. H. (2005) 'An integrated approach to consumer representation and involvement in a multicentre randomized controlled trial', *Clinical Trials*, vol 2, no 1, pp 80-7.

Larana, E., Johnston, J. and Gusfield, J. R. (1994) *New social movements: From ideology to identity*, Philadelphia, PA: Temple University Press.

Lathlean, J., Burgess, A., Coldham, T., Gibson, C., Herbert, L., Levett-Jones, T., Simons, L. and Tee, S. (2006) 'Experiences of service user and carer participation in health care education', *Nurse Education Today*, vol 26, pp 732-7.

Leach, M., Scoones, I. and Wynne, B. (eds) (2005) *Science and citizens: Globalisation and the challenge of engagement*, London: Zed Books.

Leadbeater, C., Bartlett, J. and Gallagher, N. (2008) *Making it personal*, London: Demos.

Letherby, G. (2003) *Feminist research in theory and practice*, Buckingham: Open University Press.

Letherby, G. and Bywaters, P. (eds) (2007) *Extending social research: Application, implementation and publication*, Maidenhead: Open University Press.

Letherby, G., Brown, G., Di Marco, H. and Wilson, C. (2002) *Pregnancy and postnatal experience of young women who become pregnant under the age of 20 years*, Coventry: Centre for Social Justice, Coventry University.

Lewin, K. (1951) *Field theory in social science: selected theoretical papers by Kurt Lewin*, Cartwright, D. (ed) New York: Harper Row

LGIU (Local Government Information Unit) (2008) *Out of our control? The case for better health accountability*, London: LGIU.

Lindenmeyer, A., Hearnshaw, H., Sturt, J., Ormerod, R. and Aitchison, G. (2007) 'Assessment of the benefits of user involvement in health research from the Warwick Diabetes Care Research User Group: a qualitative case study', *Health Expectations*, vol 10, no 3, pp 268-77.

Lindow, V. and Morris, J. (1995) *Service user involvement: Synthesis of findings and experience in the field of community care*, York: Joseph Rowntree Foundation.

Lister, R. (2003) *Citizenship: Feminist perspectives*, New York, NY: New York University Press.

Lovenduski, J. and Randall, V. (1993) *Contemporary feminist politics*, Oxford: Oxford University Press.

Lowes, L. and Gill, P. (2006) 'Methodological issues in nursing research: participants' experiences of being interviewed about an emotive topic', *Journal of Advanced Nursing*, vol 55, no 5, pp 587-95.

Lowndes, V. and Sullivan, H. (2004) 'Like a horse and carriage or a fish on a bicycle: how well do local partnerships and public participation go together?', *Local Government Studies*, vol 30, no 1, pp 51-73.

Lupton, C., Peckham, S. and Taylor, P. (1998) *Managing public involvement in healthcare purchasing*, Buckingham: Open University Press.

Lupton, D. (2003 [1994]) *Medicine as culture* (2nd edition), London: Sage Publications.

Macaulay, A. C., Commanda, L. E., Freeman, W. L., Gibson, N., McCbe, M. L,. Robbins, C. M. and Twohig, P. L. for the North American Primary Care Research Group (1999) 'Participatory research maximises community and lay involvement', *British Medical Journal*, vol 319, pp 774-8.

McCormick, S., Brody, J., Brown, P. and Polk, R. (2004) 'Public involvement in breast cancer research: an analysis and model for future research', *International Journal of Health Services*, vol 34, no 4, pp 625-46.

McGrath, M. (1989) 'Consumer participation in service planning--the AWS (All Wales Strategy) experience', *Journal of Social Policy*, vol 18, no 1, pp 67-89.

McLaughlin, H. (2006) 'Involving young service users as co researchers: possibilities, benefits and costs', *British Journal of Social Work*, vol 36, pp 1395-410.

McLaughlin, H. (2009a) 'Keeping service user involvement in research honest', *British Journal of Social Work*, doi: 10.1093/bjsw/bcp064, pp 1-18.

McLaughlin, H. (2009b) *Service user research in health and social care*, Los Angeles, LA: Sage Publications.

Macmillan Cancer Support (2006) *Macmillan Listening Study: The research priorities of people affected by cancer: Full report*, London: Macmillan Cancer Support.

MacVarish, J. (2010) 'The effect of "risk-thinking" on the contemporary construction of teenage motherhood', *Health, Risk and Society*, vol 12, no 4, pp 313-22.

Mansbridge, J. and Morris, A. (eds) (2001) *Oppositional Consciousness: The subjective roots of social protest*, Chicago, IL: University of Chicago Press.

Marsden, J. and Bradburn, J. (2004) 'Patient and clinician collaboration in the design of a national randomized breast cancer trial', *Health Expectations*, vol 7, no 1, pp 6-17.

Marsh, P. and Fisher, M. (1992) *Good intentions: Developing partnership in social services*, York: Joseph Rowntree Foundation.

Martin, G. P. (2008a) 'Ordinary people only: knowledge, representativeness, and the publics of public participation in healthcare', *Sociology of Health and Illness*, vol 30, no 1, pp 35-54, doi: 10.1111/j.1467-9566.2007.01027.x

Martin, G. P. (2008b) 'Representativeness, legitimacy and power in public involvement in health-care management', *Social Science & Medicine*, vol 67, no 11, pp 1757-65.

Martin, G. P. (2009) 'Whose health, whose care, whose say? Some comments on public involvement in new NHS commissioning arrangements', *Critical Public Health*, vol 19, no 1, pp 123-32.

Martin, G. P. (2011) 'The third sector, user involvement and public-service reform: a case study in the co governance of health-service provision', *Public Administration*, doi: 10.1111/j.1467-9299.2011.01910.x.

Mayer, J. and Timm, N. (1970) *The client speaks*, London: Routledge.

Maynard, M. (1994) 'Methods, practice and epistemology: the debate about feminism and research', in Maynard, M. and Purvis, J. (eds) *Researching women's lives from a feminist perspective*, London: Taylor & Francis.

Means, R., Richards, S. and Smith, R. (2003) *Community care policy and practice*, Basingstoke: Palgrave Macmillan.

Meyrick, J. (2002) *An evaluation resource to support the Teenage Pregnancy Strategy*, London: Health Development Agency.

MHF (Mental Health Foundation) (2000) *Strategies for living*, London: MHF.

Mickel, A. (2008) Changing practitioners attitudes towards young mothers, *Community Care* 7th November

Milewa, T. (1997) 'Community participation and health care priorities: reflections on policy, theatre and reality in Britain', *Health Promotion International*, vol 12, no 2, pp 161-8.

Milewa, T., Harrison, S., Ahmad, W. and Tovey, P. (2002a) 'Citizen's participation in primary healthcare planning: innovative citizenship practice in empirical perspective', *Critical Public Health*, vol 12, no 1, pp 39-53.

Milewa, T., Dowswell, G. and Harrison, S. (2002b) 'Partnerships, power and the 'new' politics of community participation in British health care', *Social Policy and Administration*, vol 36, no 7, pp 796-809.

Miller, E. J. and Gwynne, G. V. (1972) *A life apart*, London: Tavistock Publications.

Mockford, C., Staniszewska, S., Griffiths, F. and Herron-Marx, S. (2009) *A systematic review of the impact of patient and public involvement on NHS healthcare services*, Warwick: National Centre for Involvement.

Moriarty, J., Rapaport, P., Beresford, P., Branfield, F., Forrest, V., Manthorpe, J., Martineau, S., Cornes, M., Butt, J., Illiffe, S., Taylor, B. and Keady, J. (2007) *Practice guide: The participation of adult service users, including older people, in developing social care*, Stakeholder Participation Guide 17, London: Social Care Institute for Excellence.

Morison, J. (2000) 'The government–voluntary sector compacts: governance, governmentality, and civil society', *Journal of Law and Society*, vol 27, no 1, pp 98-132.

Morris, J. (1992) 'Personal and political: a feminist perspective on researching physical disability', *Disability, Handicap & Society*, vol 7, no 2, pp 157-66.

Morris, J. (1993) *Independent lives: Community care and disabled people*, Basingstoke: Macmillan.

Morris, J. (1994) *The shape of things to come? User-led social services*, London: National Institute for Social Work.

Morris, J. (1995) 'Easy targets: a disability rights perspective on the "young carers' debate"', in Social Services Inspectorate (ed) *Young Carers: Something to think about: Papers presented at four SSI workshops May-July 1995*, London: Department of Health, pp 38-62.

Mort, M., Harrison, S. and Wistow, G. (1996) 'The user card: picking through the organisational undergrowth in health and social care', *Contemporary Political Studies*, vol 2, pp 1133-40.

Mouffe, C. (2002) *Politics and passions: The stakes of democracy*, London: Centre for the Study of Democracy, University of Westminster.

Mountford, L. and Anderson, W. (2001) 'Patient and public involvement in primary care groups and trusts: central Croydon case study', draft report, King's Fund Primary Care Programme.

MPU (Mental Patients' Union) (1973) 'Declaration of intent of the Mental Patients Union', http://studymore.org.uk/mpu.htm#MPUDeclaration

MPU Hackney (1975) 'Mental Patient's Union: interviews with "Joan Martin, Val and Andrew Roberts, Austin Johnson and others" (November 1974–February 1975)', *New Humpty Dumpty Today*, nos 6 and 7, pp 6-10.

MPU Manchester (1979) *Your rights in mental hospital: A mental patients union (MPU) pamphlet*, Manchester: MPU c/o Grass Roots Books.

MRC (Medical Research Council) (2008) *Complex interventions guidance*, Swindon: MRC, www.mrc.ac.uk/complexinterventionsguidance

Naples, N.A. (1996) 'A feminist revisiting of the insider/outsider debate: the outsider phenomenon in rural Iowa', *Qualitative Sociology*, vol 19, no 1, pp 83-107.

National Centre for Involvement (2009a) Patient and Public Involvement in NHS Commissioning: Lewisham Project.

National Centre for Involvement (2009b) Patient and Public Involvement in NHS Commissioning : Kent Project.

National Health and Medical Research Council (2002) *Statement on Consumer and Community Participation in Health and Medical Research*. Canberra, Australia: Commonwealth of Australia.

National Institutes of Health Director's Council of Public Representatives (2010) www.copr.nih.gov/About_COPR.SHTM

NAW (National Assembly for Wales) (2001) *Improving health in Wales: A plan for the NHS with its partners*, Cardiff: NAW.

NCAT (National Cancer Action Team) (2008) *National Cancer Peer Review Programme: Handbook*, London: NCAT.

NCB (National Children's Bureau) (2002) *Including children in social research*, Highlight no 193, London: NCB.

NCRI (National Cancer Research Institute) (2008) *2008-2013 NCRI strategic plan*, London: NCRI.

Needham, C. (2008) 'Realising the potential of co-production: Negotiating improvements in public services' *Social Policy & Society*, vol 7, no 2, pp 221-231.

Needham, C. and Carr, S. (2009) *Co-production: An emerging evidence base for adult social care transformation*, Research Briefing 31, London: Social Care Institute for Excellence.

NHSE (National Health Service Executive) 1997) *Health Action Zones: Invitation to bid*, EL (97) 65, 30, Leeds: Department of Health.

NHSME (National Health Service Management Executive) (1992) *Local voices: The views of local people in purchasing for health*, London: Department of Health.

NICE (National Institute for Clinical Excellence) (2004) *Guidance on cancer services: Improving supportive and palliative care for adults with cancer: The manual*, London: NICE.

Nicholls, V., Wright, S., Waters, R. and Wells, S. (2003) *Surviving user-led research: Reflections on supporting user-led research projects*, London: Mental Health Foundation.

NIHR (National Institute for Health Research) (2007) Directors message 4, Patient and Public Involvement. www.nihr-ccf.org.uk/site/docdatabase/rfpb/rfpb_docs/RfPB_Directors_message_4.pdf

NIHR (2010) The NIHR School for Social Care Research, http://www.nihr.ac.uk/research/Pages/programmes_school_for_social_care_research.aspx

Nowotny, H., Scott, P. and Gibbons, M. (2001) *Rethinking science*, Cambridge: Polity Press.

Nunes, T., Pretzlik, U. and Olsson, J. (2001) 'Deaf children's social relationships in mainstream schools', *Deafness & Education International*, vol 3, no 3, pp 123-36.

Offe, C. (1985) 'New social movements: challenging the boundaries of institutional politics', *Social Research*, vol 52, no 4, pp 817-68.

Oliver, M. (1990) *The politics of disablement*, London: Macmillan.

Oliver, M. (1992) 'Changing the social relations of research production?', *Disability, Handicap & Society*, vol 7, no 2, pp 101-14.

Oliver, M. (1997) 'Emancipatory research: realistic goal or impossible dream?', in Barnes, C. and Mercer, G. (eds) *Doing disability research*, Leeds: Disability Press.

Oliver, M. (1998) 'Theories of disability in health practice and research', *British Medical Journal*, vol 317, no 7170, pp 1446-9.

Oliver, M. (2004) 'If I had a hammer: the social model in action', in Swain, J., French, S., Barnes, C. and Thomas, C. (eds) *Disabling Barriers: Enabling Environments*, London: Sage Publications.

Oliver, M. (2009) *Understanding disability: From theory to practice* (second revised edition), Basingstoke: Palgrave Macmillan.

Oliver, M. and Barnes, C. (1998) *Disabled people and social policy: From exclusion to inclusion*, Harlow: Addison Wesley Longman.

Oliver, S., Clarke-Jones, L., Rees, R., Milne, R., Buchanan, P., Gabbay, J., Gyte, G., Oakley, A. and Stein, K. (2004) 'Involving consumers in Research and Development agenda setting for the NHS: developing an evidence-based approach', *Health Technology Assessment Monographs*, vol 8, no 15, pp 1-148.

Oliviere, D. (2000) 'A voice for the voiceless', *European Journal of Palliative Care*, vol 7, no 3, pp 102-5.

Oliviere, D. (2001) 'User involvement in palliative care services', *European Journal of Palliative Care*, vol 8, no 6, pp 238-41.

Osborne, S. P. and McLaughlin, K. (2004) 'The cross-cutting review of the voluntary sector: where next for local government–voluntary sector relationships?', *Regional Studies*, vol 38, no 5, pp 573-82.

Owen, S. and Kearns, R. (2006) 'Competition, adaptation and resistance: (re)forming health organisations in New Zealand's third sector', in Milligan, C. and Conradson, D. (eds) *Landscapes of voluntarism*, Bristol: The Policy Press, pp 115-32.

Parker, S. and Heapy, J. (2006) *The journey to the interface: How public service design can connect users to reform*, London: Demos.

Participation Works (2008) *Listen and change: A guide to children and young people's participation rights*, London: Participation Works.

Paterson, C. (2003) *Consumer involvement in research into complementary and alternative therapies*, Bristol: MRC Health Services Research Collaboration.

Patton, M. (1990) *Qualitative evaluation and research methods*, London: Sage Publications.

Pawson, R. and Tilley, N. (1997) *Realistic evaluation*, London: Sage Publications.

Peck, E., Gulliver, P. and Towel, D. (2002) 'Information, consultation or control: user involvement in mental health services in England at the turn of the century', *Journal of Mental Health*, vol 11, no 4, pp 441-51.

Perkins, R. and Goddard, K. (2004) 'Reality out of the rhetoric: increasing user involvement in a mental health trust', *The Mental Health Review*, vol 9, no 1, pp 21-4.

Pestoff, V., Osborne, S. P. and Brandsen, T. (2006) 'Patterns of co production in public services – some concluding thoughts', *Public Management Review*, vol 8, no 4, pp 591-5.

Phoenix, A. (1988) 'Narrow definitions of culture: the case of early motherhood', in Westwood, S. and Bhachu, P. (eds) *Enterprising women: Ethnicity, economy and gender relations*, London: Routledge.

Phoenix, A. (1991) 'Mothers under twenty: outsider and insider views', in Phoenix, A., Woollett, A. and Lloyd, E. (eds) *Motherhood: Meanings, practices and ideologie*, London: Sage Publications.

Pickard, S. and Smith, K. (2001) 'A "Third Way" for lay involvement: what evidence so far?', *Health Expectations*, vol 4, pp 170-9.

Pivik, J., Rode, E. and Ward, C. (2004) 'A consumer model for health technology assessment in Canada', *Health Policy*, vol 69, pp 253-68.

Plowden, W. (2003) 'The compact – attempts to regulate relationships between government and the voluntary sector in England', *Nonprofit and Voluntary Sector Quarterly*, vol 32, no 3, pp 415-32.

PMSU (Prime Minister's Strategy Unit) (2005) *Transforming the life chances of disabled people*, London: HM Government.

Poll, C., Duffy, S., Hatton, C., Sanderson, H. and Routledge, M. (2006) *A report on In Control's first phase 2003-2005*, London: In Control.

Popay, J. and Williams, G. (1996) 'Public health research and lay knowledge', *Social Science & Medicine*, vol 42, no 5, pp 759-68.

Postle, K., Beresford, P. and Hardy, S. (2008) 'Assessing research and involving people using health and social care services: addressing the tensions', *Evidence & Policy*, vol 4, no 3, pp 251-62.

Powell, M. A. and Smith, A. B. (2009) 'Children's participation rights in research', *Childhood*, vol 16, pp 124-42.

Powers, S. (2002) 'From concepts to practice in deaf education: a United Kingdom perspective on inclusion', *Deaf Studies and Deaf Education*, vol 7, no 3, pp 230-43.

Price, K., Gillespie, S. and Rutter, D. (2009) 'Dedicated personality disorder services: a qualitative analysis of service structure and treatment process', *Journal of Mental Health*, vol 18, no 6, pp 467-75.

Prior, L. (2003) 'Belief, knowledge and expertise: the emergence of the lay expert in medical sociology', *Sociology of Health and Illness*, vol 25, no 3, pp 41-57.

Prout, A. (2002) 'Researching children as social actors: an introduction to the Children 5-16 programme', *Children and Society*, vol 16, no 2, pp 67-76.

Raine, P. (2001) *Women's perspectives on drugs and alcohol: The vicious circle*, Aldershot: Ashgate.

Ramon, S. (2003) 'User research: reflection and action', in Ramon, S. (ed) *Users researching health and social care: An empowering agenda?*, Birmingham: Venture Press.

Ray, M. (2007) 'Redressing the balance? The participation of older people in research', in Bernard, M. and Scharf, T. (eds) *Critical perspectives in ageing societies*, Bristol: The Policy Press, pp 73-87.

Raynes, N., Temple, B., Glenister, C. and Coulthard, L. (2001) *Quality at home for older people: Involving service users in defining home care specifications*, Bristol and York: The Policy Press and Joseph Rowntree Foundation.

RCUK (Research Councils UK) (2008) *The concordat to support the career development of researchers*, www.researchconcordat.ac.uk/documents/concordat.pdf

Reason, P. (ed) (1994) *Participation in human inquiry*, London: Sage Publications.

Reason, P. and Bradbury, H. (2001) 'Introduction: inquiry and participation in search of a world worthy of human aspiration', in Reason, P. and Bradbury, H. (eds) *Handbook of action research*, London: Sage Publications.

Reason, P. and Torbet, W. R. (2001) 'The action turn: toward a transformational social science', *Concepts and Transformation*, vol 6, no 1, pp 1-37.

Redfern, M., Keeling, J. W. and Powell, E. (2001) *The Royal Liverpool Children's Inquiry report*, London: The Stationery Office.

Rhodes, P., Nocon, A., Booth, M., Chowdrey, M. Y., Fabian, A., Lambert, N., Mohammed, F. and Walgrove, T. (2002) 'A service users' research advisory group from the perspectives of both service users and researchers', *Health & Social Care in the Community*, vol 10, no 5, pp 402-9.

Ripley, M., Sullivan, D. and Evans, J. (2007) 'The role of patient users in cancer genetic services in primary care', *Familial Cancer*, vol 6, pp 241-8.

Robert, G., Hardacre, J., Locock, L., Bate, P. and Glasby, J. (2003) 'Redesigning mental health services: lessons on user involvement from the Mental Health Collaborative', *Health Expectations*, vol 6, pp 60-71.

Roberts, A. (2009) 'Scotland the brave', *Mental Health Today*, July/August, pp 16-18.

Roberts, C. and Hindley, P. (1999) 'Practitioner review: the assessment and treatment of Deaf children with psychiatric disorders', *Journal of Child Psychology and Psychiatry*, vol 40, no 2, pp 151-67.

Rogers, A. and Pilgrim, D. (1991) '"Pulling down churches": accounting for the British mental health users' movement', *Sociology of Health and Illness*, vol 13, no 2, pp 129-48.

Rose, D. (2001) *Users' voices: The perspectives of mental health service users on community and hospital care*, London: The Sainsbury Centre.

Rose, D. (2003) 'Collaborative research between users and professionals: peaks and pitfalls', *Psychiatric Bulletin*, vol 27, pp 404-6.

Rose, D. (2004) 'Telling different stories: user involvement in mental health research', *Research and Policy Planning*, vol 22, no 2, pp 23-30.

Rose, D., Fleischmann, P., Wykes, T., Leese, M. and Bindman, J. (2003) 'Patients' perspectives on electroconvulsive therapy: systematic review', *British Medical Journal*, vol 326, no 7403, pp 1363-7.

Ross, F., Donovan, S., Brearley, S., Victor, C., Cottee, M., Crowther, P. and Clark, E. (2005) 'Involving older people in research: methodological issues', *Health & Social Care in the Community*, vol 13, no 3, pp 268-75.

Rossi, P. N. (2009) *Fighting cancer with more than medicine: A history of Macmillan Cancer Support*, Stroud: The History Press.

Rowling, L. (2007) 'School mental health: politics, power and practice', *Advances in School Mental Health Promotion*, vol 1, no 1, pp 23-31.

Roxan, D. (1958) *Sentenced without cause: The story of Peter Whitehead*, London: Frederick Muller.

RQIA (2009) Corporate Strategy 2009-12. *Informing and Improving Health and Social Care*. Belfast. Regulation and Quality Improvement Authority.

Ruel, B. (2007) 'Personal profile on pain', *British Journal of General Practice*, vol 57, no 535, p 163.

Russell, M. (1998) *Beyond ramps: Disability at the end of the social contract: A warning from an uppity crip*, Monroe, ME: Common Courage Press.

Savage, C., Xu, Y., Lee, R., Rose, B., Kappesser, M. and Anthony, J. (2006) 'A case study in the use of community-based participatory research in public health nursing', *Public Health Nursing*, vol 23, no 5, pp 472-8.

Sayce, L. (2000) *From psychiatric patient to citizen*, Basingstoke: Macmillan.

Scherer, S. and Sexton, S. (2010) *Involving service users in commissioning services*, York: Joseph Rowntree Foundation.

SCIE (Social Care Institute for Excellence) (2008) *Strengthening user involvement in Northern Ireland: A summary and action plan*, London: SCIE.

SCIE (2009) *Building user and carer involvement in social work education*, London: SCIE.

Scottish Executive Health Department (2001) *Our national health: A plan for action, a plan for change*, Edinburgh: Scottish Executive.

Sedgwick, P. (1982) *Psycho politics*, London: Pluto Press.

Serrano-Anguilar, P., Trujillo-Martin, M. M., Ramos-Goni, J. M., Mahtani-Chugani, V., Perestelo-Perez, L. and Posada-de la Paz, M. (2009) 'Patient involvement in health research: a contribution to a systematic review on the effectiveness of treatments for degenerative ataxias', *Social Science and Medicine*, vol 69, pp 920-5.

SEU (Social Exclusion Unit) (1999) *Teenage pregnancy*, London: HMSO.

Sevenhuijsen, S. (1998) *Citizenship and the ethics of care*, London: Routledge.

Shakespeare, T. (1993) 'Disabled people's self-organisation: a new social movement?', *Disability, Handicap and Society*, vol 8, no 3, pp 249-64.

Shakespeare, T. (2006) *Disability rights and wrongs*, London: Routledge.

Shaping Our Lives (2010) www.shapingourlives.org.uk/projects.html

Sinclair, R. (2004) 'Participation in practice: making it meaningful, effective and sustainable', *Children & Society*, vol 18, pp 106-18.

Sinclair, R. and Franklin, A. (2000) *A Quality Protects research briefing: Young people's participation*, London: Department of Health, Research in Practice and Making Research Count.

Sitzia, J., Cotterell, P. and Richardson, A. (2006) 'Interprofessional collaboration with service users in the development of cancer services: the Cancer Partnership Project', *Journal of Interprofessional Care*, vol 20, no 1, pp 60-74.

Slough User Led Consultation (2004) *All talk: a study of talking and mental health*. East Berkshire Mind: Slough. http://www.spn.org.uk/fileadmin/spn/user/*.pdf/All_talk_research_report.pdf accessed 04 July 2011

Smith, E., Ross, F., Donovan, S., Manthorpe, J., Brearley, S., Sitzia, J. and Beresford, P. (2008) 'Service user involvement in nursing, midwifery and health visiting research: a review of evidence and practice', *International Journal of Nursing Studies*, vol 45, no 2, pp 298-315.

South, J. (2004) 'Rising to the challenge: a study of patient and public involvement in four primary care trusts', *Primary Health Care Research and Development*, vol 5, pp 125-34.

South London and Maudsley Foundation NHS Trust (2009) *Strategy*, London: South London and Maudsley Foundation NHS Trust.

Soyez, V., Tatrai, H., Broekaert, E. and Bracke, R. (2004) 'The implementation of contextual therapy in the therapeutic community for substance abusers: a case study', *Journal of Family Therapy*, vol 26, no 3, pp 286-305.

Spandler, H. (2006) *Asylum to action: Paddington Day Hospital, therapeutic communities and beyond*, London: Jessica Kingsley Publishers.

Spicer, N. and Evans, R. (2005) 'Developing children and young people's participation in strategic processes: the experience of the Children's Fund Initiative', *Social Policy and Society*, vol 5, no 2, pp 177-88.

SSI (Social Services Inspectorate) and Audit Commission (2000) *A report of the joint review of social services in Wiltshire*, Abingdon: Audit Commission Publications.

Staley, K. (2009) *Exploring impact: Public involvement in NHS, public health and social care research*, Eastleigh: INVOLVE.

Staniszewska, S., Brett, J., Mockford, C. and Barber, R. (2011) 'The GRIPP checklist: strengthening the quality and transparency of reporting for patient and public involvement in research', *International Journal of Technology Assessment in Health Care*, in press.

Staniszewska, S., Jones, N., Newburn, M. and Marshall, S. (2007) 'User involvement in the development of a research bid: barriers, enablers and impacts', *Health Expectations*, vol 10, no 2, pp 173-83.

Staniszewska, S., Herron-Marx, S. and Mockford, C. (2008) 'Measuring the impact of patient and public involvement: the need for an evidence base', *International Journal for Quality in Health Care*, vol 20, no 6, pp 373-4.

Stanley, L. and Wise, S. (1993) *Breaking out again: Feminist ontology and epistemology*, London: Routledge.

Steel, R. (2005) 'Actively involving marginalised and vulnerable people in research', in Lowes, L. and Hulatt, I. (eds) *Involving service users in health and social care research*, London: Routledge.

Stone, E. (ed) (1999) *Disability and development: Learning from action and research in the majority world*, Leeds: The Disability Press.

Stone, E. and Priestley, M. (1996) 'Parasites, pawns and partners: disability research and the role of non-disabled researchers', *British Journal of Sociology*, vol 47, no 4, pp 699-716.

Survivors History *Mental health and survivors movements*, http://studymore.org.uk/mpu.htm, archived, under *Mental health history timeline*, in the UK Web Archive at www.webarchive.org.uk/ukwa/target/145406

Survivors History Group (2008) *Celebrating our history: Valuing ourselves: A mental health service users' conference with historians*, http://studymore.org.uk/m080529.pdf

Swain, J., Finkelstein, V., French, S. and Oliver, M. (1993) *Disabling barriers: Enabling environments*, London: Sage Publications.

Sweeney, A. (2009) 'So what is survivor research?', in Sweeney, A., Beresford, P., Faulkner, A., Nettle, M. and Rose, D. (eds) *This is survivor research*, Ross-on-Wye: PCCS Books, pp 22-37.

Sweeney, A., Beresford, P., Faulkner, A., Nettle, M. and Rose, D. (eds) (2009) *This is survivor research*, Ross-on-Wye: PCCS Books.

Talbot, M., Atkinson, K. and Atkinson, D. (2003) *Language and power in the modern world*, Edinburgh: Edinburgh University Press.

Tan, L. and Szebeko, D. (2009) 'Co designing for dementia: the Alzheimer 100 project', *Australasian Medical Journal*, vol 1, no 12, pp 185-98.

Tanesini, A. (1999) *An introduction to feminist epistemologies*, Oxford: Blackwell Publishers.

Tarrow, S. (1998) *Power in movement*, Cambridge: Cambridge University Press.

Taylor, G., Brown, K., Caldwell, K., Ghazi, F., Henshaw, L. and Vernon, L. (2004) 'User involvement in primary care: a case study examining the work of one patient participation group attached to a primary care practice in North London', *Research Policy and Planning*, vol 22, no 1, pp 21-30.

Taylor, V. (2000) 'Emotions and identity in women's self help movements', in Stryker, S., Owens, T. J. and White, R. W. (eds) *Self, identity and social movements*, Minnesota, MN: University of Minnesota Press.

Telford, R., Boote, J. and Cooper, C. (2004) 'What does it mean to involve consumers successfully in NHS research? A consensus study', *Health Expectations*, vol 7, no 3, pp 92-103.

Thomas, C. (2007) *Sociologies of disability and illness: Contested ideas in disability studies and medical sociology*, Basingstoke: Palgrave Macmillan.

Thompson, J., Barber, B., Ward, P., Boote, J., Cooper, C., Armitage, C. and Jones, G. (2009) 'Health researchers' attitudes towards public involvement in health research', *Health Expectations*, vol 12, pp 209-20.

Thornicroft, G. (2006) *Shunned: Discrimination against people with mental illness*, Oxford: Oxford University Press.

Todd, M. J. and Taylor, G. (eds) (2004a) 'Introduction', in *Democracy and participation: Popular protest and new social movements*, London: Merlin Press, pp 1-28.

Todd, M. J. and Taylor, G. (eds) (2004b) *Democracy and participation: Popular protest and new social movements*, London: Merlin Press.

Touraine, A. (1981) *The voice and the eye: An analysis of social movements*, Cambridge: Cambridge University Press.

Tregaskis, C. (2004) *Constructions of disability: Researching the interface between disabled and non-disabled people*, London: Routledge.

Treseder, P. (1997) *Empowering children & young people training manual: Promoting involvement in decision making*, London: Save the Children.

Tritter, J. Q. and McCallum, A. (2006) 'The snakes and ladders of user involvement: moving beyond Arnstein', *Health Policy*, vol 76, pp 156-68.

Tritter, J. Q., Barley, V., Daykin, D., Evans, S., McNeill, J., Rimmer, J., Sanidas, M. and Turton, P. (2003) 'Divided care and the Third Way: user involvement in statutory and voluntary sector cancer services', *Sociology of Health and Illness*, vol 25, no 5, pp 429-56.

Trivedi, P. and Wykes, T. (2002) 'From passive subjects to equal partners: qualitative review of user involvement in research', *British Journal of Psychiatry*, vol 181, pp 468-72.

Tronto, J. (1993) *Moral boundaries: A political argument for an ethic of care*, New York, NY and London: Routledge.

Turner, M. and Beresford, P. (2005) *User controlled research: Its meanings and potential*, Eastleigh: INVOLVE.

UK Clinical Research Collaboration (2011)) *Patient and Public Involvement Strategic Plan 2008-2011*, London: UK Clinical Research Collaboration www.ukcrc.org/patientsandpublic/ppi/ppistratplan/

UN (United Nations) (1989) *Convention on the rights of the child*, Geneva: Office of the United Nations High Commissioner for Human Rights.

Usher, R. (1996) 'A critique of the neglected epistemological assumptions of educational research', in Scott, D. and Usher, R. (eds) *Understanding educational research*, London: Routledge.

Valentine, G. and Skelton, T. (2007) 'The right to be heard: citizenship and language', *Political Geography*, vol 26, no 2, pp 121-40.

Waddell, G., & Burton, A.K. (2006) Is Work Good for Your Health and Well-being? Norwich, UK: The Stationary Office Cited in The Sainsbury Centre for Mental Health (2007) Work and wellbeing: Developing primary mental health care services. Briefing 34. London, UK: The Sainsbury Centre for Mental Health

Walker, A. (2007) 'Why involve older people in research?', *Age and Ageing*, vol 36, pp 481-3.

Wallcraft, J., Read, J. and Sweeney, A. (2003) *On our own terms: Users and survivors of mental health services working together for support and change*, London: Sainsbury Centre for Mental Health.

Walters, G. D. (2002) 'Twelve reasons why we need to find alternatives to Alcoholics Anonymous', *Addictive Disorders and their Treatment*, vol 1, no 2, pp 53-9.

Ward, L. and Gahagan, B. (2010) 'Crossing the divide between theory and practice: research and an ethic of care', *Ethics and Social Welfare*, vol 4, pp 210-16.

Ward, L., Barnes, M. and Gahagan, B. (2008) *Cheers!? A project about older people and alcohol*, Brighton: Health and Social Policy Research Centre, University of Brighton, www.brighton.ac.uk/sass/research/publications

Weare, K. and Gray, G. (2003) *What works in promoting children's emotional and social competence?*, London: DfES.

WFOT (World Federation of Occupational Therapists) (2004) 'What is occupational therapy?, www.wfot.org/information.asp

Whitehead, E. (2001) 'Teenage pregnancy: on the road to social death', *International Journal of Nursing Studies*, vol 38, pp 437-46.

Wilcock, A. A. (1999) 'Reflections on doing, being and becoming', *Australian Occupational Therapy Journal*, vol 46, pp 1-11.

Williams, V. (2003) *User-led research with people with learning disabilities: An introduction and practical guide for researchers & practitioners*, Exeter: Centre for Evidence-Based Social Services.

Wilson, C. Letherby, G. Brown, G. and Bailey, N. (2002) The baby brigade: teenage mothers and sexuality. *Journal of the Association of Research on Mothering* 4, 1: 101–110.

Wilson, C. (2007) 'An inappropriate transition to adulthood? Teenage pregnancy and the discourses of childhood in the UK', *Journal of the Association for Research on Mothering*, vol 9, no 1, pp 92-100.

Winter, R. (2002) 'Truth or fiction: problems of validity and authenticity in narratives of action research', *Educational Action Research*, vol 10, no 1, pp 143-54.

Women in Mind (1986) *Finding our own solutions: Women's experience of mental health care*, London: Mind.

Wright, D. N., Hopkinson, J. B., Corner, J. L. and Foster, C. L. (2006) 'How to involve cancer patients at the end of life as co-researchers', *Palliative Medicine*, vol 20, no 8, pp 821-7.

WSUN (Wiltshire and Swindon Users' Network) (1996) *I am in control*, Trowbridge: WSUN.

Wyatt, K., Carter, M., Mahtani, V., Barnard, A., Hawton, A. and Britten, N. (2008) 'The impact of consumer involvement in research: an evaluation of consumer involvement in the London Primary Care Studies Programme, *Family Practice*, vol 25, no 3, pp 216-24.

Young, I. M. (2000) *Inclusion and democracy*, Oxford: Oxford University Press.

Zarb, G. (1992) 'On the road to Damascus: first steps towards changing the relations of disability research production', *Disability, Handicap & Society*, vol 7, no 2, pp 125-38.

INDEX

Page references for notes are followed by n